The Study of Religion in Canada /
Sciences Religieuses au Canada: 6

The Study of Religion in Canada
Sciences Religeuses au Canada

The Study of Religion in Canada/Sciences Religieuses au Canada is a series of publications planned as "A State-of-the-Art Review" of religious studies in Canada. Each volume in the series covers a particular geographic region. The aim is to present a descriptive and analytical study of courses, programs and research currently being undertaken in the field of religious studies in Canada. The descriptive aspect of the study takes into account the history, nature and rationale of courses and programs, and statistics concerning enrolments and faculty involved. The analytical aspect of the study is concerned with trends and directions of programs, both projected and actual, the relationship of programs and courses to the training and research of faculty, the appeal of courses and program, and the relevance of such courses and programs to larger issues in society.

To date there has been no thorough study of the state of the art of religious studies in Canada. Information concerning religious studies has been confined basically to university and college catalogues and course information in guidance counselling offices in high schools. The descriptive and analytical aspects of this study serve to provide valuable information generally not contained in lists of courses, and will aid students, counsellors and educators in both public and private institutions.

This study, including the research it has involved and the publication of its results, was made possible by a generous grant from the Social Sciences and Humanities Research Council of Canada.

GENERAL EDITOR: *Harold Coward*   University of Victoria

ADVISORY BOARD: *Bruce Alton*   University of Toronto
Charles Anderson   University of British Columbia
Gordon Harland   University of Manitoba
Harold Remus   Wilfrid Laurier University
Louis Rousseau   Université du Québec à Montréal
Martin Rumscheidt   Atlantic School of Theology

THE STUDY OF RELIGION IN CANADA

Volume 6

Religious Studies in Atlantic Canada: A State-of-the-Art Review

Paul W. R. Bowlby

with essays by Tom Faulkner

Published for the Canadian Corporation for Studies in Religion /
Corporation Canadienne des Sciences Religieuses
by Wilfrid Laurier University Press

2001

National Library of Canada Cataloguing in Publication Data

Bowlby, Paul R. 1944-
    Religious studies in Atlantic Canada : a state-of-the-art review

(Study of religion in Canada = Sciences religieuses au Canada ; v. 6)
Includes bibliographical references and index.
ISBN 0-88920-361-X

1. Religion—Study and teaching (Higher)—Atlantic Provinces. 2. Theology—Study and teaching (Higher)—Atlantic Provinces. I. Faulkner, Tom, 1945- II. Canadian Corporation for Studies in Religion. III. Title. IV. Series: Study of religion in Canada ; v. 6.

BL41.B69 2001   200'.71'1715   C2001-901775-8

© 2001 Canadian Corporation for Studies in Religion / Corporation Canadienne des Sciences Religieuses

Cover design by Michael Baldwin, MSAID

∞

Printed in Canada

All rights reserved. No part of this work covered by the copyrights hereon may be reproduced or used in any form or by any means—graphic, electronic or mechanical—without the prior written permission of the publisher. Any request for photocopying, recording, taping or reproducing in information storage and retrieval systems of any part of this book shall be directed in writing to the Canadian Reprography Collective, 214 King Street West, Suite 312, Toronto, Ontario M5H 3S6.

Order from:
Wilfrid Laurier University Press
Waterloo, Ontario, Canada N2L 3C5

Contents

List of Tables	vii
Preface	ix
1 Introduction	1
2 The Religious Roots of the Universities in the Atlantic Provinces	17
3 Departments and Degree Programs in Religious Studies	27
4 The Curriculum in Religious Studies	89
5 Faculty in Religious Studies	121
6 Conclusion	159
Appendix 1	179
Appendix 2	189
Appendix 3	192
Appendix 4	197
Selected Bibliography	199
Index	207

List of Tables

3.1	Distribution Requirements	73
3.2	Total Volumes in Nova Scotia University Libraries	81
3.3	Library Holdings by Religion or Theme	84
4.1	Courses on Historic Traditions	114
4.2	Critical Approaches to the Study of Religions	117
4.3	Themes and Theories in Religious Studies	118
5.1	Years of University Teaching Experience	131
5.2	Retirement by Year	132
5.3	Distribution of Faculty by Rank	133
5.4	Priorities for Teaching, Research and Service	134
5.5	Allocation of Time for Teaching, Research and Service	136
5.6	Doctorates on Historic Traditions	138
5.7	Doctorates in Critical Approaches to the Study of Religion	138
5.8	Doctorates in Themes and Theories	140
5.9	Research on Historic Traditions	141
5.10	Research on Critical Approaches to the Study of Religion	142
5.11	Research on Themes and Theories	144
5.12	Teaching Historic Traditions	148
5.13	Teaching Critical Approaches to the Study of Religion	149

/ vii

Preface

This state-of-the-art review of religious studies in Atlantic Canada is part of a national review that began in 1982. Harold Coward, now at the Centre for the Study of Religion and Society at the University of Victoria in British Columbia, put together a plan to review the study of religion in the various regions of the country. To date, the studies of Alberta,[1] Quebec,[2] Ontario,[3] Manitoba and Saskatchewan[4] and British Columbia[5] have been published. With the completion of the Atlantic Canada review, the national project is finally finished.

The Atlantic region includes Newfoundland, Nova Scotia, Prince Edward Island and New Brunswick. The study is exclusively about the current departments of religious studies or comparative religion in the faculties of arts of the region's numerous universities. While this is a regional study, it is essential to point out that the four provinces do not see themselves as *a* region, preferring to emphasize the cultural and religious diversity that has made each the primary focus of its citizens' loyalty. The primacy of the provincial leads to a certain grumpiness when the four provinces are forced to be viewed as a single entity. As usual in Canada, however, economic forces, efficiency or national perceptions of the outsider lead to arbitrary groupings. In what follows we shall be looking at the academic study of religions in the degree-granting institutions of higher learning in the four provinces. As we proceed our goal is to respect the uniqueness of individual departments and their place in their respective institutional and provincial settings, while identifying and evaluating common patterns in religious studies across the region.

Universities in each of the four provinces are, in company with fellow institutions across the country, undergoing severe stresses that impact on the study of religions and its departmental infrastructure. The triple forces of diminishing university budgets, increasing enrolments and faculty cutbacks are manifestly at work. Acadia University's Department of Comparative Religion has been closed. The program at the Université de Moncton has been reduced from three full-time faculty to two, with no major. More recently, Mount Saint Vincent University has seen its full-time faculty complement reduced to one from the three who were there in 1995. In 1999, St. Francis Xavier saw its full-time faculty complement reduced from five to four and one-third. With that reduction the department lost a position specializing in comparative religions in order to accommodate an appointment in a multidisciplinary program in Catholic Studies. All of these losses carry with them a sense of foreboding about the state of the art in religious studies in the region.

The religious studies departments at Saint Mary's University, Mount Saint Vincent and Dalhousie in Halifax feel as if they have been fighting for their individual existence, especially since 1995. The metropolitan Halifax universities had to spend an inordinate amount of time endeavouring to maintain their respective existence and autonomy from both government and other universities. The end of these debates may still not be in sight. The hope is that this review can help to educate government officials and university administrators about the nature of religious studies in Atlantic Canada.

I want to thank JoAnne Schiffner who worked with me as a research assistant in 1993 before going on to graduate study at Wilfrid Laurier University. Similarly, I would like to thank Marie Bousquet who became involved in the project as a research assistant in September 1994. She has gone on to complete a master's degree in counselling at Acadia and has been combining her counselling career with part-time teaching in religious studies at Brandon University. I am also grateful to Stephanie Roil who assisted on the project database during the summer of 1998. I also want to thank Jenny Wilson, the copy editor, for her scrupulous work on the manuscript and the staff at Wilfrid Laurier University Press for the encouragement during the editorial process and for the fine production of the manuscript.

The original research and the publication of the project were supported by the Social Sciences and Humanities Research Council. After the Atlantic review came into my hands in 1993, it was supported over the next two years by the Senate Research Committee of Saint Mary's University. The Saint Mary's grants funded the employment of both research assistants while the Dean of Arts and the Saint Mary's Department of Religious Studies funded the work on the revised database. In 2000, the Saint Mary's Senate Research Committee gave me a grant to defray the costs of preparing the final copy of the manuscript. I am deeply indebted to Saint Mary's University for financial support.

Tom Faulkner of Dalhousie University worked on this project from 1983 to 1993. More recently, he has contributed the chapter on the history of the Atlantic universities and has permitted the inclusion of his presentation to the Canadian Society for the Study of Religion/Societé canadienne pour l'étude de la religion (CSSR/SCÉR) found in Appendix 1. While we have had many opportunities to disagree over the years, Tom's support and friendship have been unstinting. Like Tom, I presented a portion of this manuscript at the conference of the CSSR/SCÉR at the University of Ottawa in 1998. The paper read there was a major part of Chapter 5 and was entitled "The State-of-the-Art of Religious Studies in Atlantic Canada: An Update and an Introduction."

I want to thank Harold Coward for his patience and support during the preparation of this review. I am also grateful to my colleagues in the Atlantic region for their cooperation and assistance. My apologies to them all for the protracted delay in the completion of the review.

I would like to dedicate this book to my friend and colleague, Dr. Emero Stiegman, Professor Emeritus of the religious studies department at Saint Mary's University. In many ways his career as a religious studies professor is representative of that of many faculty in the region who founded or led departments of religious studies. His specialization was Saint Bernard, and virtually every year in his career he gave a paper at the conference of medievalists held at Kalamazoo, Michigan. In the modern undergraduate religious studies curriculum there is not a lot of room for specialized courses on Saint Bernard! As a result Emero Stiegman created courses on religion and culture. He offered, we believe, the first course on Ecology and Religion in Canada in 1973-74, and every year he taught the large-enrolment courses on "Love" and "Death." As the department's complement was cut in the early to mid-seventies, he fought for the inclusion of world religions in the curriculum as a whole. Just as important, comparative themes were included in each and every one of the courses he taught. Emero Stiegman is, to this day, an outstanding student of religions. He has continued his scholarly work into his retirement. He was a splendid teacher in religious studies and is remembered fondly, I am sure, by the thousands of students who completed his courses. Every religious studies department has a professor who, like Emero Stiegman, kept abreast of the debates about the nature of the study of religions and developed a clear vision of what religious studies can be. Like him, they had to spend a substantial part of their career fighting for that vision. Thank you, Emero. Thank you to all the faculty who fought so hard to establish religious studies in the universities of the Atlantic region.

Finally, and most importantly for me, I want to thank my wife, Anne Marie Dalton, who lived with "the project," the moods and the times of immersion required to complete it. Her love, support and encouragement were indispensable.

Notes

1 Ronald W. Neufeldt, *Religious Studies in Alberta: A State-of-the-Art Review* (Waterloo: Published for the Canadian Corporation for Studies in Religion/Corporation Canadienne des Sciences Religieuses by Wilfrid Laurier University Press, 1983).
2 Louis Rousseau and Michel Despland, *Les sciences religieuses au Québec depuis 1972* (Waterloo: Published for the Canadian Corporation for Studies in Religion/Corporation Canadienne des Sciences Religieuses by Wilfrid Laurier University Press, 1992).
3 Harold Remus, William Closson James and Daniel Fraikin, *Religious Studies in Ontario: A State-of-the-Art Review* (Waterloo: Published for the Canadian Corporation for Studies in Religion/Corporation Canadienne des Sciences Religieuses by Wilfrid Laurier University Press, 1992).
4 John M. Badertscher, Gordon Harland and Roland E. Miller, *Religious Studies in Manitoba and Saskatchewan: A State-of-the-Art Review* (Waterloo: Published for the Canadian Corporation for Studies in Religion/Corporation Canadienne des Sciences Religieuses by Wilfrid Laurier University Press, 1993).
5 Brian J. Fraser, *The Study of Religion in British Columbia: A State-of-the-Art Review* (Waterloo: Published for the Canadian Corporation for Studies in Religion/Corporation Canadienne des Sciences Religieuses by Wilfrid Laurier University Press, 1995).

1
Introduction

> The cry is all but universal across the types of institutions and regions of the country: colleagues (outside the field) and administrators "do not understand what we actually do ... their image of the academic study of religion is 'wrong' or inaccurate."
> — Ray L. Hart

What Is Religious Studies?

In the nineteenth and twentieth centuries, universities admitted many new categories of knowledge and created departments to teach them. English literature was added in the late nineteenth century. In the twentieth century universities added most of the social sciences, such as anthropology, sociology, economics and geography. In recent years, specialized, often multidisciplinary programs such as women's studies, Asian studies, international development studies and environmental studies have been added. As universities added departments and programs, others were reduced or eliminated. Thus, for the most part, the study of Christian theology as part of academic training for the Church's ministers and priests, has been moved out of the faculties of arts in universities and into seminaries.

Within the evolution of universities in the modern era, the nature and even the validity of the study of religions have been much debated. Some university faculty find it difficult to imagine that there could be valid research and teaching on the subject of religion. Religion, to such sceptics, is best understood as superstition, against which the rationality of the scientific methodologies stands as the guardian of authentic knowledge. Such prejudices about the subject of religion have thankfully diminished over time as the discipline has shown the worth of its research and teaching. That human beings have been religious throughout history is an empirical fact. That this dimension of what it is to be human is an appropriate subject of inquiry and of university instruction goes without saying.

It is the central characteristic of the study of religions in the university that it must have as its potential subject the whole spectrum of religious traditions—Hinduism, Buddhism, Islam, Judaism, Christianity, the new religious movements and the religious traditions of indigenous peoples, to list only a few. No department in Canada, let alone the Atlantic region, has the human resources to teach, and do research on, all of the religious traditions. What it must do is structure its curriculum to include introductory and advanced courses on those religious traditions that faculty are competent to teach.

Universities have increasingly recognized the necessity of internationalizing the curriculum. Religious studies stands as an exemplary model of a subject whose fundamental rationale is the study of the religions of the world. The international focus is also particularly appropriate for Canadian universities. Since 1969 there has been an official federal policy of multiculturalism in Canada which has acknowledged the new patterns of immigration and the desire of communities to preserve their culture, language and religion. Religion is explicitly included within the multicultural policy and its programs as an integral aspect of a people's culture.[1] The existence in Atlantic Canada of Hindu temples, Buddhist shrines and monasteries, Muslim mosques and Sikh gurdwaras reflects the religious faces of multiculturalism in Canada. Religious studies can be an essential component of an international curriculum. It can offer courses that teach students about the historical origins of religious communities. Research can be done to interpret the religious life of the immigrant communities for the larger society. So public universities have an obligation to include within their curricula the study of the religious traditions of the newest Canadian citizens along with the traditions of Native peoples, Christianity and Judaism.

Religious studies, like other subjects in the modern university, derives its dominant paradigm of knowledge from adaptations of a scientific method to the study of its subject matter. The application of the paradigm of a scientific model to the study of humanity is problematic for the humanities. It implies that humanity and all its various dimensions of activity or conduct can be rendered into an object over against which a subject may conduct its inquiry. The goal is to know the object according to its own fundamental assumptions. The scientific model is the controlled experiment. The question that has dominated all fields of inquiry in both the social sciences and the humanities is how to adapt the scientific methods to human subjects. Statistical studies are one method of imitating the controlled experiment. There is much, however, that statistics cannot explain. As an alternative to the analogy of the controlled experiment, the scientific method can be adapted primarily as a stance or perspective in relation to the subject to be understood. Objectivity was the name of this stance until it came to be understood just how intrusive any study was in relation to its object of understanding. The elusiveness of objectivity gives way more creatively to the deliberate, self-conscious perspective of an outsider seeking to understand what is "other."

In the study of religions textual studies have been at the forefront of the definition of the stance of the outsider. Studying religious or sacred texts involves seeking to understand the composition and meaning of those texts. Linguistic, historical, archaeological and literary-critical methods have been combined for the purpose of analyzing the texts. Thus, the Christian Bible first, and all other texts subsequently, can be studied by outsiders to any religious tradition following such methods. Such studies are by definition construed to stand outside the religious assumptions of the insider or participant in a religious faith.

Perhaps the clearest expression of the scientific approach as it applies to the study of religion was developed for the International Association for the History of Religions in 1960. R. J. Z. Werblowsky put it this way:

> *Religionwissenschaft* is an anthropological discipline, studying the religious phenomenon as a creation, feature and aspect of human culture. The common ground on which students of religion qua students of religion meet is the realization that the awareness of the numinous or the experience of transcendence (where these happen to exist in religions) are—whatever else they may be—undoubtedly empirical facts of human existence and history, to be studied like all human facts, by appropriate method.[2]

In order to implement such a definition of the field, it is understood that the curriculum of religious studies must include courses on as many religious traditions as the expertise of the faculty can allow.

Religion is, in Werblowsky's account, a generic term. The genus "religion" includes a variety of species—Buddhist, Christian, Confucian, Taoist, Hindu, Islam, Jain, Jewish, Shinto and so on. The range of species of religion is broad indeed. This understanding of the study of religion has produced the introductory textbooks on world religions. These books usually begin with a discussion of what religion is, followed by a survey of the various methods of inquiry that exist for the study of religions. The textbooks, then, provide a brief survey of the principal religious traditions of Asia, Europe and the Americas. Often not well integrated are the traditions of Africa and South America. Until recently no textbook assumed that there was any fundamental distinction between the experience of women and that of men as participants in religious traditions. Nonetheless, the textbooks have often illustrated the themes and content that frequently are the core of the curriculum of a religious studies department.

Religious studies departments do not merely teach about religions; they include a comparative aspect which is usually expressed in the form of thematic courses. There are, as we shall see, a plethora of "religion and" courses. A course on love, non-violence, ethical issues or contemporary spirituality will often include an analysis of the theme from Hindu, Buddhist, Jewish and Christian traditions. It is essential, then, in virtually all courses in a religious studies curriculum to include a comparative dimension to the discussion of a theme.

Like all subject areas and their respective scholastic disciplines, religious studies has developed its own lexicon which informs the nature of the study of religion. In the lexicon there are terms such as "ritual," "sacred text," "priest," "healer" and "shaman." The lexicon is publicly visible in the structure of knowledge employed by the Library of Congress categories on religion(s) or in textbooks introducing students to religions. These categories of religion define objects to be known and studied within the methodological approaches of the discipline. For these categories to be adequately known, it is not sufficient to explain them in terms of one religious tradition. Rather, explanation requires that the phenomenon of the sacred text, or myth, or ritual be examined with reference to examples drawn from several religious traditions. Even when courses are designed to interpret the Buddhist or Jain religious tradition, explanation of the particular aspects of religious behaviour or sacred texts usually takes the form of a cross-reference to comparable phenomena in several religious traditions.

Religious studies has been deeply affected by the contemporary debates about the paradigms of knowledge in science and in the humanities and social sciences. The feminist critiques of the authenticity of knowledge about "man" as the universal human have taken solid effect in the field in both research and teaching. The distinctive patterns of socialization for women and for men have profoundly influenced the nature of the religious traditions. Religious traditions have been a principal means of structuring and authenticating the whole range of gender roles for both women and men. That this should have been a "discovery" in the latter half of the twentieth century and that it was met with such a fierce resistance are both startling facts in themselves. However, as feminist scholars have completed in-depth research on how distinctive gender roles are, on how those roles developed and were reified into patriarchal systems, it is possible to say now that these issues are working their way into the normative lexicon of religious studies, into the classrooms of the universities and into society at large. To interpret and to understand these facts is now an integral and significant part of the task of religious studies.

No less significant has been the review of the relationship between academic study and the cultures of non-Western peoples. "Orientalism"[3] has come to name the ethnocentric ways of Western scholarship in relation to the study of cultures and religions of the non-Western world. Rooted originally in the critique of Western studies of Islam, orientalism has forced into the forefront of research and teaching the awareness that what we study has frequently been named by Western scholars, and the methodologies employed have been culturally specific to the West. As scholars from Asia, Africa and Latin America have adapted or even rejected Western methods of study, the stance of scholarly objectivity has faced its most serious critique. Both gender studies and orientalism have helped shape the realization that knowledge is humanly constructed and that its builders come with plans in hand. That startling awareness has humbled every discipline in its claims to "truth" and most particularly created a profound difficulty for claims to a universal truth. So, too, it has laid open a continuing rethinking of the scientific paradigm of knowledge itself. Humility is an academic virtue much to be espoused in Western-based study in the wake of these currents of thought.

The elementary fact is that the study of religions, like all other fields of study and disciplines in the social sciences and humanities, lives in a house that has ceased to be confident of its foundations. There is great danger in acknowledging such a situation. In the eyes of university administrators and the public, the relevance of the arts in general, not just religious studies, has become a newspaper stock-in-trade. For their critics, the arts have become in large measure something like a museum of civilization,[4] capable of displaying the elements of civilizations but puzzled about how to name and interpret those artifacts. Every room in the museum is interesting in itself, but what is its connection to the next room, to the viewer? There simply is no grand synthesis that permits us to situate our knowledge and call it truth. It is not a criticism of religion or the scholars in faculties of arts to say that there is no consensus of meaning in terms of which the parts of our knowledge make sense. It is to acknowledge that the study of religions both imitates its companion disciplines in their search for knowledge and shares with them that fundamental inability to hold information to a centre of meaning that is shared broadly in the university or in society at large.

Religious Studies in Canada

To situate the study of religions in the academy's debates about the validity of knowledge in the disciplines of the humanities and social sciences is not to ignore the distinctive shape of the debates in religious studies itself. In

Religious Studies in Ontario: A State-of-the-Art Review[5] Harold Remus has succinctly and usefully summarized the unfolding of the debates from the development of "critical inquiry" within Christianity into the development of the institutional form of religious studies in the contemporary university. Without setting out to repeat what is done well in the Ontario review, it does seem important to summarize crucial elements of the development in order that readers of this study may appreciate what has taken place in the development of the study of religion in Canada and how those developments affected religious studies in Atlantic Canada.

The field has developed two venues in which to carry forward the process of self-definition. Firstly, the Canadian Society for the Study of Religion/ Société canadienne pour l'étude de la religion was established within the Learned Societies of Canada and began holding annual conferences in the 1960s. The annual meetings have provided a consistent locus for the debate about the appropriate ways by which to study religions. Secondly, and of equal importance, in 1970 the *Canadian Journal of Theology* suspended publication and was replaced by the new journal *Studies in Religion/Sciences Religieuses*. The new journal signalled the move from a strictly Christian theological focus of inquiry and debate to the study of religions.

The new Canadian Society for the Study of Religion/Société canadienne pour l'"étude de la religion took its place at the annual meeting of the Learned Societies alongside other academic societies focused primarily on the study of Christianity, such as the Canadian Society for Church History, the Canadian Society for Patristic Studies, the Canadian Theological Society and the Canadian Society for Biblical Studies. Faculty in each of these societies could and did publish in the new journal. To further the publication of scholars in all aspects of the study of religions, these societies joined together to form the Canadian Corporation for Studies in Religion/Corporation canadienne des sciences religieuses to publish the new journal, and books by Canadian scholars in the field of religion.

Having established conventional venues for scholarly debate, there were now academic forums in which to argue the issues of methodology, philosophical assumptions and perhaps the single most important issue—the relation of the study of religions to critical inquiry within Christianity. Again, there is little point in repeating what has been well outlined by Harold Remus in the Ontario review.[6] Suffice it to say that there is no scholarly consensus on resolving the philosophical and methodological issues that distinguish theology as a Christian enterprise from the study of Christianity from the perspective of the outsider in religious studies. It is, as Harold Remus states, "the "state-of-the-art" that religious studies scholars are divided on the nature and purpose of theology and religious studies and the relation between the two."[7] What we shall see in our study of departments of religious studies in the Atlantic region are the historical factors that have made the study of Christianity the major subject of teaching and research.

The consequence of the lack of resolution in the debates about religion and theology is significant. The simple fact is that faculty who may well have been trained in one or more of the approaches to the study of Christianity and who now find themselves in religious studies departments go on doing, at least in some significant part, what they were trained to do. Biblical science is the paradigm for the study of sacred texts based in any religious tradition. Historical studies applied to churches or to Hindu communities follow an established method by which what counts as evidence and what does not is both knowable and definable. Scholars on both sides of the debate have much in common with their colleagues in literary studies or departments of history. And perhaps most importantly, teaching and research proceed in the midst of the unresolved debates. This is an essential attribute of the state of the art in the university as a whole and in the study of religions in particular. More significant, however, is the fact that the debates are a measure of the vitality in the field itself.

The University: Setting for the Study of Religions

The university exists concretely as an ordered structure representing materially *an* image of what knowledge is as Western, North American and European peoples have imagined it. Within the university the library is the most comprehensive form of the image. The classification system of the Library of Congress is used in virtually every university library in North America to organize books. This is not just a tool for their storage and retrieval. The Library of Congress classifications constitute a map of the regions and territories of knowledge. They include every subject and all its sub-categories, subdivisions and methods of inquiry. Universities replicate portions of that image in their academic departments. From physics and chemistry to history, philosophy, sociology and religious studies, we can see a catalogue of the subjects that faculty teach and do research on and that students are able to study.

No university includes departments for all of the subjects represented by the map provided by the Library of Congress classification system. Nor can a library acquire anything but a very modest fraction of the books listed on the Library of Congress map. Research libraries like the Library of Congress and some of the libraries at the largest universities in Canada attempt to hold in their collections all, or at least the majority of books published. No such library exists in Atlantic Canada.

In the same way, then, that particular libraries can house only a fraction of the books published, so, too, can the actual curriculum of any particular university and its departments or programs be only a fraction of what could be taught. Every university is an imperfect image of the sum of knowledge. Nonetheless its task is to provide the setting in which students and faculty can explore human knowledge to the widest extent possible. To do so it must be organized and structured to enhance both teaching and study.

Departments, faculties of arts, science and commerce and the university Senate are structures of the university whose role is academic governance. Thus the modern university is divided into faculties of arts and science, and professional faculties such as commerce, law, medicine and the health sciences. The faculty of science organizes the study of the sciences into departments such as physics, biology and chemistry. A faculty of medicine, law or commerce provides the institutional setting for professional study in each of these areas, often requiring for admission that students have first graduated with a degree in arts or science.

Usually the largest single faculty in the university is the Faculty of Arts, which houses departments teaching courses in both the humanities and the social sciences. This division generally places the departments of history, philosophy, religious studies, English and modern languages in the humanities, and anthropology, geography, sociology, political science, psychology and economics in the social sciences.

The purpose of the organization of the university into faculties and departments is to oversee the degree-granting programs and standards of the university. Through the academic departments housed within them, universities hire faculty to teach students, to conduct research and to establish the institutional criteria for validity of success in courses and in research. Departments and programs are staffed by faculty who have themselves been trained in universities and have for the most part graduated with accredited doctoral degrees. While the minimum academic degree required for university teaching is a Master of Arts or Science, it is inconceivable now that a person would receive tenure in a university without completing a doctorate.

Departments and programs in all faculties exist with the approval of an academic Senate. Once degree programs and courses are approved, the professors oversee the content and requirements for a student's specialization in a subject. Every time a Faculty of Arts and a Senate approve a new course or regulations for a degree program, something important is said about the place of the department involved and its subject in the overall education of students. The Senate is making a statement about what counts as knowledge and what is therefore appropriate for inclusion in a degree offered by the university.

All of these university structures provide the material setting in which religious studies exists. Religious studies departments bring into the university a multidisciplinary approach for the acquisition of knowledge about how human beings have been, and continue to be, religious. To that end religious studies departments undertake to teach about as many religious traditions as it can and in doing so, use tools from both the humanities and the social sciences. From the perspective of the humanities it approaches the study of religion philosophically, historically, theologically or textually, using literary-critical and historical methods. When it approaches the study of religion in one or more of the social-scientific ways, it employs the methodologies of anthropology, ethnology, archaeology, psychology or sociology.

The department selects the faculty who, in turn, set out a curriculum of study for undergraduate, and where approved, graduate study. In both research and teaching about the religions and human religiosity, the pedagogical task is to train students as thoroughly as possible as to how to study. Both teaching and research rest upon the foundation of the faculty's education at the graduate level. For faculty, their continuing place in the university is measured, for the purposes of acquiring tenure and promotion, principally by their skill and productivity in teaching students and by continual development of their research in the field.

Put negatively, it is not the task of religious studies courses to train people to *be* religious or to provide training for professionals who wish to serve in religious institutions. Such tasks are properly part of the work of a religious community as a service for its own people, either lay or professional. Thus a theological school for Christian churches trains its students for the priesthood or lay ministry.

Put positively, religious studies departments, like all departments in a Faculty of Arts, teach students descriptively and analytically about the breadth of their respective fields. Further, a religious studies department will, like any other department, teach students about diverse critical assumptions and methods that have been employed to interpret religions and the ways in which human beings have been religious.

In summary a religious studies department, from the point of view of a university, is an integral part of its particular map of human knowledge. The department offers courses that are constituent parts of the requirements for a university degree. It is made up of faculty who teach and do research on religions and of students who either major in the field or choose to do an elective as part of their degree program.

Religious Studies in Canadian Universities

Religious studies in Canada has not emerged from a vacuum. The study of religions originated in Canadian universities in a form that focused almost entirely on the study of Christianity. For the most part the study was in departments of theology, particularly in universities founded by churches. Such departments understood their function to be to teach about the Bible, the history of Christianity, and the history of theology and the debates that have fractured the Church through the centuries. Many Canadian universities were founded by churches that understood education to be one of their principal social functions. This fact is evident in the four Atlantic provinces.

The University of Prince Edward Island is the product of the amalgamation of Christian colleges and the reformulation of the university into a public institution without any religious affiliation. Universities such as St. Thomas, St. Francis Xavier and Saint Mary's were founded and maintained by Roman Catholic dioceses, while Mount Saint Vincent University was founded by the Sisters of Charity. Acadia University was founded by the Baptists and the University of King's College by the Anglican Church. Mount Allison was founded by Methodists and continued its church connection with the United Church of Canada.

As religiously founded universities became secularized and publicly funded, departments of Christian theology frequently became religious studies departments. This was the case at Saint Mary's University and Mount Saint Vincent University. At St. Francis Xavier University, the Department of Theology retained that name until 1997. Even in those departments that were renamed, many of the faculty originally appointed and tenured in the theology department continued their appointments in the religious studies department. This virtually ensured that the curriculum remained predominantly Christian.

It is, then, a historical fact that the vast majority of religious studies departments in the Atlantic region are heir both to the significance of Christianity in their respective universities and to the emerging definition of religious studies as a field of study. In virtually every department, faculty expanded the curriculum to incorporate more and more of the approach characteristic of the emerging field of religious studies. The progressive addition of faculty trained in religious studies departments and in world religions is the product of deliberate choices made within the departments and reflects an ongoing awareness of the scholarly debates about what constitutes the meaning of the study of religions.

Only three universities in the region were not sponsored by churches. In the case of the University of New Brunswick, its charters expressly excluded the teaching of religion in order to avoid fractious denominational controversies. Dalhousie University has always seen itself as a public university, even though many leading Protestants were among its founders and academic leaders. In Newfoundland the education system was until 1998 protected constitutionally as both Christian and denominationally administered. There were Roman Catholic school boards and one Protestant board, inclusive of all denominations, with each administering its own schools. Memorial University of Newfoundland was the exception to this denominational pattern. The university was from its inception a public university without religious affiliation.

Memorial University of Newfoundland and Dalhousie established departments for the study of religions. Despite this secular setting, Memorial's Department of Religious Studies continues to have a dominant focus on biblical studies and church history, in large part because of the denominational school systems and their need for teachers of religious studies. In the Comparative Religion Department at Dalhousie the chosen emphasis has been on developing all its religious studies courses with a multi-religious content. We shall examine the reasons for these very different strategies for interpreting what religious studies is in Chapter 3.

Early Surveys of Religious Studies in Canada

Charles P. Anderson edited and wrote the first surveys of religious studies in Canada.[8] and noted in the 1969 *Guide*, "the rapid development of Religious Studies in Canada."[9] The survey listed courses in Canadian universities at both undergraduate and graduate levels, but offered little or no analysis of the expansion of departments and their courses. In a subsequent *Guide,* published in 1972, Anderson wrote an introductory essay on religious studies in English-speaking Canada.[10] Michel-M. Campbell[11] wrote an essay on the study of religions in French-Canadian universities. Between them they noted several emerging patterns in the continued expansion of religious studies in Canada. Many of the themes that they noted provide a kind of benchmark by which to see in perspective the characteristics of religious studies as it emerged in Atlantic Canada.

The historical record clearly shows that religious studies courses in Canada proliferated during the 1960s. Universities with departments of theology or programs called "Religious Knowledge" renamed them "Religious Studies." Anderson noted the renaming of seven departments during the period 1969-72.[12] While a change of name does not produce immediate and substantive changes in the curriculum, it does set in place a new set of criteria for what will be taught and how it will be presented. What followed from the decision to change the name was an obligatory debate about the place of Christian theological courses and methodologies in the newly named department. Anderson made clear that the long-standing argument, which ranged from total opposition to all theological courses and methods in religious studies to an acceptance of at least some theological courses as an integral part of religious studies, had its origins in the period that saw "religious studies" emerge as the principal name for the new study of religions in universities in Canada.

The debate continues to this day, though the perspectives of some of the participants have given the argument a radically different cast. From the 1950s through the 1980s the principal opponents were Christian theologians and historians of religion arguing about what disciplines should be included within religious studies. Ironically, we now find the argument carried forward by Muslims, Buddhists[13] and feminists who are trained both as theologians and historians of religion. Theology has taken on a multi-religious meaning. It is possible to argue for the legitimacy of a Buddhist or Muslim insider's perspective having *a* place in the religious studies curriculum along with that of the Christian theologian and the comparative historian.

With the new name in place the principal obligations of the new undergraduate departments of religious studies were to find ways to integrate a diversity of methodologies of study and to expand the courses offered about the world's religions. In Anderson's description of a typical department there were about twenty-five courses listed in the university calendar.[14] The introduction to religious studies was typically a course on world religions or on history and methods in the new discipline. Advanced courses were divided between Eastern and Western traditions, and others dealt with contemporary moral or ethical issues. Initially the dominant characteristics were "Christian in content, implicitly theological across most of the curriculum."[15] Anderson noted the dominance of the Christian inheritance and "a definite trend toward giving the non-Christian religions greater attention."[16] Greater attention, however, did not extend much beyond the introductory level. The number of advanced courses on non-Western religious traditions was relatively few. However, the baseline requirement to introduce such courses was in fact imposed by the transformation of programs into religious studies departments. Furthermore, the courses on "existential" themes and the development of methodologies from the social sciences more and more accentuated the distinctive characteristics of the curriculum of a religious studies department. Significant increases in the number of courses in this area very frequently afforded the opportunities to hire new faculty trained in religious studies graduate programs.

The transformation of religious studies between 1967 and 1972 was nowhere more evident than in the number of faculty teaching and doing research in the field. Anderson noted that "on the national scale, there were about 140 faculty members of religious studies and theology departments in 1967; at present there are approximately 220."[17] Overall this represented a 63 percent increase. This figure needs to be qualified, however. Thirty-one faculty at the University of Toronto who were counted in the religious studies program were also members of the various theological colleges affiliated to the university. Omitting the thirty-one faculty at the University of Toronto, there was still a 25 percent increase in religious studies faculty nationally during the period.

A further indication of the growth in religious studies on a national scale was the number of universities offering a major or honours degree in religious studies. "In 1967, 40 percent of the English-speaking and bilingual universities offered a major or an honours program in religious studies or theology; in 1972 this figure stood at nearly 70 percent."[18] Finally, Anderson showed the dramatic increase in the total number of courses offered annually in religious studies. This number rose from 180 in 1967 to 450 in 1972.[19] He estimated that the enrolment in those courses had risen from approximately 7,500 to 17,000 by 1972.[20]

All of Anderson's work points to the huge increase in religious studies as a discipline in Canadian universities. The Atlantic provinces participated in the dramatic growth in the study of religions during the period in a variety of ways, as we shall see. In the region church-founded universities were in some cases becoming public institutions, funded from the provincial tax base. This fact led many institutions to look at how religion was to be taught, if at all, within these newly constituted universities.

Departments of Religious Studies in Atlantic Canada

There are twelve religious studies departments included in this review:
- one at Memorial University of Newfoundland;[21]
- one at the University of Prince Edward Island;
- four departments in New Brunswick at Mount Allison, St. Thomas University and the Université de Moncton. The religion major has been suspended at the Université de Moncton. Two full-time faculty remain, one of whom was tenured in 1998. The Atlantic Baptist University in Moncton was chartered in 1996 and offers an undergraduate major in religious studies and biblical studies. In 1998 St. Stephen's University in St. Stephen, was chartered to teach liberal arts and ministry. It does not offer a religious studies program and is not included in this study;
- five departments in Nova Scotia at Dalhousie University, Mount Saint Vincent University, St. Francis Xavier University and Saint Mary's University.

There is a major program at University College of Cape Breton where the religious studies and philosophy departments have been merged. The Acadia Department of Comparative Religion, while included in this study, was closed in 1995.

There are other degree programs and divinity schools in the region, which are not included in this review:
- There are three theological schools:[22] Queen's College, Memorial University of Newfoundland (Anglican), Acadia Divinity College in Wolfville, Nova Scotia (Baptist); and the Atlantic School of Theology in Halifax, an ecumenical professional school training priests and laity for the United, Anglican and Roman Catholic churches.
- At St. Francis Xavier there is a newly created, multidisciplinary program in Catholic Studies with one faculty member currently on a term contract funded by an endowment.

Memorial University of Newfoundland has the largest religious studies department in the region in terms of total enrolments, total number of full-time faculty and its degree programs, which include a full undergraduate major and honours, as well as the only master's degree in religious studies in the region. In the three Maritime provinces, the departments range in size from one to five full-time faculty members: one at Mount Saint Vincent University and at the University College of Cape Breton; two at the Université de Moncton and Dalhousie University; three at Mount Allison University and the University of Prince Edward Island; four at Saint Mary's and St. Thomas Universities, and five at St. Francis Xavier University.

With the exception of the Université de Moncton and the virtually unused major on the books at the University College of Cape Breton, all of the departments offer a major or a concentration in religious studies. If universities offer a minor option in a degree program, then the minor is normally available to students where there is a major in religious studies.

The State-of-the-Art Review

It is of the essence in this review of the state of the art of religious studies in the Atlantic region that the field is defined both by the history and culture of the universities and by the continuing evolution of the field of religious studies. Such a thesis implies that the state of the art of the field is affected by four principal factors: the founding heritage of the institution in which the religious studies program exists; the fate of that founding heritage as universities became publicly funded institutions and how that affected the place of religious studies in the degree requirements; the location of religious studies in the degree requirements of the institutions; and the evolution of its relation to the national and international state of the study of religions.

To take my own institution as an example: When it was a Jesuit-administered university, there was a department of theology with a faculty complement of eight. A theology or Bible course was a degree requirement within the structure of a Nova Scotian three-year degree program. When the institution became independent of the Archdiocese of Halifax, it immediately dropped the degree requirement of a course in theology and indeed, over the next four years, cut the department of religious studies from eight faculty to four. Until 1975 it even went so far as to deny students the opportunity to choose a religious studies course as a humanities elective as required for the first-year basic arts faculty requirements. The case for acceptance of a religious studies course to fulfill the basic degree requirements was made not with reference to the Christian heritage of the institution, but with reference to the national and international literature on the study of religion, which requires the comparative study of religions as an essential component of a department. Ultimately that argument prevailed and religious studies came to be recognized as a department like any other within the Faculty of Arts.

Taken together, then, the four factors outlined are the key to a description of the state of the art of religious studies in the Atlantic region. They provide the essential background for the formation of the major in religious studies and the honours and master's degree requirements in the field.

Notes

1 *An Act for the preservation and enhancement of multiculturalism in Canada* (C-18.7, c. 31). The *Multiculturalism Act* endorses the International Covenant on Civil and Political Rights, which "provides that persons belonging to ethnic, religious or linguistic minorities shall not be denied the right to enjoy their own culture, to profess and practise their own religion or to use their own language."
2 Cited in Harold Remus, William Closson James and Daniel Fraikin, *Religious Studies in Ontario: A State-of-the-Art Review* (Waterloo: Wilfrid Laurier University Press for the Canadian Corporation for Studies in Religion/Corporation canadienne des sciences religieuses), 32.
3 Edward Said, *Orientalism* (New York: Pantheon Books, 1978).
4 Cf. George P. Grant, "The Academic Study of Religion in Canada," in *Scholarship in Canada, 1967: Achievement and Outlook*, edited by R. J. Hubbard. Symposium presented to Section 11 of the Royal Society of Canada in 1967 (Toronto: University of Toronto Press, 1968) 59-68; also "Faith and the Multiversity," and "Research in the Humanities," in George P. Grant, *Technology and Justice* (Toronto: House of Anansi Press, 1986).
5 Remus et al., *Religious Studies in Ontario*, 19ff.
6 Ibid., 24-34.

7 Ibid., 33.
8 C. P. Anderson, *Guide to Religious Studies in Canada/Guide pour les études religieuses au Canada*. (Canadian Society for the Study of Religion/société canadienne pour l'étude de la religion, 1969) and *Guide to Religious Studies in Canada/Guide des sciences religieuses au Canada* (Corporation for the Publication of Academic Studies in Religion in Canada, 1972).
9 Anderson, *Guide*, 1969, v.
10 C. P. Anderson, "Religious Studies in English-Speaking Canada 1967-72," *Guide*, 1972, 7-19.
11 Michel-M. Campbell, "Notes sur la conjoncture des sciences religieuses au Canada français depuis 1967" in Anderson, *Guide*, 1972, 21-40.
12 Anderson, *Guide*, 1972, 13.
13 For example, see Rita M. Gross, *Buddhism After Patriarchy: A Feminist History, Analysis, and Reconstruction of Buddhism* (New York: State University of New York Press, 1993) and Wendy D. O'Flaherty, *Other Peoples' Myths: The Cave of Echoes* (Chicago: University of Chicago Press, 1995).
14 Anderson, *Guide*, 1972, 11.
15 Ibid.
16 Ibid.
17 Ibid., 14.
18 Ibid., 15.
19 It is not possible to determine whether or not Anderson was referring to courses that were two semesters in length or whether the statistic is a mixture of one-semester courses with two-semester courses.
20 Once again the statistic is difficult to interpret precisely if the enrolments were derived from a mixture of two-semester and one-semester courses. If some of the courses were two semesters in length, the student count, when combined with the number of students enroled in one-semester courses, would be inflated.
21 Sir Wilfred Grenfell College in Corner Brook, Newfoundland, is a semi-independent college. Religious studies has one faculty member there, but he is also identified as a member of the department at Memorial University in St. John's. Appointment, promotion and tenure decisions for the person at Grenfell College are made through the department in St. John's.
22 For the purposes of this review the focus is on undergraduate and graduate programs in religious studies.

2

The Religious Roots of the Universities in the Atlantic Provinces

by Tom Faulkner

> I'd rather have a department of pornography than a department of religion at this university.
> — Anonymous

Introduction

In the eighteenth century a remarkable transformation occurred in Western civilization. To a significant extent, intellectual life and religious life parted company, like two streams rising from the same source but flowing in opposite directions down the slopes of a continental divide. One current was Apollonian, understanding itself as cool and rational, carrying with it the universities; the other was Dionysian, given more to the romantic and the emotional, carrying with it the Christian churches. The bifurcation was not absolute, but it left religious intellectuals with a certain amount of explaining to do. In an earlier period Tertullian might be dismissed for asking what Athens has to do with Jerusalem—after all, people could say, he finished as a heretic. But for the past 200 years the situation has been different. It is true that not all modern intellectuals obey Voltaire's order, "Écrasez l'infâme!"[1] But then, neither has there been any doubt in anyone's mind that his synecdoche implies religion.

Western civilization continued to be both intellectual and religious despite this tendency to distinguish the rational mind from the pious heart, and even to set them over against each other. In the British and French colonies that were to become the Maritime provinces of Canada, however, people of European descent felt an urgent need to establish a familiar civilization in an unfamiliar and unfriendly wilderness, isolated by a sea voyage of six weeks to three months from its European original. That urgent need led people to put a great deal of energy and resources into founding religiously based universities as one of their first priorities. In 1789 the Revolution that was intended to realize Voltaire's hopes was being launched in France, but in the Maritimes the region's first institution of higher learning was being founded under the pious motto, "Deo legi regi gregi."[2] And settlers fresh off the boat from Scotland seemed almost as eager to open libraries that would presently mutate into divinity colleges as they were to get the first crop planted in Maritime soil.[3]

The Maritime region of Canada has seen a surprisingly large number of post-secondary institutions founded and maintained over the years—so surprising that educational reformers regularly raise the possibility of cutting down the sheer number of them through amalgamation. Sometimes the reformers have succeeded in their aim; more often they have been frustrated by those who favour maintaining their institutional independence. Nevertheless the history of Maritime universities and colleges is a history of progressive secularization and merger. By contrast the history of higher education in Newfoundland constitutes yet one more proof that Newfoundland is a province *pas comme les autres*.

I would like to suggest that there are six institutional clusters of universities and colleges that can be helpfully considered together:
- the Halifax cluster (5)
- the Nova Scotian Catholic cluster (2)
- the Maritime Baptist cluster (4)
- the New Brunswick cluster (4)
- the Prince Edward Island cluster (1 hybrid)
- the Newfoundland cluster (3)

The Halifax Cluster

Halifax is the metropolitan centre of the Canadian Maritimes, and it exerts a seemingly magnetic pull on everything around it, including universities and colleges. Founded in 1789, King's College was established first in Windsor, Nova Scotia, forty kilometres away from Halifax. But when it faced bankruptcy in 1923, the Carnegie Foundation successfully persuaded the university to move to Halifax to reside on the edge of the Dalhousie campus, in return for paying

King's outstanding debts. The lesson that university federations are generally not money-savers, but instead are possible only when the partners are enticed into cooperation by increased grants seems to have been lost on provincial policy-makers, who continue today to propose rationalization through consolidation without cash bonuses.

Dalhousie University also started as a rural institution: its original incarnation, the Pictou Academy, was established 100 kilometres from the present site of the university, and its founder was the Reverend Thomas McCulloch, a Presbyterian minister. Officially Dalhousie is a secular university, but that condition stemmed less from convictions rooted in the Enlightenment than from the fact that McCulloch was unsuccessful in persuading the Methodists, Baptists and Anglicans to merge their denominational colleges into one provincial university capable of attracting public funding. When Dalhousie was founded in 1818, its initial funding came from government sources—the proceeds of a raid on an American customs house during the War of 1812—but the necessity of keeping the government from appearing partial to Presbyterians ensured that Dalhousie would be nominally independent of any church. Informally, however, the Presbyterian connection at Dalhousie has been surprisingly long-lived. Until the end of the 1940s the university president was always a Presbyterian or United Church divine; until the late 1970s the only people named to senior administrative posts also happened to be United Church laymen of Presbyterian descent.

Thomas McCulloch also founded Pine Hill Divinity Hall, recognizing as he did the utility of training clergy on this side of the Atlantic rather than depending upon Scottish seminaries to generate the necessary recruits. Through a series of migrations Pine Hill found its way to Halifax, where in 1975 it became the Atlantic School of Theology (hereinafter "AST"), a fusion of three seminaries (Anglican, Catholic and United Church) preparing candidates for ordered Christian ministry. In the early 1990s the provincial government again considered the virtues of amalgamating universities, particularly within the Halifax metropolitan region, but AST declared itself opposed to being added to Dalhousie University, as did the Nova Scotia College of Art and Design. The Technical University of Nova Scotia was, however, merged with Dalhousie.

The Atlantic Institute of Education, another free-standing post-secondary institution, had already been merged with Dalhousie a decade earlier. By 1997 a metropolitan region that had contained seven independent institutions of higher learning had seen the seven become five. Two of these remaining campuses were formerly Catholic universities specializing in undergraduate education.

Mount Saint Vincent University was founded as a women's academy in 1873 by the Sisters of Charity of Saint Vincent de Paul and first granted degrees in 1914 through an affiliation with Dalhousie University. This cooperation across denominational boundaries is somewhat surprising, considering that Dalhousie's founder was a Presbyterian divine who had written theological texts hostile to the Catholic tradition: *Popery Condemned* (1808) and *Popery Again Condemned* (1810). But by 1914 the Reverend Thomas McCulloch had been dead for seventy years, and Canadians at war were well disposed to grant support to an institution that would continue to the present day to hold the reputation of being the one Canadian university that particularly serves the interests of women.

What is more surprising is that the Sisters of Charity who maintained the university did not enter into a cooperative effort with Saint Mary's University, the Catholic college that had been granting baccalaureate degrees to men in Halifax since 1852. But the times were not propitious: Saint Mary's had been struggling to survive for half a century when it was taken over by the Irish Christian Brothers in 1913, and furthermore there was a historical rivalry between the two religious orders, both of which were involved in teaching. The Sisters apparently found it easier to cooperate with Dalhousie's secularized Presbyterians than with the Christian Brothers until 1925 when Mount Saint Vincent University was provincially chartered as an independent university. Meanwhile in 1940 the Jesuits succeeded the Christian Brothers as the managers of Saint Mary's University, and they remained in charge until 1970 when Saint Mary's was laicized by the provincial government.

Saint Mary's University remains proudly independent, however, and is fiercely opposed to amalgamation with Dalhousie, whose campus border lies closer to Saint Mary's than parts of the Dalhousie campus lie to each other. Why has Saint Mary's remained independent? When bankruptcy threatened following the Second World War, the Archdiocese of Halifax mortgaged the properties of parish churches in large part to help the Jesuits keep the campus open, despite a direct order from the Vatican not to risk the loss of Halifax's Catholic sanctuaries.[4] The commitment to maintain Saint Mary's as an independent university has deep roots in the memories of its graduates.

The Nova Scotian Catholic Cluster

Founded in 1890 by the Eudist Fathers as part of the *renaissance acadienne*, Université Sainte-Anne has remained at Church Point, Nova Scotia, and was secularized by the provincial government in 1971, just one year after Saint Mary's University in Halifax was laicized. This small French-speaking university has never had a department of religious studies, but its ties to a minority community with a strongly Catholic character are clear.

Equally clear are the ties between the Catholic community of Nova Scotia and St. Francis Xavier University, a college chartered in 1853 in Antigonish, Nova Scotia, by a bishop rather than by a religious order. The special connection to the Catholic community was further strengthened by the Antigonish Movement headed by Father Moses Coady, binding St. Francis Xavier to the farms and fishing villages of eastern Nova Scotia through the university's extension program.

St. Francis Xavier spawned a secondary campus in Sydney on Cape Breton Island in 1951, and this offspring was joined with the Nova Scotia Eastern Institute of Technology to become the independent, degree-granting University College of Cape Breton in 1982. The University College of Cape Breton is remarkable for the formal connection between itself and the provincial government's Department of Education, which has an influence over its curriculum that some faculty members consider dangerous to university autonomy and academic freedom.

If the secular government appears to some to pose a threat to academic freedom at the University College of Cape Breton, the faculty of St. Francis Xavier are demonstrably unconcerned over possible church influence on their Catholic campus today. When the papal encyclical *Veritatis Splendor* was issued in 1993, it triggered vigorous opposition from seventy Catholic theologians and ethicists holding posts in Quebec universities, but it was barely noticed at St. Francis Xavier where little discussion was heard and no alarms were raised.[5]

The Maritime Baptist Cluster

The disengagement between Catholic educators and the Church hierarchy has been a dance whose pattern is gradual and, to a large extent, graceful. This stands in contrast to the pattern of the dance in which Baptist educators and the Baptist Church authorities have engaged—perhaps because the magisterium is clearer in Catholic circles, while the peculiar importance that Baptists attach to "liberty" makes the relationship between educator and hierarchy more difficult for them than it is for Catholics.

No fewer than three institutions of higher learning have been generated by Maritime Baptists, a number far out of proportion to their share of the general population of the region. In 1828 Baptists who included in their number some former Presbyterians from Halifax founded Horton Academy in the town that was later to take the name of Wolfville, Nova Scotia. In 1841 it became

Acadia College and in 1844 it began to offer studies in divinity, even admitting women to the undergraduate programs in 1880. The college became Acadia University in 1884 and offered its first divinity degrees in 1911. In 1966 provincial legislation reduced the proportion of members of the Board of Governors appointed by the Baptist Convention from 100 percent to 39 percent, and within two years the Baptist Convention made the decision to establish an independent degree-granting institution under its auspices. The institution was named Acadia Divinity College, and it was primarily intended to continue the education for Baptist ministry that had once been conducted within Acadia University.[6]

Meanwhile, what had started as a Bible college catering to the needs of Maritime Baptists who harboured some concerns that Acadia University might be becoming too worldly became the Atlantic Baptist University in 1996. The Atlantic Baptist University, located in Moncton, continues to enjoy a friendly but informal relationship with Acadia University and with Acadia Divinity College, sending a significant number of its students on to those two institutions.

One might include a fourth university in this Baptist cluster, if one expands the category of "Baptist" to "evangelical Protestant": St. Stephen's University was chartered in 1998 and seeks to provide a baccalaureate education that is largely Protestant, and useful to those wishing to enter church work in conservative denominations and extra-ecclesial organizations such as Varsity Christian Fellowship. It operates out of two small buildings in St. Stephens, New Brunswick, and has no department of religious studies; but religion provides the key element in its curriculum of liberal arts and ministry preparation.

The Baptist or evangelical universities have been more eager than most to affirm their distinctive character within a secular university system. But that has not kept them from participating actively in the larger system. It was Watson Kirkconnell, a distinguished Baptist layman and president of Acadia University, who served as the architect of the first system of grants from provincial governments in the Maritime provinces to universities. Until his day, such grants often came with political strings attached; on his initiative the grants were awarded on the basis of a formula that prevented, or at least minimized, political interference.[7]

The New Brunswick Cluster

The University of New Brunswick was chartered as the leading provincial university in 1859, but it developed out of King's College, a New Brunswick rival to the King's College founded by Anglicans in Windsor, Nova Scotia. Interestingly, the New Brunswick rival spawned a provincial university whose charter explicitly forbids "the teaching of religion"—in 1859 widely understood to be a reference to sectarian Anglicanism, but in the twentieth century interpreted as referring to all forms of religion. Consequently, the University of New Brunswick, the province's largest institution of higher learning, has no department of religious studies.

However, following the Second World War, a small Catholic institution named St. Thomas University, relocated to the edge of the University of New Brunswick campus, where its strong program in religious studies attracts considerable interest from University of New Brunswick students. St. Thomas University originated as a secondary school founded by the Roman Catholic Bishop in Chatham, New Brunswick, during the 1860s, becoming a degree-granting institution in 1934. Its federated status gives it a formal relationship to the University of New Brunswick without destroying its independent identity.[8]

French-language higher education is centered in the three campuses of the Université de Moncton, whose principal campus is located in Moncton, New Brunswick. Its oldest roots go back to Collège Saint-Joseph, established in Memramcook in 1864 by the fathers of the Congrégation de Sainte-Croix[9]—the same religious order that founded Notre Dame in Indiana. The university's charter sets a minimum for the number of faculty members who can constitute a department, and hence religious studies has been merged with philosophy in the Faculty of Arts.

Mount Allison University originated as a boys' academy, founded in 1839 by Methodists in Sackville, New Brunswick. It became a college open to men of all religious traditions in 1858 and graduated the first woman baccalaureate in the British Empire in 1875. An unusually fine institutional history written by John Reid tells the story of the decades-long tug-of-war between faculty at Mount Allison who preferred to cultivate an undergraduate program that emphasized high academic achievement by a few and United Church supporters of the institution who preferred to see the university serve the community by opening its doors to everyone who wanted an education.[10]

The Prince Edward Island Cluster

The University of Prince Edward Island is a public, non-denominational institution that is the product of a union in 1969 of St. Dunstan's University (originating as a Catholic college founded in 1855) and Prince of Wales College (founded as a non-denominational college in 1834 but widely regarded by Islanders as "the Protestant college"). The tensions between some Catholics and Protestants over what might appear to be the region's most successful amalgamation in higher education may be gauged by reference to a short book describing the event called *Church Politics and Education in Canada*. It was written by Frank MacKinnon, a distinguished educator who was the outgoing principal of Prince of Wales College at the time of the amalgamation. MacKinnon intemperately characterized the merger as the worst example of Catholic malice since the Inquisition.[11]

The Newfoundland Cluster

Religion and higher education took a different course in Newfoundland than they did in the Maritime provinces. Until 1925 the only institution of higher education in "Britain's oldest colony" was Queen's College, a theological seminary founded in 1841 by the Anglican Church. As a gesture of Anglican commitment to ecumenical theological education, Queen's was closed when A.S.T. opened in 1975, but Queen's reopened in 1982, then entered into formal cooperation with A.S.T. to offer joint programs in the late 1980s.

Considering the distinctive history of education in Newfoundland, it is not surprising to see a denominational school flourish for such a long period. For, until the provincial referendum of 1995 produced a majority of 54 percent in favour of ending church control of the provincial school system,[12] the public schools in Newfoundland were managed by twenty-seven denominational school boards whose religious identities were protected by the Terms of Union that brought Newfoundland into the Canadian Confederation in 1948. For centuries Newfoundlanders had been accustomed to their schools being run by churches on behalf of the government. When it finally came time to found a university in the province, the economies of scale dictated that this keystone to a thoroughly denominational school system must be a single, non-denominational, provincial institution of higher learning. The mouldbreaking foundation of Memorial University of Newfoundland was made possible in part by naming the institution in honour of the Newfoundland soldiers who had died in the First World War. In particular Newfoundlanders remembered the incredibly bloody fate of the Royal Newfoundland Regiment at the Battle of the Somme, when hundreds of men went over the top and died under machine-gun fire within a few minutes.[13] Only a human catastrophe of such magnitude could furnish the symbol necessary to legitimate Newfoundland's first non-denominational school.

The tenacity of the religious tradition in Newfoundland education is suggested by the fact that, when Memorial University of Newfoundland opened a second campus on the other side of the province in 1975, the new institution was named after a famous Christian missionary, Sir Wilfred Grenfell.

Notes

1. "Smash the disreputable!"
2. King's College—now the University of King's College—is the oldest institution of post-secondary education in Canada. Its motto translates thus: "For God, the law, the king, the people."
3. Laurie C. C. Stanley, *The Well-Watered Garden: The Presbyterian Church in Cape Breton, 1798-1860* (Sydney, NS: University College of Cape Breton Press, 1983).
4. J. Brian Hanington, *Every Popish Person: The Story of Roman Catholicism in Nova Scotia and the Church of Halifax, 1604-1984* (Halifax, NS: Archdiocese of Halifax, 1984), 212-7.
5. President James Lawless, Private communication, St. Francis Xavier University, October 1994.
6. *Acadia Divinity College Calendar*, 1983-84, 5.
7. Tom Sinclair-Faulkner, "Watson Kirkconnell and the Practice of Tolerance." *Touchstone* 5/1 (January 1987): 40-42.
8. *Catholic New Times*, 4 December 1988, 9.
9. *Université de Moncton 1982-1984. Renseignements généraux*, 21.
10. John G. Reid, *Mount Allison University: A History to 1963*. 2 Vols. (Toronto: University of Toronto Press, 1984).
11. Frank MacKinnon, *Church Politics and Education in Canada: The P.E.I. Experience* (Calgary, AB: Detselig Enterprises, 1995).
12. John DeMont in *Maclean's*, 18 September 1995.
13. John Keegan, *The Face of Battle* (New York: Viking Press, 1976), 369 and passim.

3
Departments and Degree Programs in Religious Studies

> The study of religion is a meditation on cultural difference, the deep differences in what is ultimately valued. — Stephen D. Crites

Religious studies departments plan the requirements for a major, minor and honours degree program. They also plan how their subject can be developed and integrated into the general degree requirements of the humanities and social sciences of the Faculty of Arts and the university as a whole. The starting point for an understanding of the state of the art of religious studies is a comprehension of the place of religious studies within the universities of which it is a part and of each religious studies department's contribution to the Bachelor of Arts degree.

The Formative Traditions of Universities

Religious studies is a hotly contested field with many subjects, methods, assumptions, philosophies and theologies. No department in the Atlantic region ignores that fact. What departments are doing in their respective programs is defined by several formative elements:
- the department's faculty, each with specific scholarly training;
- the university's history and often very different contemporary culture;
- the scholarly field of religious studies both nationally and internationally; and
- the community at large.

These four formative elements are consistent with the 1990 study "scribed" by Stephen Crites, who observed that our consultants amply confirmed our initial impression of the enormous programmatic diversity in this field. In the details of specific programs the local ethos is of overriding importance: how a department developed over the past few decades, what specialties are represented on its faculty, how the student body is constituted, what the institutional traditions and expectations are, and the like. If we, or the AAC [American Association of Colleges], were ever tempted to think that we might prescribe programmatic details for the entire field, our consultations would have crushed such an illusion.[1]

These observations about the diversity of the degree programs offered by departments of religious studies reflect a predominant contextual characteristic of the departments of religious studies in the Atlantic region. With the exception of the Department of Comparative Religion at Dalhousie University and the Department of Religious Studies at Memorial University of Newfoundland, every department of religious studies has evolved out of a department of theology, or had its origin in a university founded by a religious community or church.

The emergence of religious studies departments was dependent upon the vision of those faculty who looked beyond the theological, quasi-seminary styles of curricula. They saw the necessity for undergraduate programs in publicly funded institutions which were not tied to any particular Christian denomination or Christian theological perspective. There was risk in this vision because the theology programs frequently had large enrolments. Students were obligated to include courses in biblical studies, church history or Christian theology as part of their undergraduate degree programs in the religious universities. The transition to public institutions and to religious studies removed that advantage from the newly constructed religious studies departments.

The department at the University of Prince Edward Island provides a textbook example of this process. In the late 1960s the province's colleges were united to form the publicly funded University of Prince Edward Island. In 1969, in the new institutional setting, the religious studies curriculum was shaped by the clerical faculty from St. Dunstan's University and the faculty from Prince of Wales College. The first step was to make the faculty ecumenical, which in reality meant adding to the Roman Catholic professor one who was Protestant. With a retirement from among the original faculty, it was possible to add a biblical scholar trained at McMaster University's department of religious studies, where, in addition to a specialization in biblical studies, graduate students were required to minor in an Asian religious tradition. This allowed the program at the University of Prince Edward Island to expand its offerings in biblical studies and in world religions. With a further retirement in 1991, the department hired a person specializing in East Asian religious traditions. Since 1991 the department has remained stable at three full-time faculty. As the faculty are members of a religious studies department, religious affiliation has disappeared as a criterion for hiring.

In the Prince Edward Island example, we see a three-step process in the evolution of religious studies departments: the existence of an exclusively Christian faculty; movement to an ecumenical faculty; and the hiring of faculty specializing in world religions. Departments still reflect these successive stages in the composition of their faculty and the content of their curriculum. These stages reflect the local history and community that supported the university. They further illustrate the ongoing engagement of the faculty with the debates about the fundamental characteristics of religious studies as both multidisciplinary and multicultural in focus.

A departmental study done in 1989 in preparation for an external review of religious studies at the University of Prince Edward Island prepared the ground for an appointment following a faculty retirement. The report stated: "The particular shape of the religious studies program arises from a blending of the conventional definition of the discipline and the special talents and interests of the department's members."[2] It is significant that the report then defined the relationship between the department's curriculum and the conception of religious studies as an international field of study:

> Most religious studies programs today attempt to address four broad areas, which could be defined as follows: Biblical Studies; Western Religious Tradition (primarily Christian thought and history); Eastern and/or Comparative Religion; and Religion in Modern Society (usually within a social-scientific framework).[3]

The report then went on to identify each of the three members of faculty by name and their general areas of contribution to the courses in the curriculum so defined.

The rationale for what the department does in its curriculum now is determined by several factors. There is the limitation imposed by the number of faculty. With only three faculty, the department must design its curriculum to permit each professor to teach his or her specialization and supplement those courses with a selection of others designed to cover the field of religious studies. In the departmental study, therefore, the strength of the curriculum was understood to be its breadth; its weakness was understood to be its lack of depth, particularly at an advanced level of study for majors.

That is to say, courses and requirements for a major or concentration are integrated into the larger service commitment of the department. It is virtually impossible with three faculty and the demands of the university degree requirements to focus religious studies around a curriculum principally designed for majors. Rather, aiming for breadth in the curriculum allows the introduction of elective courses oriented toward the undergraduate population as a whole. The department, in turn, gains substantial enrolments in its courses.

The history of religious studies at the University of Prince Edward Island also illustrates a common fact about religious studies in the Atlantic region. Substantial change in what constitutes the breadth of the department's course offerings can be achieved only as a department is allowed either to add faculty to its complement or to replace retiring faculty. Only with new appointments can a department change the fields of specialization that make up the department. In the first new appointment in the department at the University of Prince Edward Island, the person hired was trained not in theology, but in a religious studies department in Canada. He had a specialization in biblical studies and had studied world religions at the graduate level. In 1991, a second appointment, again from a Canadian graduate school, permitted the employment of a specialist in the Chinese and Japanese religious traditions. This not only strengthened the courses in comparative religious studies but allowed the development and strengthening of an Asian studies program as well.

The pattern at the University of Prince Edward Island is borne out in almost all of the departments in the region, with variations to be expected as the departments evolve in their particular institutional and provincial settings. Departments rethink most clearly and decisively what religious studies is to be at their institution at those moments in their history when new appointments are made. The comparative, multireligious and multidisciplinary character of religious studies as a subject plays a very significant role in the case made for new faculty. In addition to the perceived requirements of the discipline, the individual universities exercise a decisive influence on the priorities for new appointments.

In what follows, then, I want to look at various departments of religious studies to establish a case-by-case account of what their priorities for religious studies appear to be and measure those priorities against what I am arguing is the general pattern illustrated by the department at the University of Prince Edward Island.

Religious Studies in Roman Catholic Universities[4]

There are four universities in the Atlantic region that were founded either by Roman Catholic dioceses or by religious orders. St. Thomas University in Fredericton, St. Francis Xavier University in Antigonish and Saint Mary's

University in Halifax were founded by local Roman Catholic dioceses. Mount Saint Vincent University in Halifax was founded by the Sisters of Charity.

St. Francis Xavier and St. Thomas universities both maintain by charter strong links with their local diocese and the Catholic tradition. St. Francis Xavier's Department of Religious Studies was the last department in the region to change its name from theology to religious studies. Its curriculum remains very theological in its structure and content. In contrast, St. Thomas University's department has moved dramatically to create areas of study including a very strong curriculum in Islam, Mi'Kmaq[5] and Maliseet religions, Hinduism and other world religions, while maintaining Christian, particularly Roman Catholic courses serving the local student constituencies and the Fredericton community.

Mount Saint Vincent University had until 1998 a religious studies department in which the emphasis was on biblical studies, explicitly understood as the Old and New Testaments, and on a Christian focus for the teaching of comparative religion. Since its secularization, Mount Saint Vincent University has become the only university in Canada to identify itself as dedicated primarily to the education of women. Shortly after this, the first of three retirements of the faculty in religious studies occurred. These resulted in the reduction of the department to one full-time faculty member, whose specialization was religion in Canada and gender and religion.

Of the four universities, Saint Mary's has adopted a respectful but distant relationship with its founding tradition. While the archbishop of Halifax remains the university's chancellor and its charter describes the university as a "Christian University," the actual role of that definition in the university's decision-making is marginal. For the religious studies department the transition to a public institution meant the loss of four faculty between 1969 and 1975 leaving a continuing faculty complement of four full-time professors.

It is fair to say that Saint Mary's University's evolution as a public institution and the retirements at Mount Saint Vincent University in the wake of secularization brought about major crises for religious studies. In light of these facts, I shall review the departments at Saint Mary's and Mount Saint Vincent first, then St. Francis Xavier and St. Thomas universities.

Saint Mary's University

Saint Mary's was founded in 1802 as a boys' high school. While there were gaps in the continuity of its educational programs, it was legally recognized by the province of Nova Scotia in 1841. From 1913 to 1940 the Christian Brothers of Ireland administered and taught the academic programs of Saint

Mary's, and from 1940 until 1970 the Society of Jesus managed the university for the Archdiocese of Halifax. The legislature of the province of Nova Scotia enacted the current charter of the university in 1970, placing the ownership of the university in the hands of a Board of Governors and academic supervision with the Senate.

While under the leadership of the Society of Jesus, the university's theology department offered required courses on the Bible and theology to undergraduates. After 1970 the theology department saw the required courses dismantled as degree requirements. The department responded with a planned restructuring of its curriculum and renamed the department as a religious studies department. In the newly conceived department there were three areas of focus: "Religion in Western Civilization," "Religion in Contemporary Society" and "History of Religions (Comparative Religion)."

No sooner were the new department name and curriculum put in place than the religious studies department became the focus of an administrative decision to dismiss several faculty in the university and in religious studies in particular. The debate that ensued led to an external review of the department, which affirmed the new curriculum as appropriate for a public university. In the midst of this controversy seeds were planted that resulted in Saint Mary's University becoming the first unionized university in Canada. Unionization, however, did not prevent the reduction of the religious studies faculty complement.

Reduced enrolments frequently justify the reduction of faculty complements. Reductions in enrolment can also be planned. Thus, the arts faculty decided that religious studies courses would not count at all toward the general Bachelor of Arts requirements for students in their first year. The department's courses could only count as electives in a student's degree program. Predictably enrolments plummeted, creating the conditions under which the administration could reduce faculty in the department. Despite the efforts of the department's faculty to make major changes in curriculum and pedagogy, by 1973, the departmental allotment had been reduced to six faculty and by 1975, further reduced to four, its current allotment. It took intensive lobbying before religious studies courses were included as part of the humanities requirement for first-year students. By 1975, then, the courses of the religious studies department were treated on par with those of all other humanities and social science departments in the arts faculty.

The members of the department of theology had initiated the ecumenical phase of the transition from a strictly Roman Catholic faculty prior to the university becoming a public institution. Three of the eight faculty in 1970 were not members of the Roman Catholic Church. Among them was a new faculty member, Dr. Manabu Waida from the University of Chicago, trained by Mircea Eliade in comparative world religions. In the attempts to cut faculty in the department, it was the newer, untenured faculty, including the comparative religions expert, whose positions were at greatest risk. By 1975 there were three faculty whose appointments had originated in the theology department and one who graduated from a graduate program in religious studies in Canada.

From 1970 onward the mandate of the department was to offer a major and an honours and to provide service or elective courses within the university's degree programs. Students from the faculties of commerce, arts and science could take electives in religious studies. From the founding of the first multidisciplinary program in Asian studies in the early 1970s, religious studies, with at least one member of faculty trained in comparative religion, provided cross-listed courses in Asian studies. With the development of new programs in international development studies, Atlantic Canada studies, women's studies and environmental studies, the department contributes courses and faculty time, including supervision of honours and masters degree theses.

In the late 1980s the department revised its organization of courses to reflect more accurately the interests and specializations of its four faculty. The curriculum continued to have three areas, but they were renamed. The first was Comparative Religion, defined as the study of the specific religious traditions, but not including Christianity. The second was the Christian Tradition, defined to acknowledge the historic role of the Roman Catholic Church in the university and the community. This area is supported by external funding for an unpublicized chair in religious studies. To date the external funding has donated $1.5 million to the university in equal support of the chair and the Roman Catholic chaplaincy. The third curriculum area was called "Thematic Studies in Religion" and included courses that set out to compare the views of various religious traditions and non-religious views on issues of contemporary society. It also includes courses on the various methodologies in the study of religions, ranging through psychology, sociology, anthropology, classics and the hermeneutical debates within the study of religions itself. This threefold structure for the curriculum continues at Saint Mary's to this day.

In 1993, the department made its first new appointment since 1975. With the retirement of Dr. Emero Stiegman, the department advertised for a position in religion and culture and appointed a new member of faculty, Dr. Anne Marie Dalton, to develop the area of religion and ecology as well as offer courses on gender, development studies and religion. In 1995, Dr. Lawrence Murphy, the last Jesuit teaching at Saint Mary's, retired. His replacement, was Dr. Magi Abdul-Masih, hired to teach courses on Christianity and Roman Catholicism. With these appointments, the department maintained an important continuity with its past while transforming the department's gender balance and opening new areas of cooperation with various coordinated programs in the university. In addition to contributing courses in Asian Studies, and Atlantic Canada studies, the two new appointees offered courses in conjunction with environmental science, international development studies and women's studies. The effect on the department of two retirement replacements has been to put the crises of the 1970s finally to rest. The department also extended its offerings in Islamic studies by inviting Dr. Jamal Badawi of the Management Department to offer courses each year, with the hope that he might be transferred full-time to Religious studies.

The Religious Studies department at Saint Mary's finally appears to be confident of its place in the university and is looking forward to new possibilities of expansion and cooperation with colleagues at Mount Saint Vincent and elsewhere.

Mount Saint Vincent University ("The Mount")

Mount Saint Vincent University[6] was founded as an academy in 1873 by the Sisters of Charity. Its original task was to educate novices. By 1914 the mandate had expanded and an agreement with Dalhousie University permitted two years of post-secondary education at the Mount to be followed by the completion of the degree at Dalhousie. In 1925 the Mount became provincially chartered as a degree-granting institution called Mount Saint Vincent College. In 1966 the legislature passed the current charter, which changed the name of the university to its present form and instituted a lay Board of Governors to oversee the university along with the corporation of the Sisters of Charity. The ownership of the university passed to the Board of Governors from the Sisters of Charity in 1988.

With the change in 1988 came the current mission statement of the university:

> Mount Saint Vincent University is concerned primarily with the education of women. It provides a strong liberal arts and science core and selected professional disciplines. It is dedicated to promoting academic excellence and an environment characterized by a Catholic tradition and a high degree of personalized education. The major objectives of the university are: ... the continuing development—intellectual, moral spiritual, physical—of those sharing in its life; and service to the community through its programs, resources, and facilities.[7]

The focus on the education of women gives the Mount a unique place among the universities in Canada. It is the only university dedicated primarily to the post-secondary education of women. In turn that mission is seen to be supported by the Catholic tradition as represented by the founding order, the Sisters of Charity.

In a departmental study prepared for an external review, the religious studies department identified its history and academic mandate very closely with the categories of the university's mission statement. In doing so the department saw its own history and development focused around the teaching of the Christian scriptures and theological, if not pastorally grounded, courses. The focus had derived originally from the department of theology and was carried forward into a religious studies department which retained all three of the theological faculty. From 1970 onward the focus of the department was on biblical studies and the Christian tradition in particular, but with a shift in methodological approach. The study asserted that a deliberate and conscious effort was made to integrate "diverse methodologies and specialties into a relatively coherent program devoted to the newly maturing study of religion/ Christianity."[8]

In its argument, the department contended that the field of religious studies incorporated the study of Christianity as well as that of other religious traditions. The general task was to "understand religions on their own terms."[9] As a result the focus in the department could continue to be on Christianity, since that was the tradition in which the faculty were trained. The report argued that the Christian focus of the curriculum did not need to be understood any longer as doing "theology" but as an attempt to understand the religious experience under consideration.[10]

The Mount's distinction between theology and courses taught about Christianity in religious studies was grounded in studies that have animated the meetings of the Canadian Society for the Study of Religion/Société canadienne pour l'étude de la religion and the Canadian journal *Studies in Religion/ Sciences Religieuses* and the state-of-the-art reviews of religious studies in Quebec and Ontario. In making its case the department carried forward a debate that has been a constant in the field for the better part of the last thirty years. Those who see no place for theological reflection in religious studies departments and advocate only the methodologies of a humane, scientific study of religion are ranged against those who insist that the study of Christianity, and within that study, Christian theological reflection can and should be a constituent part of the overall curriculum of a religious studies department. It is clear that in the study at the Mount these academic debates played a role in the process of defining the study of religions for the department of religious studies. At the same time, the proposal to continue a Christian focus in the curriculum made the department much narrower than it needed to be. Furthermore, it is clear that the department maintained a pastoral concern for its students both inside and outside its courses. At the Mount the effect of the training and orientation of the three faculty who were in religious studies from the 1960s to their retirements in the 1990s meant that there was an emphasis on the Roman Catholic tradition in the academic content of the academic courses and in the non-credit courses offered each year for laity.

In its study the department argued that "if the program has a focus or a centre, it is "Christianity and Personal Development."[11] Such a focus was tied to the university's mission statement which, as we have seen, speaks of the continuing development of the intellectual, moral and spiritual qualities of the community. Since there were only three faculty, all of whom were hired into a theology department, the focus so described conformed to their respective academic training and gave to the department's curriculum a clear, but narrow, sense of direction.

In the report by the external review that followed the departmental study, the reviewers agreed with the focus of the department and commended it for its endeavours. Unfortunately the reviewers were drawn principally from theological schools, and there was very little by way of input from the perspective of the debates in religious studies that could help the department plan for the necessary changes required to broaden the focus of the department.

Since 1996 Mount Saint Vincent's Department of Religious Studies has faced a crisis. The department has seen all of its original faculty members retire, one in 1995, one in 1996 and a third at the end of December 1998. To date only one of those three faculty has been replaced. Whether or not additional faculty will be hired remains an open question. What is starkly evident is that retirements, combined with the university's decision not to replace departing faculty, have been disastrous for religious studies. The ongoing financial crises of universities in Nova Scotia have resulted in a situation in which religious studies is at risk at the Mount. One faculty member, no matter how talented, cannot deliver a whole program for students. Even the increasing number of students in the past two years has not yet been a sufficient reason to rebuild the department, in the face of the competing claims of other departments for more faculty.

Recognizing the danger inherent in three closely timed retirements, the departments of religious studies from Saint Mary's University and the Mount began conversations in 1995 that led to a formal agreement to work together to offer their programs.[12]

Most of the universities in metropolitan Halifax in the mid-1990s were looking at ways to cooperate in order to forestall a government-initiated amalgamation. This was particularly true of the smaller universities, such as the Mount and Saint Mary's and the other specialized universities in the city such as the Nova Scotia College of Art and Design. In a report written by the deans of arts of the metropolitan universities, religious studies was identified as at risk, due to several retirements both at Mount Saint Vincent and at Saint Mary's,[13] and the report therefore selected religious studies as the *only* academic program in metropolitan Halifax that could be closed. The report was quickly repudiated at both the Mount and Saint Mary's, but it made the discussions about cooperation appear to be very important. The agreement between the two departments to cooperate was viewed as a way to ensure the continuing viability of their respective programs.

At the heart of the agreement was the goal of harmonizing programs at the two universities and exchanging faculty to teach courses at the two institutions. To date the agreement has not had any significant implementation although it remains an active possibility. It is very difficult to develop exchanges of faculty time and teaching when there is only one member of faculty in religious studies at the Mount. The difficulty is further complicated by the commuting distance between the two universities.

What is important for the future of the department at the Mount is the most recent redefinition of its mandate and stated purposes. The department is now staffed by Dr. Randi Warne, whose training is in religious studies, not theology, and whose particular specialization is in the issues of gender and the study of religions in Canada. As a result of this new appointment, the description of the department's mandate has been dramatically changed to one that locates the study of all religious traditions in the context of historical and gender studies, and places greater emphasis on the methodologies of the study of religions.

This change in direction creates the potential for several important initiatives. First, it situates the department within the mandate of the university as primarily a women's university. Secondly, it reopens the possibility of increased cooperation with the department of religious studies at Saint Mary's because Dr. Warne's specializations have no parallel at Saint Mary's. Thirdly, it places the department clearly and strongly in the religious studies field. Whether or not Mount Saint Vincent University will recognize the significant changes as sufficient reason to rebuild the department of religious studies remains to be seen.

St. Francis Xavier University

At St. Francis Xavier the origin of the study of Christianity dates back to 1853 and the founding of the university and the seminary that was to train clergy for the diocese. The seminary closed in 1861 but courses in theology continued to be offered in the university. However, the courses had a somewhat checkered history until 1908-09, when the university began to require students to take courses on Christian doctrine for their degree and to pass examinations on the subject. The courses differed from the norm for courses offered by other departments, however: fewer class hours were required and the results in the courses were not counted as part of a student's average for the degree.

In 1964 a new theology requirement was implemented, which required all Roman Catholic students to take two full-year theology courses as part of their degree. Normally these courses were to be taken during the first two years of degree study. In 1966 the university listed "Theology" in the calendar and subsequently moved to establish a department by that name.

Preparations for changing the name of the department from "theology" to "religious studies" were laid in 1993 through a formal, external review of the department. The full report of the reviewers was not released for this review. Rather, a summary was provided by the department chair, Burton MacDonald, in the form of a memo regarding the change of name of the department[14]. The external review noted that a religious studies department normally offers courses on the social-scientific study of religions and on world religions. In addition to these types of courses, the department should offer "extensive offerings in biblical studies and in philosophical theology."[15] The reviewers invited the department to review its orientation in its teaching and courses:

> The department, at the request of the ARP [Academic Review Panel] was asked to consider, in its deliberations on its orientation, the point that the distinction between a Department of Theology and a Department of Religious Studies is not made primarily by the topics covered but by the vantage point from which they are covered. Theology is usually done within a confessional setting, by people who are reflecting on and explicating beliefs which they openly profess and hold in common. Religious Studies is, by definition, more disinterested with regard to confessional commitments and examines religious beliefs and practices as an aspect of human culture.[16]

The fact that the Academic Review Panel reviewing the Department of Theology at St. Francis Xavier in 1993 asked the department to implement such a reorientation indicates the centrality of the university's and the department's identity as a Roman Catholic university. This is confirmed in the 1993 university calendar in which the university's newly formulated strategic plan states:

> The strategic plan confirms the Catholic character of the University and points to ways in which we will build on our Catholic heritage. At the same time, it re-states our policy of openness to students and staff of all religious backgrounds, of intellectual freedom, and the students, faculty and staff are treated equally regardless of religious conviction.[17]

In such a university the theology department appropriately held to the view from the 1960s to the early 1990s that its role was primarily theological, "the rational reflection on Roman Catholic tradition and practice"[18] as Burton MacDonald phrased it in his memo.

What followed from the external review was an argument for a change in name to clarify for students what the department was about and to clarify for the university that a change in name to "Religious Studies" did not require a total revision of the place of the department in the purposes of the university. That argument was made using Ray Hart's 1991 study[19] in which he observes that

> religious studies in higher education ranges from theological studies in small, church-related schools to broadly based religious studies in public or "secular" universities; and from small teaching-oriented liberal arts colleges to research-oriented universities (including graduate studies in religion).[20]

After protracted debate within the Department of Theology and within the governing academic structures of the university, the department was renamed the "Department of Religious Studies" in 1997. Burton MacDonald concluded that the name "Religious Studies" incorporated theology and the other elements of the departmental program including comparative religion courses and therefore more accurately conveyed what the department was in the university. Under the new name, the department could continue maintain its strengths in "biblical studies, moral theology and world religions."

The extended debate about the change of departmental name at St. Francis Xavier indicates that the Department of Religious Studies is committed to combine courses appropriate to the institution's Roman Catholic heritage with at least some courses on the scientific study of the Christian Bible and also comparative religion. The argument developed here is similar to the one made in the departmental study and external review of religious studies at Mount Saint Vincent University. The focus on Christianity within the religious studies department at St. Francis Xavier has been borne out in its recent appointments. In the department there are now two faculty who are specialists in biblical studies, one in comparative religion,[21] one in philosophical, moral theology and one in the philosophy of the social-scientific study of religion.

The intended contrast between religious studies and theology was accentuated in 1997 with the introduction of a multidisciplinary program in Catholic Studies separate from, but dependent on, religious studies for many of its courses. In 1998 there was one faculty member appointed to the program on a contractually limited basis. What is clear in the early stages of its existence is that the program in Catholic Studies would not have sufficient courses to offer a major concentration without those housed in the religious studies department.

For the religious studies program, the existence of Catholic Studies permits a clearer separation of the Christian component of its curriculum from the religious studies component. However, that clarity is entirely dependent upon the religious studies program expanding its world religions courses, strongly developing courses on various comparative themes, and developing the social-scientific study of religions. After the early retirement of the comparative religion specialist in 1999, the department lost two-thirds of the position in this critical area to the Catholic Studies program. Nonetheless, the new appointment primarily in Catholic Studies is a tenure-stream position attached to the Religious Studies department. This fact further confuses the potential for a clear distinction between the two programs. It appears to leave the full-time faculty complement of the department intact while denying it the ability to meet its most minimal requirement, a position dedicated to a strong comparative approach to the study of world religions.

St. Thomas University

St. Thomas University was founded in 1910 by the Roman Catholic Bishop of Chatham, New Brunswick, as a secondary school and junior college. It was chartered by the province as a university in 1934 and moved to Fredericton in 1964. It shares a portion of the campus of the University of New Brunswick. In its mission statement in the 1998-99 calendar it stated:

> St. Thomas University is a small, Catholic institution whose central liberal arts program is complemented by professional programs in education and social work. St. Thomas University takes pride in, and seeks to nurture its Catholic and humanistic heritage, its concern for social issues, its interaction with the community beyond the campus and its sensitivity to the needs of individual students.[22]

The statement continued:

> We are a liberal arts institution whose roots are in the faith and tradition of the Roman Catholic Church. We continue under its sponsorship. We provide an atmosphere hospitable to faith, in which the academic study of the Roman Catholic tradition and the experience of Christian life may be pursued with respect and freedom and where non-Catholic faculty and students are recognized and supported as full and equal participants in the university community.[23]

This mandate arose out of a context very closely connected to the religious studies department. The department was staffed by four clergy in 1976. Two lay faculty were in place by 1978, one of whom was specialized in the religious traditions of Asia. The Roman Catholic courses in the curriculum were for the most part taught by academic clerical appointments, but by the late 1980s it was becoming more and more difficult, given the shortage of priests for churches, for the department to count on such appointments. From the mid-1980s forward two major revisions to the curriculum were drafted which maintained a significant component of the curriculum dedicated to the Catholic studies and the expansion of the program into the teaching of comparative religions and specific world religions.

For the religious studies department there followed from the mission statement of the university a clear mandate for a curriculum that had as one of its central themes "the academic study of the Roman Catholic tradition . . . pursued with respect and freedom."[24] The department therefore offered "a core of courses . . . that focused on the Christian, and more specifically, the Roman Catholic tradition."[25] Having made this a major portion of its mandate, the department did not see the necessity of requiring Roman Catholic students to take its courses, and requested the removal of the university requirement that "one full course in religious studies is required for Roman Catholics."[26] This change in policy permitted the department to fulfill its wider mandate arising from the field of religious studies, and, endorsed by the university Senate, to teach courses that were about other religious traditions.

To clarify exactly how to hold together the two aspects of its mandate the department conducted an elaborate study leading toward an external review and a major revision to its curriculum overall. The study also identified the need for an additional full-time faculty appointment. The case for the new appointment required a full explication of what religious studies is and how the department intended to implement its twofold mandate.

The key document explaining the rationale of religious studies was "The Religion Major: A Report" by Stephen D. Crites, cited above. Out of this report one theme predominated. "The study in depth of *religion* requires that the student have more than a superficial acquaintance with at least one other tradition, in the context of its attendant culture. It requires a knowledge of at least two traditions to study religion in depth."[27] To this statement the department brought the Canadian public policy term "multicultural" and argued that the study of one tradition such as the Roman Catholic tradition required an understanding of cultural settings and "the place of Roman Catholicism in the family of humankind's religious traditions."[28] In turn the department located this rationale for its multicultural curriculum in religious studies in the connection between the theory of a multicultural society and the liberal arts curriculum that was also central to the university's mission statement and overall degree program.

The department articulated the argument for its particular combination of courses on Roman Catholicism and multicultural studies of selected world religions, most clearly in the following:

> While the field of religious studies as an independent academic discipline is itself relatively new, it stands on the shoulders of the oldest: theology. The discipline of theology has constituted a significant part of the religious studies department in the past and will continue to be a major element in the future. This is consistent with our commitment to inclusive discourse and the principle that theology is a complementary aspect of religious studies.... For theology, the "queen of the sciences," to take its place as a respected member of the larger Religious Studies Department at St. Thomas University is recognition that scholars in both theology and the study of religions share a common concern—the need and capacity of human beings, by both rational and trans-rational experiences, to make sense of their lives. The products of creating meaning, whether articulated through stories, rituals and texts or through architecture, sculpture, painting, music and poetry, are the data of religious studies. Grappling with the process of creating meaning in other cultures and in our own is at the heart of what we do as students of religions. It is also, it seems to us, at the heart of the liberal arts.[29]

St. Thomas, then, joins the Mount, Saint Mary's and St. Francis Xavier in a commitment to preserving the historic, founding tradition as a central and integral part of its curriculum. St. Thomas, as we shall see in some detail below, has a much broader interpretation of the place of the multicultural or comparative in its overall approach to the study of religions than, for example, St. Francis Xavier. It has two faculty who are trained in comparative religions, one of whom has actively developed a specialization in the religious traditions of Native peoples. Both philosophically and in terms of its sophisticated plan for its program, St. Thomas has a uniquely clear appreciation of what it is doing and why. It has set as its priority the engagement between the broad religious studies formulations of itself as a field of study and the particular institutional context in which those formulations are adapted and modified to fulfill the institutional mandate.

The department's argument for a definition of a religious studies department that combines courses on the founding tradition of the university with courses on diverse religious traditions shows the extent to which a self-reflective department engages routinely with the conceptions animating the discipline or field of study internationally and the concrete situation of the department in a particular institution.

Religious Studies in Protestant Universities

The Roman Catholic Church was not the only church to found universities in the Atlantic region. The Baptist Church founded Acadia University in Wolfville, Nova Scotia, and more recently the Atlantic Baptist University has been chartered by the province of New Brunswick. St. Stephen's University was also chartered by the province as a university with the declared mandate of the training of lay ministers. Also in New Brunswick, Mount Allison University, with its Wesleyan Methodist roots, was established as a degree-granting institution in 1858 by the Methodist Conference. From 1875 onward there was a faculty of theology and some of its members served within the university's Faculty of Arts. These Protestant universities all offered courses on the Bible and on Christian theology during their formative periods. Subsequently some of these universities became the setting in which religious studies departments were established. Along with the Roman Catholic universities, the Protestant universities held that an integral aspect of a good education was the study of theology and in particular the study of the Bible. In what follows we shall review only those universities which have developed religious studies departments.

Acadia University

In December 1992 the Programme Review Committee for the Department of Comparative Religion of Acadia University submitted its report to the Senate Curriculum Review Committee. The result of the ensuing discussion was the effective closure of the department in 1995 and the allocation of its faculty to other departments. "Comparative Religion" remains listed in the university calendar with the equivalent of four two-semester courses—World Religions, Introduction to the Bible, Ecology and Religion, the Bible as Literature and Readings in Biblical Literature—officially listed under that title. Other courses are available through the departments of history, classics, philosophy and sociology. The C. B. Lumsden Chair of Religious Studies, established in 1984, continues to be held by Dr. Bruce Matthews, and scholarship money remains available for students who minor in comparative religion. Ironically the number of courses in comparative religion from all departmental sources has increased rather than decreased due to the addition of a historian who specializes in China. Overall enrolment in the courses from all departmental sources is as high as, or higher than it was, when the department existed.

The Department of Comparative Religion at Acadia was established as a department of religious studies in 1969 by Dr. J. R. C. Perkin, soon to be dean of arts, and ultimately president of the university. The reduced teaching load carried by Dr. Perkin and the fact that one member of the department regularly taught at least one course in the philosophy department meant that the total number of courses actually taught by the full-time members of the department was the equivalent of the full-time teaching load of two faculty, not three.

The Department of Comparative Religion appeared to have many important assets. It received a strong evaluation of its potential from its external reviewers if the faculty allotment were raised to three full-time faculty. It had an endowed chair and large student enrolments in the department's courses. Such assets ought to have strengthened the case for the department's continued existence. However, the fact that the department had lost two members, one to administration and ultimately retirement, and the other to the department of philosophy, conspired against its continued viability. Neither the Faculty of Arts nor the university would support replacements for the full-time faculty. With one and one-third full-time faculty the department could not meet the criteria established by the Arts Faculty Planning Committee, which required as a definition of viability the "demonstrated ability of a Department or a Faculty to offer a four-year programme of study (such as an honours programme or double major)."[30] On the basis of this criterion the Department of Comparative Religion was unable to offer a four-year degree program, and it was closed. Dr. Bruce Matthews continued to hold an endowed professorship in religious studies from within the department of history. A program in comparative religion remains and it is possible to do a minor concentration in the area. There is no longer a major or honours concentration in the Faculty of Arts. Students do take the courses listed as electives.

The Atlantic Baptist University

The Atlantic Baptist University was chartered by the New Brunswick legislature in 1996. Its history, however, goes back to the 1940s when the United Baptist Convention founded the United Baptist Bible Training School. In its early history the Training School functioned as a Bible college and as a high school. In 1970 the name was changed to reflect the continuance of the Bible college and the addition of the first two years of a liberal arts program. The remaining two years were added with the most recent charter, and the university was established with a new campus and buildings on the outskirts of Moncton.

In its mission statement, the Atlantic Baptist University calendar describes the university as a "Christ-centered university committed to providing a high quality educational experience grounded in the preeminence of Jesus Christ."[31] The university offers a liberal arts education and complementary professional and general educational programs. In addition, "the University is committed to the growth of the whole person: spiritual, intellectual, personal/ social and growth in physical well-being. This is done in an environment in which the Christian faith is integrated with further study, life-long learning, leadership and service."[32]

The university is affiliated with the Coalition of Christian Colleges and Universities Study Programs, permitting off-campus exchange programs. Within its academic programs, the university offers students two majors in the field of religion, one in biblical studies and a second in religious studies. The overwhelming majority of the courses deal with Christianity either as the study of scripture or as the study of Christian church history and theology. There are courses on Eastern philosophy, the psychology and the sociology of religion in the religious studies major but the majority of courses follow theological or seminary-type curricula.

The Atlantic Baptist University has approximately twenty full-time faculty and another eight adjunct faculty. While many of the faculty have doctorates, at the time of writing, all were appointed on one-year contracts. The university is exploring the development of a tenure system for full-time appointments in order to establish the grounds for recognition by the Association of Universities and Colleges of Canada. Without such recognition, the university's courses are not accepted for transfer credit to other universities, nor are its degrees recognized for admission to graduate programs.

Since the university does not receive any provincial government funding, it is free to maintain its programs as it sees fit. While instruction in biblical studies, post-Reformation church history and the social sciences is well represented in the courses, the program offers minimal teaching the religions of the world. More importantly all courses in this program are taught on the assumption of the primacy of Christianity. While the major in religious studies exists in name, it does not meet the minimum standard for such a title. It would be more accurate to name the major "Christian Studies."

St. Stephen's University

St. Stephen's University was chartered by the provincial legislature in 1998. It is a very small university with approximately fifty full-time students doing a Bachelor of Arts program, and another fifteen doing part-time degrees. In addition, the university offers graduate-level Bachelor of Ministry and Master of Ministry degrees. The mission statement of the university states:

> Through a dual emphasis on character formation and academic excellence, the University seeks to develop men and women who model servant leadership in the world. St. Stephen's is a caring community of disciples seeking to be obedient to Jesus, who is the Way; of scholars seeking to articulate a unified world-view centered on Jesus who is the Truth; of servants seeking to love god and neighbor through Jesus, who is the Life."[33]

The university calendar lists eight full-time faculty including the librarian, four of whom are listed as having doctorates. Part-time and visiting faculty include four people with doctorates, one Ph.D. candidate and others with one graduate degree. "The integrated approach to the Liberal Arts is rooted in biblical Christianity, is academically challenging and is alive to contemporary issues. The program includes two terms of travel and study abroad and is designed to develop in every student an appreciation of the history, philosophy and cultures of the world in which we live."[34] There is no religious studies or comparative religion concentration in the liberal arts program; however, there is a concentration in "Biblical and Ministry Studies." In addition, there are cultural studies, literature studies, historical studies and philosophy, all of which are focused on themes associated with Christianity in the West.

Unlike the Atlantic Baptist University there is no major in religious studies at St. Stephen's. It is clear that the primary emphasis at St. Stephen's is to train students from within a committed Christian environment for both lay and ministerial activities.

Mount Allison University

While many universities and departments of religious studies in Canada can speak of their history since the 1960s or perhaps the post-Second World War era, it is one of the attributes of the universities in the Atlantic region, that there are several whose history is both long and distinguished. Such is the case with the Mount Allison University and its department of religious studies. In its academic planning submission dated January of 1991, the department of religious studies spoke of the key dates in its history: 1843, then 1859, 1926, and entering its modern phase in 1960 and 1972.

Departments and Degree Programs 47

Mount Allison had its beginnings as the Wesley Academy of 1839, which was succeeded by Mount Allison Wesleyan College in 1859. With the founding of the United Church of Canada in 1926 the college's theology department of theology moved to Halifax, leaving behind the undergraduate programs. Throughout this history there was a continuous emphasis on the academic preparation of lay people and on pre-theological studies. Such a context permitted the founding of a department of religion in 1960 and its renaming in 1968 as the department of religious studies.

Founded by the Wesleyan Methodist Conference, the college, from its inception as a non-degree-granting institution, offered courses such as "Evidences of Christianity." With degree-granting authority conferred in 1859, the university offered the biblical language courses which were also taught in the seminary programs and a variety of courses about Christianity and natural theology. Biblical studies courses were central to the university curriculum. Even after the theology department left Mount Allison in 1926, students were still able to do one year of seminary studies at Mount Allison and to include biblical and theology courses in the undergraduate Bachelor of Arts degree program.

With the inception in 1960 of the Department of Religion, subsequently called the Department of Religious Studies, something new emerged. The pattern of departmental development was determined first by the continuation of faculty whose expertise was in Christian theology and biblical studies. There followed successive changes in areas of expertise and training consistent with the priorities first of the local university and community. The most recent additions to the department in the late 1990s brought a full-time specialist in Asian religions and a biblical scholar who will teach courses on Islam and Judaism. These changes were both progressive and evolutionary. They reflect the pattern of change at most of the departments where appointments have been possible and where departments have chosen to ensure that the comparative component of the curriculum receives a high priority.

Until 1960, the program at Mount Allison was explicitly understood to be dealing with Protestant Christianity in the Methodist, United Church tradition. Once the department became focused on the study of religions, the faculty and the program became engaged in the discourse on the modern academic study of religions. Christian courses, at least in theory, were shifted in context from a setting in which the scriptures and the theologies were examined as part of the rational exploration of faith to a setting in which Christianity was one of the religious traditions among many included in the curriculum. As such, it was to be studied using the critical and historical methods applied to other religious traditions. In theory the department adopted a rationale rooted in the modern study of religions. Its academic planning submission stated:

> The study of religion deals with the deepest and most basic questions of human existence: the meaning and purpose of life, relations with a divine presence and power, the shaping of culture and society, interpersonal relations, and ultimate human destiny. A programme of religious studies at the university level will seek to examine the various religious traditions, taking a historical and critical approach and utilizing the insights and advances of modern scholarship. It will be concerned with the Judaeo-Christian tradition, but also with all the major world faiths; with the origins and history of religious traditions, but also with the live issues and contemporary concerns of religion today. A rigorous, liberal education of high quality cannot afford to neglect religious studies.[35]

This statement is important for it shows how the department engaged in the debate between its Methodist past and its academic present. It is clear that it gave priority to the traditions of the university within the United Church of Canada, seeing that as the core to which the study of world religions was added.

The three faculty in the department worked through the elements of the debate about the nature of religious studies to devise four streams for their program that acknowledged both the past and the academic training of the faculty. Three of the streams—biblical studies, Christian theology and the history of the Christianity—show the dominance of the historical setting and the specializations of the faculty. A fourth stream, world religions, shows the integration of the comparative, world religions component into the curriculum.

Speaking to the criticism that the program privileged the position of Christianity, the department argued that this critique constituted a reverse bias against the founding traditions of the very universities that house the comparative and the scientific studies of religions. It was also difficult to imagine that the decisions taken in the 1960s to hire and tenure specific professors could or should be negated in order to change the faculty and their specializations.

What is remarkable both at Mount Allison and elsewhere in the region is the extent to which faculty extended their teachable subjects to include both new areas of comparative study and new methodologies in order to address the kind of challenges posed by the debates with the scholarly societies for the study of religions. Other strategies were also employed at Mount Allison to expand the curriculum. Part-time faculty were found with specializations in Asian religions. Finally, as retirements did take place, new areas of specialization in both Islam and Hinduism were brought into the department. While change may be seen to be slow, the need for it cannot abrogate such fundamentals in the university as tenure.

Religious Studies in Non-Denominational Universities

Paralleling the historical fact of the Christian universities in the region is another university culture which has focused the study of religions rather differently. At one extreme the University of New Brunswick (including its Saint John campus) is prohibited by charter from teaching religion. As we have seen, however, the presence on the Fredericton campus of St. Thomas University and its Department of Religious Studies has permitted the University of New Brunswick to give academic credit to some religious studies courses without contradicting its charter by offering courses on religion in its own curriculum. Such a solution is not characteristic of the other non-denominational universities in the region.

Very different from the University of New Brunswick are Memorial University of Newfoundland and Dalhousie University in Halifax. Both have established departments of religious studies or comparative religion. Neither of these institutions has an explicit religious connection to any church. The venerable Anglican university, King's College, is located on the campus of Dalhousie University. Unlike St. Thomas University, it does not have a religion program. Many of the students at King's finish their degree programs primarily through courses offered at Dalhousie. As we shall see, the non-religious founding of a university does not necessarily mean an open mind about the study of religions in the university curriculum.

Memorial University of Newfoundland

Memorial University was not in any sense a religiously based university. The public university existed, however, in the midst of an education system that was run by churches. The demand from the various religious denominations was for teachers trained in Christian scripture and tradition to teach religion in the schools. In the face of the demand there was a consensus that there ought to be a religion department at Memorial. Those who were initially hired to develop the curriculum insisted on a non-denominational curriculum and faculty for the department of religious studies.

The first step in the development of the study of religions at Memorial was a program listed in the university calendars of 1966-68 as "Theological Studies." There were only three courses in the program. Religious studies as a department appeared in the 1968-69 calendar, with Dr. Morley F. Hodder newly appointed as head of the department. The public lecture inaugurating the Department of Religious Studies was given in October of 1968 by Langdon Gilkey of the University of Chicago.

With the appointment of Dr. Hodder and the formation of a religious studies department there was a fierce defence of the principle that the study of religions at Memorial must not be governed by any one church. The initial faculty appointments in theological studies were from three churches—the United, the Anglican, and the Roman Catholic—to which was added faculty to teach the essential component of comparative religion. In a letter nominating Dr. Hodder for the title of professor emeritus in 1997, members of the department remembered the vision he had brought to the establishment of the department:

> Dr. Hodder's distinction lies in his vision to create and maintain a Department of Religious Studies that reflects and values religion not as an instrument of sectarian power and self-assertion but as a forum where humanitarian values and human insights are allowed to flourish among those who teach and learn.[36]

The letter continues:

> During his tenure as head and Professor, he also developed pedagogical emphases and a curriculum by which prospective teachers in the school system would have the opportunity to study not only the beliefs and practices of Christianity but also those religions of other cultures and regions. He thus contributed greatly toward globalizing the cultural vision of Newfoundland and Labrador students.[37]

The emerging discipline of the study of religions in Canada was an effective support for such a vision of religious studies at Memorial. This was especially evident in the department's decisions to hire new faculty who were graduating from new doctoral programs in Canada such as that at McMaster University. The emphasis on biblical studies and church history was established early to meet the broad needs of the community, and gradually the faculty diversified, with specialists hired to teach Chinese language and religious traditions. The introduction of a master's program served the need of the school system for advanced training for teachers.

Memorial University now has the largest religious studies department in the region. The department did not have to contend with the issues associated with the religious universities, but it certainly had to contend with the sectarian splits in the community and particularly in the school system. This was a variation on the pattern in the Protestant and Roman Catholic universities in the rest of the region. Once again, however, it points to the balancing act required of religious studies departments as they take seriously the needs of the local university culture and community in constructing degree programs and a curriculum.

It is difficult to imagine exactly how the recent secularization of the school system in Newfoundland is going to affect religious studies. One might be tempted to speculate that over time there will be a diminished need for the emphasis on biblical studies and the study of Christianity. Should multicultural immigration expand into Newfoundland, there may well emerge a greater need for comparative and sociological studies of religions. What is important is that the fundamental principles established from the outset of the program will stand the department in good stead.

Dalhousie University

Dalhousie University in Halifax had no religion department or program until the early 1970s. Historically Roman Catholics did not attend Dalhousie in any number until after the Second World War. The absence of Roman Catholics and some Protestant denominations among the student body may well have been rooted in the Dissenter and Catholic laws inherited from the imperial colonial law and carried forward by custom as much as by legalities. Both the Baptist Church, a Protestant dissenting tradition, and the Roman Catholics founded their own universities because their members could not easily obtain what they deemed to be an appropriate education in the "public" universities of the region.

Nonetheless, the fact that the tradition at Dalhousie did not include the study of religion was qualified by the presence of the independent King's College, originally with its Anglican seminary, on the campus. Along with the classics department that the studies by Charles Anderson[38] correctly identified as offering numerous courses on Christianity in the West, it can be said that Dalhousie actually offered its students numerous courses about Christianity prior to the founding of the Department of Comparative Religion.

In 1973 after "an acrimonious debate"[39] a Department of Religion[40] came into existence. It was developed through the university committee structures by Dr. Ravi Ravindra from the Department of Physics. The first appointment to the Department was Dr. Wilfred Cantwell Smith, one of the most eminent scholars in the field of religious studies. Subsequently the department added Drs. Ravindra and Faulkner to its full-time complement. When Dr. Cantwell Smith returned to Harvard, no full-time replacement was allowed by the university and the complement has remained at two full-time faculty since.[41]

The Department of Comparative Religion is the only one in the region planned from its inception to be a department reflecting a particular understanding of the field of religion. At Dalhousie all courses are understood to be taught comparatively within courses on traditions such as Hinduism or Christianity and within thematic courses such as "Religion and Story" or "Religion and War." The curriculum is hierarchically structured, beginning with courses on the traditions and culminating in a thematic, comparative seminar. In its understanding of itself both as a "religion" department and as a "comparative religion" department, the fundamental place of the study of religions is understood to be an integral aspect of liberal education.[42]

Dalhousie's departmental plan is no less shaped by its context than are the programs at the other universities in the region. Two examples will illustrate how this is so. The department's historical sketch sets out the parties in the "acrimonious debate" that preceded its establishment:

> We are inclined to see opposition to the proposal as rooted in Enlightenment suspicions of clerical interference in academic freedom, while support for the department came from two sources. On the one hand there were those who responded to the evanescence of interest in religious studies during the 1960s with a sober conviction that religious phenomena of all kinds are fit subjects for academic study, and on the other hand there were those who had some hope that opening a department of religious studies would add weight to current studies of Christianity.[43]

In this account there was only a very small perceived need to acknowledge the Christian heritage of the community at large, while there was a pre-eminent need to identify the program with the conventions of post-Enlightenment analysis of religion and the fascination with the subject in the 1960s. The dominant methods of textual study based in biblical science, the theories of the history of religions or the Chicago School, and of course the important theoretical contributions of Wilfred Cantwell Smith himself, fitted the university and its academic priorities for the study of religions.

The context of institutional culture was even more evident in the discussion of the department's change of name to the Department of Comparative Religion. In the departmental history, the understanding of "religion" in the Catholic universities provided the comparative foil for the change, along with careful attention to the popular student perceptions of the meaning of the terms. Of comparative religion a hypothetical student is reported to have said, "Oh, that means that you don't favour one religion, eh?"[44]

In response to the institutional culture at the student level and at the level of the faculty, administration, and Board, the department's mandate was to undertake the "comparative and historical study of religion"[45] and in doing so to identify its mandate in particular with the term "comparative religion." The historical sketch reflected on the origins of this term in the following way:

> Its historical roots are found in the foundation of the Department of Comparative Religion at the University of Chicago in 1892, which was itself associated with the world Parliament of Religions which met during the Columbian Exposition of 1893, the first occasion on which representatives of all the world's major religious traditions came together to meet and understand each other, rather than to proselytize each other. (Dalhousians will be interested to know that George Munro Grant, one of those associated with the financial rescue of Dal in the late nineteenth century, represented Canadian Protestants at this gathering).[46]

The intent of the argument was to get the university to understand the appropriateness for the institution of the comparative study of religions through a series of overlapping identifications. A model of the discipline, the Chicago school, is linked to a historic figure in the university's history. In other words, the historical characteristics of Dalhousie and the theory of what comparative religion is are mutually compatible. Indeed, following the insight of Stephen Crites noted above, every instance of the study of religions, indeed of any discipline in the university, is subject to *a* privileged self-understanding.

Summary

These brief descriptions of the departments of religious studies or comparative religion in the region illustrate a general thesis. Every department involved in the study of religions carries on a discussion about how best to design and implement a program in religious studies for its particular institution. The discussion has many participants. It is carried on internally at each university and involves the issue of the relationship of the study of religions to the particular university and its culture or tradition. This discussion involves faculty administrators and students. It is continued within the professional debates about the discipline at academic conferences and meetings. No less important the debate involves segments of the larger community within which the university is situated and to which it is in some sense accountable. Every program is able to give its particular emphasis and point of view to these discussions in ways that can be heard and understood by students, colleagues and the community at large. In the same way as the Crites report argues that " 'Religion,' to be sure, is a construct of academic study"[47] so too I would argue that the forms which religious studies or comparative religion take within any given university is a construct, the result of the discussions about what it means to study religions appropriately in any given historical context and within a particular institution and its community.

Having considered the history and characteristics of the departments of religious studies in the region, it is now necessary to situate these departments within the work of the university—in this case the design of the arts degree within which a religious studies major or honours degree exists in order to see how these arts degree programs shape religious studies.

Types of Bachelor of Arts Degrees

The culture of a university is defined at least in part by its admission policies. The standard admission requirement of universities in the Atlantic region is completion of Grade 12 with a minimum acceptable average. The admission standards vary from virtually open admission of students with a 65 percent average to much higher requirements that set limits to enrolment with higher standards for admission. For example, in the 1995 rankings in *Maclean's* magazine,[48] in the primarily undergraduate category, Mount Allison ranked highest with an 84.8 percent average admission standard from grade twelve. Close behind was Dalhousie with 81 percent, Acadia with 80 percent, the University of Prince Edward Island with 80 percent and St. Francis Xavier with 79 percent. Mount Saint Vincent followed with 78 percent and Saint Mary's with 76.5 percent. Memorial University of Newfoundland, Université de Moncton and St. Thomas did not participate in the *Maclean's* evaluations that year. These averages did not indicate what the lowest admission standard was at any of these institutions.

The effect of relatively open admission is to create a complex body of students ranging from the outstanding to those who are not sufficiently skilled to cope with a university education. Further complicating the picture are the adult students whose motivation and experience in the working world often transform their lack of formal preparation into high achievement.

Admission to the Bachelor of Arts degree from Grade 12 is the foundation on which the universities in the Atlantic region build their regulations. It is striking therefore that there are major differences between the Bachelor of Arts requirements in the four Atlantic provinces. In Newfoundland, Prince Edward Island and New Brunswick the Bachelor of Arts requires completion of the equivalent of twenty credits (forty half- or one-semester credits) for a degree. That is, the minimum normal duration of a degree is four years of study beyond Grade 12. Nova Scotia is the exception to this. There, the basic Bachelor of Arts degree requires fifteen credits (thirty half-credits) and three years to complete.

The anomaly of the Nova Scotian degrees was originally caused by the awarding of advanced standing credits for Grade 12 courses by the universities. In effect, for many years, Grade 12 in Nova Scotia constituted both the normal admission standard to university and the requirement for the first five credits of a twenty-credit university degree. All institutions have now stopped awarding these advanced standing credits at the time of admission, but continue the practice of awarding a Bachelor of Arts degree based upon successful completion of fifteen credits or the equivalent in half-credits. As will become evident as we examine the general Bachelor of Arts requirements for the major or area of concentration and then the specific requirements for a major in religious studies, this fundamental anomaly in the Nova Scotian universities has a significant effect on what can be accomplished within the framework of the shorter degree program.

Several Nova Scotian universities have begun to address the anomaly of the three-year Bachelor of Arts degree by introducing what is called an Advanced Bachelor of Arts degree. It requires a minimum of four years to complete and twenty credits or their equivalent. Institutions offering this "Advanced" degree program include Acadia, Dalhousie, Mount Saint Vincent University, St. Francis Xavier and, more recently, Saint Mary's University. It goes without saying that the euphemism "Advanced" simply brings the degree programs into line with the norm across the Atlantic region and North America: four years and twenty two-semester credits or forty one-semester credits following completion of an academic Grade 12.

General degree requirements differ from university to university but ensure that students have a significant breadth of study at the undergraduate level. Memorial University of Newfoundland recently revised its general degree requirements and established a series of core requirements in its twenty-credit (40 one-semester credits) degree program. The core includes a requirement in English, a second language, numeracy/science, humanities (two courses exclusive of English), social sciences (two courses from two disciplines), and research/writing. In these core requirements, religious studies is located in the humanities. Requirements such as a second language or an introductory course may be applied toward the completion of a major or a minor. At Memorial, therefore, one of the department's courses in Hebrew or Mandarin can be taken as a core requirement and also count toward the major. Religious studies also offers courses that meet the core requirement in research/writing. Such a course can be taken as a core requirement and also count toward the major. However, there is an upper limit to the number of courses that can count as core requirements and toward a major. Such limits prevent students from having too narrow a focus of study in the completion of these requirements. To the foundation of the general degree requirements students must add a major and electives in order to complete the degree.

While Memorial has an elaborately defined set of core requirements for its twenty-credit degree in arts, other universities have a variety of requirements at the general level. The university may, for example, stipulate only a bare minimum of required courses. The University of Prince Edward Island requires one course in English and a completed major in a department or program for the degree. In New Brunswick, where the usual degree requirement is completion of the equivalent of twenty credits, Mount Allison requires that students take at least one course in each of humanities, social sciences and sciences, and a major concentration, and that they include in their course selection at least eight courses at the third-and-fourth year levels.

St. Thomas University permits a major to take up half of the total twenty credits, and requires students to complete eight courses at the third- and fourth-year levels. In the first year students must complete five courses, with two from the humanities and two from the social sciences. An alternative to the first-year distribution requirement is the Aquinas program which permits students to consolidate three of their five first-year credits and pursue a multi-disciplinary thematic program offered by three or more faculty. Annual enrolment in the Aquinas program is limited to thirty-six students.

In Nova Scotia, where the normal requirement for a Bachelor degree has been fifteen credits, the setting of degree requirements involves striking a balance between stipulating the requirements for a major, permitting some electives and including general degree requirements in a program that is five full credits less than elsewhere in the region. Dalhousie University requires an arts student to complete a humanities course, a life or physical science course, a social science course and a language and a writing course for which there is a minimum quantity of written assignments. An introductory course in the Department of Comparative Religion qualifies for this requirement. Within this structure "at least four and no more than eight credits in the area of concentration (major) must be beyond the 1000 level including 2 beyond the 2000 level."[49] This provision allows students to take most or all of their elective courses at the introductory level. In turn, that permits a major program, such as the comparative religion, to be designed hierarchically and with prerequisites because the large-enrolment courses can all be at the first-and-second year levels of a student's degree program.

In contrast to these degree requirements at Dalhousie, Mount Saint Vincent University requires that nine courses be at the second-year-level or above, and Saint Mary's University requires that eight of the fifteen credits required for the degree must be at the second-and-third year levels or above.

The effect of these requirements is to make virtually every student take electives beyond the first-year level and as a result departments are required to offer open elective courses. Both the religious studies departments therefore have an open course structure with no prerequisites permitting students to take all courses except those specifically designated for majors. The degree requirements effectively prevent the departments from implementing a hierarchical program with introductory courses providing the large-enrolment elective courses.

In addition to the required courses at the third- and fourth-year levels, both universities have general degree requirements. At Mount Saint Vincent University it is recommended but not required that students take one full credit in the humanities, the social sciences, the natural sciences and a language. At Saint Mary's, students must complete the equivalent of one full English course, two different social science courses, one humanities course other than English, and a mathematics/science/basic logic or language course.

The "advanced" degree at St. Francis Xavier University sets out to ensure breadth in a degree program in quite a different way from other universities in Nova Scotia. The university requires that students follow a course pattern in each of the four levels of study. Students must take a "major subject" and a "minor subject" in pairs of courses. Over the duration of their degree, students must complete four electives. In addition, students in the "Advanced" major must submit a research report in their major subject.

It is already clear that the Nova Scotian universities impose serious limitations on all of their academic departments as long as the fifteen-credit degree is continued. Ending this anomaly, however, is easier said than done as it raises serious political issues, both with students who do not wish to see their degree programs lengthened or costs increased and with the provincial government which does not want to deal with the opposition such a change is likely to bring. Nonetheless, the universities will have to make the change to bring their degree programs into line with those of universities in the other Atlantic provinces, not to mention the rest of North America.

The Religious Studies Major

The design of a major program in religious studies is the concrete expression of a department's view of what religious studies is. The requirements for the major provide the structure that tells students what they are required to know about religions and religious traditions in order to receive a Bachelor of Arts degree with a major. In order to offer a major, a department must have a sufficient range of courses from the introductory level through to the advanced level and therefore must have sufficient faculty and library resources to be able to sustain student study.

For most academic departments in the university the major is also a principal source of course enrolment. That is, the students who declare a major commit themselves to taking a range of courses beyond the introductory level in the field of their major. Requirements can range from the minimal of a set number of courses to a series of courses covering various areas in a department's curriculum such as world religions, biblical studies, ethics or methods courses. Some departments construct these requirements in a hierarchical series of courses that require students to meet a prerequisite for each level. Others, especially those that have open enrolments in their courses, design the major around distribution requirements and usually have only one or two courses at the most senior level which are exclusively for religious studies majors.

At a number of universities in the region, religious studies faculty have concluded that it is not possible to offer a major or, if there is a major approved by the Senate, not to allow students to register for the completion of the major. Acadia University closed down its major in comparative religion in 1995. Courses in comparative religion continue to be offered but through other departments. A similar decision, though with a different rationale, was taken at the University College of Cape Breton and at the Université de Moncton. With one faculty member at the University College of Cape Breton in 1994 and two at Université de Moncton, the view was that there were not enough faculty resources to offer students the opportunity to complete a major in the field of religious studies. The decision means that students may include elective courses from religious studies in their degree while majoring in other subjects.

A major in religious studies is offered at Memorial University of Newfoundland; the University of Prince Edward Island; the Atlantic Baptist University, Mount Allison University and St. Thomas University in New Brunswick; and St. Francis Xavier, Mount Saint Vincent, Saint Mary's and Dalhousie universities in Nova Scotia. The approach to the structure of the major at each of these universities is quite distinct, and several of the programs have gone through various revisions to their structure, either in preparation for external reviews or because there have been significant changes in the department's faculty.

There are three crucial points to be made about the structuring of requirements for the religious studies majors in the Atlantic region. First, it makes a substantial difference if the major is planned for a twenty-credit degree or a fifteen-credit degree as in Nova Scotia. Secondly, a university's overall degree requirements impact substantially on the way in which the major is constructed. Finally, how a department decides to provide the introductory courses and elective options for the university degree requirements has a major impact on the resources available for the major program within a department.

Always at issue within the religious studies departments of the Atlantic region is the maintenance of a balance between ensuring that the overall enrolments in the department are comparable on a per capita basis with those of other departments in the Faculty of Arts and providing the required courses for the major in the department. This balance is not easy for departments, and the outcome frequently involves faculty in overload teaching, often without remuneration, to ensure that the major is available to students. Overload teaching may include directed reading courses, special topics courses, honours thesis direction, honours courses and specialized courses exclusively for the major students on such topics as methods and theory.

The strategies employed by departments differ according to the way in which they decide to fulfill their service function within the arts faculty. Departments must decide between a strategy that is based on an open curriculum in which students from the university may take any course in religious studies at virtually any level as an elective and one that limits the service courses or electives to the first and second years, beyond which students must meet prerequisites before taking advanced-level courses. Usually this means that only majors or students doing a minor can enter the courses at the advanced level. Some departments have worked out a middle ground on this issue by combining two levels of a course on the same topic in the same classroom. Such a strategy requires different assignments for the two levels.

The decision to opt for an open structure is usually tied to the perceived need to maintain and enhance overall enrolments in the department. The number of declared majors in many religious studies departments does not warrant many courses, if any, exclusively for them. Department size—that is, the number of faculty—is not a determinant in this issue as the largest department in the region, at Memorial, has dropped the system of prerequisites, while one of the smallest, at Dalhousie, with two full-time faculty, maintains a program for majors tied to prerequisites. As was the case with the negotiation between theological history and the religious studies field of subjects, it would appear that local context is a major contributing factor in the decision as to which strategy to employ.

Memorial University of Newfoundland

The degree program at Memorial is based on the completion of twenty credits. Religious studies offers a major that requires students to complete twelve one-semester religious studies credits of which five must be at the 3000 level and one at the 4000 level. The department also offers special concentrations in religious studies for students who are simultaneously fulfilling the requirements for education faculty degrees. The requirements for a concentration range from six to eight credits depending on the degree program. The department also offers an eight-credit minor in religious studies.

The religious studies department opted to remove the structure of course prerequisites for its major in 1997-98. Even though Memorial's department is the largest in the region, it could not guarantee that all of the required courses, particularly at the introductory levels, could be offered in any given year.

Explanations for the breakdown of the prerequisite system varied. Department faculty took administrative leaves, sabbatical leaves or research leaves or obtained other course reductions for other reasons. Course releases meant that individual faculty were not able to offer the required courses for the early stages of the major. The unintended effect was that student access to more advanced courses was limited or removed. That meant that students were not able to complete their major in the required sequence. As a result, the department at Memorial decided to revise the structure of the major to exclude prerequisites. In making the decision it was understood that academic counselling of majors would be the basis for ensuring that students completed the major with an adequate breadth and depth in their program.

In the revised program, the introductory-level courses cover the religions of the world, religion in the modern world and Christianity in Western civilization. In addition, slightly more focused courses are offered on the millennium, East Asian religions and creation stories. Language courses in Mandarin and biblical Hebrew meet the requirements for a language in the arts degree as well as providing a language option for majors. All these courses provide a variety of substantive introductions to major areas of the religious studies curriculum.

The second or 2000 level of courses is designed to offer the opportunity to be introduced to major portions of the field such as world religions, Christian thought and history, biblical studies, religious ethics and modern culture. The third and fourth levels of courses are stated in the university calendar to be dependent upon the introductions and a cumulative knowledge of the subject matter in the field of religious studies. The program does not offer a keystone course or a seminar for majors but puts the focus on the sub-fields of the department outlined in the second or 2000 level of courses. Directed reading and special topics courses are available in each of the sub-fields.

The field of religious studies is represented by the four course areas: world religions; Christian thought and history; biblical studies; and religious ethics and modern culture. Students must complete half of the major at the third-year level or above in three of these four areas. The risk in this distribution requirement is that students could exclude world religions and concentrate entirely on various aspects of Western traditions.

University of Prince Edward Island

The degree program in arts at the University of Prince Edward Island is based on a semester system. Students normally take ten courses a year, five in each semester, and complete forty half-credits for the degree. The forty credits are translated into credit hours, three for a one-semester course and six for a course that is taught over two semesters. Students must complete 120 credit hours for their degree, of which a minimum of forty-two is devoted to the completion of a major.

Religious studies majors must complete the two introductory courses entitled "Religion and the Person: An Introduction to the Study of Religion" and "Religions of the World." After the introductory-level courses, students may select their courses for the major as they wish, but they must complete one of the fourth-year tutorial or seminar courses. The fourth-year courses include "Special Studies" or special topics courses, a course entitled "Practical Theology" and a third called "The Comparative Study of Religion."

In the 1996-98 two-year calendar, the department published a revised description of the major. Introduced at that time were four areas of study, and students were required to take two courses in each of the areas. The first area was an introduction to the study of religions and included a survey of world religions and a newly revised course, "Introduction to the Study of Religion." The other three areas, at the second- and third-year level included "Biblical Studies and Western Religious History" (six courses), "Eastern Religions and Comparative Religion," (nine courses) and "Contemporary Religion and Interdisciplinary Studies" (ten courses). Not listed in these three areas but countable in the religious studies major and minor were nine cross-listed courses from classics, history, fine arts, philosophy and sociology/anthropology.

Selected courses in religious studies have prerequisites. Of the thirty-two courses listed in the 1996-98 calendar, nine courses had prerequisites. For those courses, the requirement could be met by one of the introductory courses or one course in religious studies or by the permission of the instructor.

The majority of religious studies courses were open-enrolment courses which simultaneously served the majors in the department and the students seeking an elective.

Mount Allison University

Mount Allison requires that students complete twenty credits (or up to forty half-credit equivalent credits) for the Bachelor of Arts degree. Students must complete at least one full course in each of humanities, social sciences and sciences. Of the twenty credits, thirteen are required for a major or "area of concentration." Students may complete the major in a departmental program, or from a combination of three departmental programs or they can design their own major with the dean's approval.

Most students take electives at the introductory level. In 1994, these courses included "Introduction to the Christian Bible," "Religions of the Near East" and "Religions of the Far East." Three courses with prerequisites were also recommended for students seeking a one course elective: "World Religions and World Concerns," "The Bible as Literature" and "Faith and Doubt."

By 1996 there had been a revision of the first-year courses. Religious studies participated in offering the general humanities courses designed to be "introductions to all of the humanities disciplines."[50] The new courses were on biblical studies and world religions. The new multidisciplinary format was a positive collegial approach to the problem of the first year. It provided a natural progression from an introduction to the departments and subjects in the university to an introduction to the field of religious studies and its approach to the study of religions. After the two years of introduction permitted by a four- year degree, the department could design its area of concentration and honours program around smaller seminar courses in the final two years of a the student's program.

For the area of concentration, students were advised to build a core of six or seven courses in religious studies proper and supplement that with selections from the cross-listed courses in other departments. Students were also advised to concentrate their major in one of the three areas of the curriculum: biblical studies, world religions or the Christian Tradition. This strategy was criticized by the external reviewers for the apparent privilege it gave to the courses on the Bible and Christian tradition. The vast majority of the department's courses were in these areas.

In its response to the criticism that the major was unduly focused on Christianity, the department argued that the three full-time faculty members share a basic vision of religious studies. This involves approaching each religious tradition with critical empathy, so that a serious attempt is made to allow the tradition to speak for itself in its own terms, and each tradition is subject to critical assessment by its own standards and from the vantage point of other traditions.[51]

This approach to teaching and to the design of a degree program centred on critical empathy acknowledged three crucial factors. First, it located the focus of the major in the areas of specialization and research of the faculty tenured in the department. Secondly, it permitted the major to reflect the Methodist and United Church traditions of the university and the student body. Thirdly, it allowed the comparative and world religions component in the major to reflect the fact that it had been developed by faculty whose specializations were primarily in Christianity. The department at Mount Allison has not been the only small department that has struggled to expand its major into new areas without the benefit of hiring specialists on Islam, Buddhism or Hinduism, to mention only three. The external review of the Mount Allison department recommended that, as faculty retired, the department should diversify its faculty expertise and, in the new appointments completed in 1998, that had been done.

The department redefined the three areas around which to structure its degree to include Eastern Religions (Far Eastern Traditions, e.g., Buddhism, Confucianism, Hinduism, Shintoism), Western Religions (Near Eastern Traditions, e.g., Christianity, Islam, Judaism) and Religion and Culture.[52] Within these new categories the department proposed that "each full-time faculty member would teach courses in at least two areas."[53] The department also agreed with the reviewers that the major required more courses in specific religious traditions. With the new appointments once again this recommendation is being developed.

What is striking in the comparison of its earlier degree programme and the recommendations of the department in the wake of the external review is the dramatic movement of the department in new directions. There is a real commitment to develop the world religions component of the major by making an appointment in the area and to link the study of the Far East and Near East with the ways in that the religions of these areas are represented in synagogues, mosques and temples in the region.

The department has approached the task of reconstituting itself and its major with skill and clarity of purpose. It has maintained its program in a way that perpetuates a place in the curriculum for courses reflecting the institutional heritage while initiating the changes required to acknowledge the central criteria of the field of religious studies.

The Atlantic Baptist University

The Atlantic Baptist University requires students to complete a four-year degree. Within that degree students may pursue a major or a double major. In the field of religion there is a major both in religious studies and biblical studies. The two majors are described in the calendar under religious studies as follows:

> The B.A. in Religious Studies is designed to allow the student to study the phenomenon of Christianity from different perspectives: with respect to its origins, with respect to its historical manifestations, with respect to its making philosophical assertions, comparatively and social-scientifically.
>
> The B.A. in Biblical Studies is designed to give students the opportunity to study the Christian Bible literally, historically and theologically. Knowledge of the Biblical languages is an indispensable requirement of this major. The second-temple period will also be a subject of study for this major, since knowledge of this period is important for understanding the New Testament.[54]

Religious studies represents one of the largest degree programs in the new university. Of the 120 credit hours required to graduate, forty-two are devoted to the completion of a major, which translates into fourteen courses in religious studies. The core introductory courses for both religious studies and biblical studies are the same. Students must take courses on the Old Testament and the New Testament and two courses on basic Christian thought. The other required course is the senior seminar in religious studies and biblical studies. It is not clear if this course is common to both majors or is taught separately depending on the major. Both religious studies and biblical studies have distribution requirements as part of the major. In religious studies students must take at least one course from three of these four perspectives: historical, philosophical, comparative and social-scientific. Religious studies students must complete six credit hours in philosophy and psychology or sociology in order to complete the major. Biblical studies students must complete a biblical language course and two history courses on the ancient world and the Greco-Roman world. Both majors require that students complete at least five of the fourteen credits at an advanced level appropriate to the third and fourth years of study.

It is clear that the religious studies and biblical studies majors are almost entirely centred on Christianity. The use of the name "religious studies" is in this respect a misnomer. It is a program in Christian studies. The comparative or world religions courses that are available are not sufficient in number nor are they taught by instructors trained in comparative study. It would be a great service to the students to rename the programmes appropriately.

St. Thomas University

The major in religious studies at St. Thomas University is part of a twenty-credit degree program requiring four years for full-time students to complete. Each student in the Bachelor of Arts program is required to have a major. The major may occupy up to half of the total credits completed for the degree.

A student has a number of options in the first year. In the normal stream, students divide their courses between the humanities and the social sciences. Religious studies is part of the humanities. In addition, students may enrol in the Aquinas program that has a limited enrolment of thirty-six students. Students in this program take two courses from the first-year options and the equivalent of three courses in the Aquinas option. In these three courses the goals are to form

> [a] learning community of no more than 36 students and three or more professors to study, from a cross-disciplinary perspective, a particular theme of interest in the liberal arts. Students' time will be flexibly scheduled so that in place of nine class hours per week, seminars, tutorials, full classes, and independent and group work will be scheduled as appropriate.[55]

In the external review report[56] the reviewers noted the heavy participation of the religious studies faculty in the Aquinas program, a fact that led them to support the need for additional full-time faculty in the department.

Beyond the first year of study students must declare a major either in a department or in an interdisciplinary program. Six full credits or twelve half-credits are required to complete the religious studies major. In its own study the department set out its learning goals and in doing so made ample use of Stephen Crites' *The Religion Major*. For example, they cited the Crites report's argument that a student should

> master a number of critical methodologies applicable to the study of religion and to other fields in that they may be working as well. They gain insight into various dimensions of contemporary civilization, not only through direct study of aspects of the current scene, but through the perspective gained by knowledge of other times and places. They discover the rhetorical and the experience-shaping power of symbol systems and the social roots out of that symbol systems grow.[57]

The department interpreted this view of the study of religions in the context of an understanding that the world in which students live is socially constructed. So understood, the stated goal of the study of religions at St. Thomas is to be relevant to the real world in that students must live. The department stated:

> While we are concerned that our students leave university with an appreciation for the variety of amazing religious expressions, we are as concerned that they be able to ask the questions they will need to ask to live fully as human beings; and to discover responses to those questions that allow them to feel they have a voice in the intellectual conversations that include their questions. We understand our task as empowering students to ask their own questions of meaning and value and to discover how to find appropriate responses in the academic conversations that make our lives as scholars so rich and exciting.[58]

With these goals in mind the department submitted a complete revision of its major program and departmental curriculum in preparation for an external review. The program placed the introduction to the study of religions at the second-year level. The courses were designed to introduce students to the basic tools for studying any religion—the study of ritual and the study of sacred texts. The New Testament introduces students to the study of texts.

At the third-year level there are five categories or "streams" of courses. The first is entitled "World Religions" and includes the department's courses on the historic traditions. These range from Hinduism and Buddhism, Judaism, Islam and Christianity through Native American Religions such as the religions of the Mi'Kmaq and Maliseet of Atlantic Canada and the Northeastern United States. Two characteristics of this category are of special note. First, Christianity is taught as one of the world's religions. Secondly, St. Thomas University has a Native studies program in which the Department of Religious Studies is an active participant. Indeed, the department is the only one in Atlantic Canada to offer courses on the religious traditions of the Native peoples of North America and of the Atlantic region in particular.

The second category is entitled "Ethics" and deals with ethical issues and theories of moral development, as well as Islamic ethics. The third category is entitled "Themes and Issues" and has courses on women and religion, death and dying and psychology of religion.

The fourth and fifth categories are entitled "Roman Catholic Traditions" and "Western Christian Traditions." While Christianity is taught as one of the world's religions, it is also taught under these two categories at the advanced level. There is an important distinction between these categories relating both to their methodologies and to the fact that for many years the department at St. Thomas has hired clerical instructors from the Fredericton diocese to teach theological and biblical courses. In one category Christianity is taught as one of the religions and in the others it is taught in a way that visibly and transparently serves the Roman Catholic diocese and student body. The clarity of the distinction between the categories provides both approaches with integrity. Courses under the "Roman Catholic Traditions" rubric cover theology, ecclesiology and New Testament studies. Under "Western Christian Traditions" the focus is on biblical studies, and ecumenical studies of interreligious dialogue.

At the fourth-year level the department has an integrative seminar centred on the scope of and methods in religious studies.

Out of the 1994 revision of the major and the departmental curriculum came a major that requires six full credits or their equivalent in half-credits. Students must include the general introductory course, both the second-level "tools" courses and the integrative seminar. Beyond that the students may select six half-credits from the five categories. Students are urged to obtain academic counselling to assist them in selecting courses, but there is no requirement that they choose elective religious studies courses in world religions, for example. The system, therefore, does permit students to focus on Western religious traditions and Christianity to a considerable extent.

The documentation included in the departmental study and the application for additional faculty following the external review was the most extensive of any department's in the region. The department is to be complimented for the remarkable way it argued for both the essentials of the study of religions on the religious studies side of the equation and the theological studies fundamental to the mission of the university and to the Roman Catholic community it serves.

St. Francis Xavier University

In the 1993-94 calendar of St. Francis Xavier University, there was a department of theology that offered a major in one of three degrees, "the B.A. with major (3 or 4 years), the B.A. with Advanced Major (4 years) and the B.A. with Honours (4 years)."[59] The major offered in each of these degree programs required that students complete six courses in the major subject. Students were also required to complete a three- or four-course minor in a subject, two courses in two or three other subjects and two electives. Students in the three-year program had a reduced load in the minor, and the two-course requirement and had fewer electives.

In 1998 St. Francis Xavier abandoned the three-year, fifteen-credit Bachelor of Arts degree. For that reason this review will focus on the "Advanced" twenty-credit degree. In 1997 the Department of Theology was renamed the "Department of Religious Studies." The "Advanced" major or four-year degree in religious studies sets out a number of core requirements: students must apply to the department for admission to the major and must possess an average of 60 percent (approximately a C minus); once admitted, they must maintain a 65 (C) average in the major and produce a research report/senior paper.

Religious studies at St. Francis Xavier does not have a distribution requirement built into the structure of its major. Students must complete six credits, and in the "Advanced" degree, they must complete a fifty-page thesis. For the honours degree, the students must complete ten credits and maintain a B average or better.

In 1999 the specialist teaching world religions, Islam and Hinduism in particular, took early retirement. The department was not allowed a full-time replacement in comparative religion but had to share an appointment with the multidisciplinary Catholic Studies program. Once again faculty trained in other areas have had to step into the gap and offer some advanced courses in comparative religion. The loss of a full-time person in the area of world religions was a critical loss coming just at the point when the department was beginning to redesign its curriculum and major as a religious studies department.

The priority given to the Catholic Studies program over the fundamental requirement of the religious studies program for at least one full-time specialist in world religions suggests that both the university and the department must quickly determine the relationship between these two programs. The department must set out clearly its understanding of the field of religious studies and how it sees itself implementing that understanding as new retirements occur. There is a great advantage to a clear distinction between Catholic Studies and Religious Studies. What the department must now do is make clear what its fundamental priorities are for its mandate, its curriculum and, most importantly, its areas of specialization for future appointments.

Mount Saint Vincent University

Despite the retirement of all the faculty who were in the department at Mount Saint Vincent in 1994-95, the major in religious studies remains on the books and is offered with considerable success. With a combination of overload teaching and part-time teaching assistance, the department and its one full-time faculty member, Dr. Randi Warne, maintain the major with a distinct and unique emphasis. World religions, gender and religion, and religion in Canada are now at the centre of the curriculum, replacing a more pastoral, biblical and theological emphasis.

Despite these changes, the major in religious studies has not yet changed in any significant structural way. The department offers a major within the arts faculty's three degree programs: the fifteen- and twenty-credit Bachelor of Arts with major and an honours degree. The Religious studies major consists of six full-course credits or the equivalent in half-credits. As part of the major, the department requires students to complete three introductory courses on the Old Testament and the New Testament and a half-credit course on world religions. Beyond that students must complete at least two full courses at a senior-level. The "Advanced" degree (twenty course credits) changes these requirements only by increasing the number of senior-level courses to three from two in the fifteen-credit program. Both majors require 65 percent average.

Mount Saint Vincent has a distribution requirement for its arts degree. Students must obtain one credit in English and take one course in each of four areas of study: language communication and symbolic system, natural sciences, social sciences and the humanities. Just as important, the university specifies that nine of a student's fifteen credits must be completed at the second-year level of study or higher, with at least three of those nine at the tertiary level. The impact of this regulation is significant for religious studies as it means that students must take electives at both of these levels. As a result, religious studies does not have prerequisites on its courses in order to accommodate students requiring electives. This affects the major, as students taking only one course in religious studies are in the same courses with the majors who have taken several. The solution has been to offer the majors in religious studies selected topics courses, directed readings and the "Advanced" course entitled "Great Religious Thinkers." All of these courses are numbered at the 4000 level. Such courses are offered as overloads by individual faculty. While such courses mean that the student receives individual attention from the instructor, it does not provide them with the corporate or seminar experience of study.

Saint Mary's University

In 1994-95 the religious studies department at Saint Mary's offered a major only as part of the fifteen-credit Bachelor of Arts degree. The Faculty of Arts did not institute an "Advanced" degree or twenty-credit program until 1996-97. When the four-year degree was introduced, no change to the department major was permitted. The agreement in the Faculty of Arts was that the four-year, "Advanced" degree should enable students to do double majors, do dual degrees in arts and science or arts and commerce or take more electives. Departments agreed not to add more required courses for the major. In addition to the major, the religious studies department offers an honours degree in religious studies.

The issue of the continuation of the fifteen-credit degree is a perennial topic of discussion in the Faculty of Arts. The faculties of commerce and science have both implemented four-year degrees. However, none of the faculties of arts in the universities in metropolitan Halifax have removed the three-year degree program, probably out of fear that doing so alone would affect enrolment by diverting students to the universities that continue to offer the three-year degree. One can only hope that all the universities will eliminate this anomalous degree soon.

At the introductory level the Faculty of Arts requires students to complete distribution requirements which include one full course or its half-course equivalent in English, basic logic in philosophy or a natural science or a language; one humanities course other than English, and two courses in the social sciences. These requirements, usually completed in the first-year, are supplemented by a requirement that all students must take eight full credits at the second- and third-year levels or above. This means that students must take electives beyond the introductory level. It further means that all departments must provide courses for students wishing to take electives at advanced levels. Religious studies at Saint Mary's, along with the history department, has opted to leave all courses free of prerequisites so that they can be taken as electives. Students must have at least a C minus cumulative quality point average to graduate.

A major in the fifteen-credit degree program may include a minimum of six and a maximum of eight credits. In religious studies students must complete six and one-half credits for the major. In 1994-95 all of the tertiary-level courses in religious studies were double-numbered. That is, each three hundred level course also had a four hundred number. Admission into the four hundred level course was exclusively for majors in religious studies. Each major student had to complete two full credits at the four hundred level. The four hundred courses had distinct course requirements, usually involving additional reading and writing assignments and group work, with the major students separate from the students taking the course at the three hundred level.

The department also had a distribution requirement that obligated students to take courses in three course areas: Comparative Religion; the Christian Tradition; and Thematic Studies. The department had one half-credit keystone course for majors and honours students that was numbered at the four hundred level—a seminar on hermeneutical issues in the study of religions. In 1998 the department introduced a second keystone half-credit course for the majors, and now requires students to take a course on theory and methods in the study of religions. The department also advises majors that they may count one course in a classical or Asian language as one of their six and one-half credits.

The use of a double-numbering system for the religious studies major is unique in the region. Its strength is the system's capacity to maintain a balance between the specialized requirements at the advanced level and the department's need to maintain large-enrolment elective courses in order to maintain overall enrolment levels. The weakness of the system is that it is work-intensive. Combining two courses into one requires additional preparation, both for the regular class meetings and for the additional time specifically for the majors outside class. It also did not satisfy the need of the majors to take courses together. A remedy for that has been the addition of the two senior seminars exclusively for major and honours students. Despite its difficulties, the department has generally viewed the system as a success.

Dalhousie University

The Department of Comparative Religion has a major program in the three-year Bachelor of Arts degree and the four-year "Advanced" degree. In the fifteen-credit degree students must complete one foreign language course, a social science course, a life or physical science course, a humanities course and obtain a credit in a designated writing course. Seven credits must be completed at the second-year level or higher. Most of these latter courses are done within a major which requires between four and eight credits to be beyond the 2000 level. In the twenty-credit degree program the total number of credits at and beyond the second-year level increases to twelve. In the major, or area of concentration, six and not more than nine credits must be beyond the primary level. The distribution requirement in both degrees requires that students must take at least one credit in two subjects other than their major.

Within these two degree structures the major follows essentially the same pattern. Within the fifteen-credit degree the major is completed in the equivalent of only five full courses, while in the major within the "Advanced" degree, the area of concentration is completed in six courses. The program is highly structured, with electives concentrated in the two introductory first-year courses. Beyond that level even second-year courses require the permission of the instructor for admission.

In the second year of the major in comparative religion the courses are all half-credits or one semester in length and are focused on the major religious traditions of the world. Students must take two of the three courses on the religions of the West and similarly two of the three courses on the religions of the East. These courses offer the foundation for the higher levels of the curriculum and support the department's claim that all of its courses are comparative.

Beyond the two levels of introduction to comparative religion the department requires either two or three credits or their half-credit equivalents at the tertiary level, and one half-credit of these must be the "Topics in Comparative Religion" course offered only to majors. All courses at these levels have prerequisites based on the second-year level of study.

The pressure caused by trying to maintain this highly structured program with only two full-time faculty is immense. The topics course is taught as an unpaid overload by one of the two faculty. Despite repeated attempts to increase the total faculty complement through the five-year cycles of external reviews, the department has not been successful. These pressures also explain in part the department's decision not to explore cooperative programs with the departments at Mount Saint Vincent University and Saint Mary's University. The faculty are to be commended for their enormous effort in helping make the program work.

Distribution Requirements

One of the most interesting challenges for any religious studies department is to develop a structure that compels students in the major to study diverse aspects of the field of religious studies. Distribution requirements clearly reveal the areas of expertise in the department and are the result of hard thinking about those aspects of the entire field of religious studies that can reasonably be implemented in the major program. Table 3.1 presents an overview of the areas covered in religious studies departments of the region.

Distribution requirements for the major are the only means of ensuring that students do not focus on one or two areas of study. The systems implemented set minimum levels for the students and their major programs.

In those departments where there is no distribution requirement, other techniques may be implemented to force students to diversify their course programs. Probably the most important is course counselling for the majors. Every department does this, but it is even more crucial if students are not required to take courses that they might not otherwise choose.

The Religious Studies Honours Degree

The honours degree has a long and distinguished history in Canada. It is a twenty-credit degree normally requiring a minimum of four years to complete. It may require an overall average of B or better in all the courses taken

Table 3.1
Distribution Requirements[60]

University	Area One	Area Two	Area Three	Area Four	Area Five
Memorial University of Newfoundland	World Religions	Biblical Studies	Christian Thought and History	Religion, Ethics and Modern Culture	Honours language required
University of Prince Edward Island	Introductory Courses	Biblical Studies and Western Religious History	Eastern Religions and Comparative Religion	Contemporary Religion and Interdisciplinary Studies	
Mount Allison University	1995 Biblical Studies	1995 World Religions	1995 Christian Tradition		
	1998 Western Traditions	1998 Eastern Traditions	1998 Religion and Culture		
Atlantic Baptist University	Historical	Philosophical	Comparative	Social-scientific	
St. Thomas University	World Religions	Themes and Issues	Roman Catholic Traditions	Western Christian Traditions	Ethics
St. Francis Xavier University	1994 Theology Required courses in Christian tradition only				
Mount Saint Vincent University 1995	Bible	Christianity and Personal Development	Ethics	Themes Service and cross-listed courses	Great Religious Thinkers or directed study
Saint Mary's University 1998 Theory and Methods	Comparative Religion	Thematic Studies	Christian Tradition	Majors Seminar	Honours Seminar
	Classical or Asian Language				
Dalhousie University	Introductions to the study of world religions and religion	One or two credits in Asian religions	One or two credits in Western religions	Special Topics course for majors	

Departments and Degree Programs 73

for the degree, but it certainly requires a B in all courses in the major area of the honours degree. This degree is normally the minimum requirement for admission to a graduate school.

The honours undergraduate degree in religious studies is available at Memorial University in Newfoundland; Mount Allison, the Atlantic Baptist universities and St. Thomas in New Brunswick and Saint Mary's University in Nova Scotia. All of these programs require an honours paper or thesis for completion of the honours degree. The Memorial and the Saint Mary's Honours degrees require at least one course in a classical, biblical or Asian language. Memorial is somewhat more specific in its language requirement, stipulating that "candidates will normally be required to have a reading knowledge of a language basic to their area of specialization."[61] Memorial offers Hebrew and Chinese as part of its full-time courses. Where departments do not offer languages within their programs, such as at Saint Mary's University, they depend on language or classics departments or even sister institutions for their introductory and advanced courses.

The honours degree with a major or concentration in religious studies involves relatively few students in the region. In general, students do not enter the honours program until they have completed ten or more credits in their degree program, and then it is usually only students who see themselves as going on to graduate work. The honours degree option is not the norm even for excellent students. Students need active encouragement to embark on an honours degree.

Memorial University's honours degree requires the completion of forty-five credits overall, of which twenty must be in the area of specialization. A double honours that combines religious studies with another area of study is also possible. The university requirements specify that "all candidates are required to have completed not fewer than two courses in English AND two courses in each of two of the following: a second language, History, Mathematics."[62] In addition students must complete a comprehensive examination in their area of specialization and an honours research essay.

Mount Allison University offers an honours degree in religious studies and joint honours in conjunction with the departments of English, Greek, history, philosophy and sociology/anthropology. Each of the combined honours degrees, with its requirements, is described in the university calendar. The core requirements for the honours in religious studies include the general introductory courses taught for the humanities, a world religions course, and a course on Christianity at the second-year level. Beyond these introductory courses, students must complete the equivalent of seven full courses in religious studies and an honours thesis.

The honours program at the Atlantic Baptist University is distinguished from the major only by the inclusion in the student's program of an honours thesis and a six-credit-hours (two-semester) course. As is normally the case, students are required to maintain a B minus in any religious studies course, a cumulative grade point average of 2.84[63] with no mark below a C minus in any university course.

The honours degree at St. Thomas University that was in the university calendar in 1994-95 had as its goal "two major objects: 1) to explore the relationship between Christianity and other religious, anti-religious or ideological traditions, and 2) to explore the relationship between theology and religious studies."[64] The program required nine credits in religious studies, of which five had to be at the third- and fourth-year levels. Beyond the introductory level, students had to complete one course in Christian theology and one in world religions, an honours seminar and a thesis course. The department recommended that students wishing to go to graduate school aim to have a reading knowledge of French and German and a classical language appropriate to their intended area of study.

The revised honours program, which was in draft in 1995, is built on the developmental principles of the major. Students progress from the general introduction, to the basic tools courses, to the five categories of courses, to the fourth-year scope-and-methods course. In addition to these requirements for the major, the department offers an honours seminar and an honours thesis course, both of that are full-credit courses. Overall, students must maintain a 3.0 (B) in their major.

Saint Mary's University offers an honours degree that requires students to complete ten and one-half credits in religious studies. Student must include the distribution requirements, the two 400-level courses, and, as of 1998, complete both the majors seminar and the theory and methods course. Building upon the foundation of the major requirements, honours students must complete a classical or Asian language requirement, two additional full-course electives at the 400-level and the honours seminar in which they write an honours paper or thesis.

In general, then, the honours degree requires a higher level of overall performance both in the degree requirements as a whole and in religious studies in particular. Most departments build their honours requirements on the foundation of the major, with the clear understanding that the additional requirements are designed to prepare students for graduate study in the field.

Minors or Concentrations in Religious Studies

A minor within a bachelor's degree provides recognition that a student has completed a series of courses in a single subject or area but normally less than the total number required for a major. Whereas a major frequently requires the equivalent of six and one-half credits in a fifteen- or twenty-credit degree program, a minor requires approximately four full credits. Departments rarely have a distribution requirement for the completion of a minor concentration. Students may simply take any four full credits or their equivalent to complete the program. All departments offering a major in religious studies offer the possibility of completing a minor in the subject.

Graduate Degree in Religious Studies

In religious studies the only masters degree program in Atlantic Canada is at Memorial University. Enrolments have averaged around twenty students. Early enrolment in the M.A. program was from local teachers upgrading their professional training. More recently the enrolments have come from national applications. Admission to the Memorial program requires an honours degree or its equivalent. It is anticipated that full-time study will permit completion of the degree in two years while part-time study will result in students taking up to five years to complete the degree.

The undergraduate curriculum has four general areas of study: biblical studies; world religions; Christian thought and history and religion; and religion, ethics and modern culture. Graduate thesis areas, as outlined in the 1998 revision to the calendar, are a considerable expansion of the four areas. This expansion was intended to better reflect the expertise of individual faculty in the department. Thus students may write theses in the following areas: "Hebrew Bible/Old Testament, New Testament, Judaism, East Asian Religious Traditions, the History of Christianity, the Religious History of Canada, the Religious History of Newfoundland and Labrador, Medieval Religious Thought, Religion and Culture, New Age Religious Movements, Christian Ethics and the Philosophy of Religion."[65]

The department needs proof of proficiency in any language required for the completion of the degree program. Four courses are required, of which three are mandatory: RS6100 Interpretations of Religion; RS6120 Studies in Religious Texts; and RS6130 Studies in Religious Movements and Institutions. For the fourth course students may select from a series of topics a course corresponding to the area in which they intend to write their thesis.

Discussions took place during the research phase of this review, which indicated that both the department and the graduate administration at

Memorial would like to develop working relations with other departments in the region. Such an arrangement could permit a student to fulfill a residency requirement at Memorial and complete some course work and thesis supervision using faculty elsewhere in the region. This possibility was mentioned to all the departments in the region. Unfortunately no student has been found to date to assist the development of this exciting opportunity.

Religious Studies as Service Departments

For departments of religious studies, student enrolment is the bread and butter of their existence. To that end they offer service and elective courses either as introductory courses for first-year students or as courses at the more advanced levels. We have seen the crucial role that the particular university degree requirements play in a department's conception of how to meet its service function. In turn, determining how to maintain enrolment levels frequently affects how the major is delivered to students. For example, the departments at Mount Saint Vincent and Saint Mary's do not have prerequisites for any courses. Memorial University has recently revised its program to remove prerequisites. At Saint Mary's the decision not to implement prerequisites was determined by the degree structure. The three-year degree requires students to take the majority of elective courses in their degree program at the junior or senior level. In arts that means that eight of the fifteen credits must be at the junior or senior level. Electives such as religious studies must be available to service that demand in degree programs in science, commerce and arts. By contrast, degree requirements at Dalhousie permit students to take many more introductory-level courses in their degree requirements. Therefore the department can have large first-year courses and can implement prerequisites and a more hierarchical structure for its program.

At Mount Allison the department has become an integral part of the humanities introductory courses as a way to fulfill its service responsibility. At St. Thomas University, the Aquinas program is dependent on the religious studies faculty for essential components such as the tutorials and individual supervision.

It is a measure of the vulnerability of religious studies programs that they can be preoccupied by the demand to meet enrolment expectations. On the other hand it is a measure of the sense of realism in the modern university that maintaining adequate enrolments plays a significant part in the maintenance of the department and the field.

Religious Studies in Multidisciplinary Degree Programs

Because religious studies is a broad multidisciplinary subject in its own right, departments have participated widely in various multidisciplinary, interdepartmental or inter-faculty programs. Comparative religion courses at Saint Mary's and the University of Prince Edward Island include essential courses for Asian studies programs. At Dalhousie introductory comparative religion courses are included as part of the university writing courses. Also at Dalhousie and Saint Mary's universities, faculty have been or are in executive positions in their respective international development studies programs and participate as thesis directors or as readers of M.A. and Honours degree theses. At St. Francis Xavier University the new major program in Catholic Studies could not exist without religious studies because the majority of its courses are based there. Further, one of the religious studies courses with the highest enrolment at St. Francis Xavier is the course in health ethics which is cross-listed with the School of Nursing. Similarly, at Mount Saint Vincent the course on business ethics is an integral component of the commerce degree. Asian studies, women's studies, foundation year or special introductory year programs such as the Humanities courses at Mount Allison or the Aquinas program at St. Thomas University are all examples of programs that would have difficulty operating without the active involvement of religious studies faculty and the courses based in the religious studies departments. For Memorial, one of the essential ingredients of the degree programs was the dual degree that combined a B.A. and a B.Ed. Students completed a major or concentration in religious studies as part of their B.A. and then used their training to qualify to teach religion in the school system.

Active involvement of faculty both as teachers and as administrators of multidisciplinary programs brings enrolment advantages and curricular disadvantages. Frequently such involvements have serious effects on the ability of small departments to offer the courses essential to their own program. Course reductions to compensate for administration of departments and programs limit the number of courses in religious studies. Depending on the location of the university, finding part-time replacements may be difficult, especially in cases where the courses involve non-Western religious traditions, and Judaism or Islam among Western traditions.

Nonetheless, the dimension of a department's curriculum that is involved in both multidisciplinary programs and requirements for other faculties or departments is becoming increasingly important to university administrations, which view these types of inter-program support, the contribution of administrative time, committee involvement, honours and master's degree thesis reading and supervision as components of the activity of a department and its faculty. Such factors in turn come into play in renewal appointments and tenure decisions as well as being factors in the decisions about retirement replacements.

Library Holdings in Religious Studies[66]

The library is the central resource in the university for both teaching and research. No university can function without a library, and no department can hope to offer a major or honours degree without the necessary library resources to do so. While the World Wide Web, the Internet and on-line sources of information have opened up new vistas of information for immediate retrieval, these sources have not yet supplanted, and likely never will, the essential role of the book and the journal in the university library. University and national libraries with their book and archival collections are the repository of the cumulative recorded memories and content of our traditions. Such libraries, as we argued earlier, provide us with the "image" of knowledge as we understand it, and with that, a system by which we can study what is our own culture and, more and more, study that of other peoples.

There are major university libraries in Canada, such as those at the Universities of Toronto, McGill, Laval, Alberta and British Columbia, which are repositories for major collections sufficiently large to support both undergraduate and graduate programs. There is the National Library, as well as the various national and provincial archives that hold important research resources. There are international libraries, the catalogues of which can be accessed through the Internet and from which faculty can borrow books through interlibrary loan arrangements. The effect of these interconnected systems of library access is that no university library, no matter how small, is totally isolated from larger libraries and all the research resources they hold.

No university library, no matter how large, can hope to hold even a fraction of the total published material in English and other languages. As the federal and provincial governments have cut university budgets, libraries have faced the dual reality of precipitous escalations in costs for journals and books and diminishing budgets for acquisitions. Libraries are desperately trying to purchase what they can in support of the various fields that university Senates have authorized for incorporation into university curricula. No matter how libraries are connected both nationally and internationally, the local library is the fundamental resource for students and teachers. Few universities in Atlantic Canada can even come close to matching in size and diversity the collections at the largest universities in Canada. Yet their importance is beyond measure to the people who use them on a day-to-day basis.

There is an old adage, perhaps less cogent in the days of the Internet than it once was, that the most efficient research method is to browse in the library. But to employ that method you have to know where to browse, and it is the Library of Congress organization of books that permits such browsing. "BL" and "BT" mark the starting and ending points of the library that deals with religions. Reflecting the religions predominant in the North American setting, most of these sections are used to organize books on topics about Christianity. Other religions such as Hinduism and Buddhism and the books about religion are grouped under "BL." Judaism, and to a lesser extent, Islam are classified and refined in separate areas within the overall range.

The holdings that are actually catalogued in the Atlantic region reflect the history of the institutions and their primary commitment to undergraduate education. Only Memorial University of Newfoundland, Dalhousie University, and the University of New Brunswick set out to provide comprehensive undergraduate and selected graduate library holdings in arts, science and professional programs. The majority of the universities and their libraries exist to service the undergraduate courses that are being taught by the particular university. The library acquisitions policies serve the particular departments and their needs for teaching and to a lesser extent faculty research. The holdings of a library make possible an education that goes far beyond the course textbooks and into the breadth and depth of the range of information and arguments about any subject.

In 1995, the two largest library collections in the region were at the University of New Brunswick (1,067,621 volumes) and Memorial University of Newfoundland (1,057,313 volumes). The holdings of both these libraries exceed those of the next rank by some 250,000 books. St. Thomas University shares a campus with the University of New Brunswick and also shares library facilities. It is striking therefore that, while the University of New Brunswick has no religious studies department or program, the holdings in religious studies are nonetheless substantial—approximately 56,000 volumes. That number almost parallels the holdings on religions at Memorial University, where the largest department of religious studies and the only graduate program in religious studies exist.

The total holdings of the University of Prince Edward Island are 285,000, with some 14,900 in the field of religion. Dalhousie University's total holdings in 1994 were approximately 750,713 overall, of which some 39,400 dealt with religions. The University of King's College, located on the Dalhousie campus, has a separate library with some 90,000 volumes, of which some 5000 are catalogued under the subject of religion.

The Dalhousie and Kings libraries are located in metropolitan Halifax, where all universities have collaborated for years both to computerize their holdings and to make all of them available through a single computerized catalogue called "Novanet." This collaborative initiative of the Halifax universities has now been expanded to include virtually all provincial universities, giving students access to any book in any university library in the province. More and more, the acquisitions policies of the universities are coordinated to limit duplication in book and especially journal orders. Nova Scotia university libraries, then, deserve to a considerable extent to be viewed as a single library system. The holdings for Nova Scotia and its Novanet system are presented in Table 3.2.

Table 3.2
Total Volumes in Nova Scotia University Libraries

Institution	Place	Total Volumes (1994)	Total in Religion
Acadia University	Wolfville	633,134	33,200
Atlantic School of Theology	Halifax	69,387	69,387
Dalhousie University	Halifax	750,713	39,400
Mount Saint Vincent University	Halifax	117,000	6,100
Nova Scotia College of Art and Design	Halifax	27,000	
St. Francis Xavier University	Antigonish	589,341	30,900
Saint Mary's University	Halifax	306,170	16,000
Technical University of Nova Scotia	Halifax	64,000	
University College of Cape Breton	Sydney	290,000	15,200
University of King's College	Halifax	90,000	5,000
Université Sainte Anne	Church Point	88,300	4,600
Totals		3,025,045	219,787

In the university system in Nova Scotia considerably less than 10 percent[67] of the total holdings in the Novanet catalogues are in the areas of religious studies and the divinity schools taken together. Given the size of the religious studies programs and the modest student enrolments in the divinity schools the library holdings are quite substantial. These holdings reflect the religious origins of most of the institutions.

Despite the overall holdings in the region, and in metropolitan Halifax in particular, the budget for new acquisitions in religious studies departments is severely limited. For example, over the last twenty-five years the department at Saint Mary's has had a library purchasing budget that has increased from $3,600 per year in 1975 to slightly over $6,000 in recent years. This must cover all standing orders, journals and book purchases for all of the course areas in the university. Such limited purchasing power makes it very difficult to keep collections up-to-date across the many areas of study for undergraduates and research by faculty.

The effect of the centralized and computerized catalogue in Nova Scotia is very substantial, primarily for the metropolitan universities and the three religious studies departments there. Students and faculty have access to the books in all the university libraries from numerous terminals in the libraries or from computer laboratories. Obtaining books is another matter. The reality, of course, is that students infrequently move beyond their own campus, and the greater the distance to a library to obtain a book the less likely it is that students will make use of such a resource. Delivery systems within the Nova Scotia system now make that "reach" a little less dramatic and everything that much more accessible for the motivated student.

These 1994 statistics for total holdings overall and in religion in Nova Scotia give an idea of the overall resources in the region's library system. Equally interesting is information about those holdings that are on specific religions. There, as one might anticipate in universities that often were founded by Christian religious communities, the preponderance of library holdings is in the area of Christianity generally and biblical studies in particular. This is illustrated by the fact that the largest holdings were at universities that had a theological school (Acadia and Memorial) as part of the larger university or were at an independent theological school (the Atlantic School of Theology).

In 1998, Douglas Vaisey, Head of Reference Services at Saint Mary's University, prepared an overview of the library holdings at different universities that relate to specific religions of the world and selected categories in the study of religion. In what follows, then, I want to focus on the holdings that reflect the comparative study in the field only at those institutions where there is a religious studies department. However, there are several difficulties connected with reading the statistics that need to be kept in mind. The Department of Religious Studies at St. Thomas University has its library holdings at the University of New Brunswick. To show the holdings for St. Thomas requires that the statistics reflect the holdings at the University of New Brunswick. In Newfoundland there is no way to differentiate the holdings for the Department of Religious Studies at Memorial from those for Queen's College. Finally, while Acadia University has chosen to close its undergraduate degree program in comparative religion, its holdings in the comparative areas are significant and are included in Table 3.3. It should also be remembered that Acadia Divinity College is still located on the campus of Acadia University and in the statistics the preponderance of books in the area of Christianity will reflect that fact. Finally, the categories chosen are deliberately arbitrary and do not preclude books appearing within several of the categories. Rather, the approach is to imagine an undergraduate searching for books using the most general categories and to see how many titles would emerge.

The totals show that the overwhelming preponderance of books is on Christianity. Sixty percent of the titles are in this area of the study of religions. In contrast, less than six per cent of the reported holdings (5.77%) deal with Bahai, Buddhism, Hinduism, Islam and Judaism taken together.

It is difficult to conclude that a proportion of holdings of less than 6 percent in non-Western religions shows a slow but important transformation in acquisitions policy. It is clear that the historic emphasis in acquisitions policy was designed to serve theology departments or religious studies departments whose curricula were predominantly Christian. Nonetheless, at the major libraries in the region, there does appear to be a recognition of the necessity to expand the areas relating to world religions. Given that one of the major budgetary policies in the universities has been to hold library budgets down and to force departments to cut journals and limit acquisitions, it is going to take a long slow transformation of library holdings to reflect the requirements of comparative study by departments and the increasingly multicultural realities of the culture at large.

There are a number of special library collections in the Atlantic region.[68] Both the Acadia Divinity College and the Atlantic School of Theology have special collections dealing with Baptist Church history, and that of the Presbyterian, Methodist and United churches, respectively. All of the universities archive their own institutional documents such as senate minutes and the like, and frequently faculty donate papers to the university which then become part of the archival collection. Of special note for the study of religions are the following special archive collections:[69]

- The Winthrop Packard Bell Collection of Acadiana housed at the Ralph Pickard Bell Library at Mount Allison University.

Table 3.3
Library Holdings by Religion or Theme

Library Holdings	Acadia	Dal	King's	Memorial	Mt. Allison	Mt. Saint Vincent	St. Francis Xavier	St. Mary's	St. Thomas UNB	UPEI	Totals
Bahai	16	23		34	24	8	4	8	36	23	176 or .05 %
Buddhism	281	728		936	525	89	93	996	452	314	4,414 or 1.37%
Christianity[a]	11,423	46,622		30,250	23,020	13,219	8,521	18,865	35,321	8,589	195,830 or 60.65%
Ethics	1,749	12,386		4,622	1,307	3,715	2,155	5,250	4,401	1,795	37,380 or 11.58%
Hindu & Jain	127	558		836	166	140	157	935	327	142	3,388 or 1.05%
Islam	266	1,690		1,498	277	169	148	751	512	179	5,490 or 1.7%
Judaism	503	816		1,518	313	228	169	446	799	285	5,077 or 1.6%
Religion	2,485	10,048		6,310	3,269	2,032	1,488	5,523	5,904	2,187	39,246 or 12.15%
Religious	2,519	7,056		5,325	2,102	2,954	1,304	3,457	5,087	1,503	31,307 or 9.7%
Theosophy	19	254		39	5	28	40	98	48	13	544 or .17%

[a]Christianity=categories of Catholicism, Christianity, Christianity, Church, churches, theology.

- The Edgar and Dorothy Davidson Collection of Canadiana housed at the Ralph Pickard Bell Library at Mount Allison University. The focus of the collection is on Maritime history with the Methodist Church a special area of interest.[70]
- The Prince Edward Island Collection housed in the Robertson Library of the University of Prince Edward Island. "The collection includes current and retrospective material published on Prince Edward Island written by Islanders or about the Island."[71]
- The J. J. Stewart Collection at the Killam Memorial Library, Dalhousie University. This collection focuses on Nova Scotia and includes books and pamphlets and the first translations of the Christian Gospels into Mi'Kmaq.[72]
- The Beaverbrook Collection of Rare Books in the Harriet Irving Library of the University of New Brunswick. The collection includes important works on "sixteenth and seventeenth century religious reformers."[73]
- The Bray Collection and the Kingdon Collection at the University of King's College Library, University of King's College. The focus of the Bray Collection is "Christianity; Bible—criticism and interpretation," while the Kingdon Collection focuses on "Christianity; Theology, Doctrinal; Anglican Communion; "In 1907 it was regarded as the best Anglican theological library in private hands in Canada."[74]
- Université Sainte-Anne has developed a research institute and archive in support of Acadian studies with a special emphasis on Acadian religious traditions.

In addition to these special collections there is a relatively new Internet-based collection of materials for the study of religions in Newfoundland and Labrador. Hans Rollmann has personally set up the Web site: (http://www.ucs.mun.ca/˜hrollman/index.html). Of it he writes: "It's actually not an archive but a Newfoundland and Labrador Collection. It contains materials (literature and sources, no originals though) that will help students in their research on NF and Labrador religion, primarily those who take my two courses on Religion in Newfoundland and Labrador: 1. Beginnings to 1800; 2. 1800 to the Present. In addition to the Internet resources, there is a room that stores student papers on religion in Newfoundland and Labrador and it is equipped with a microfilm/microfiche reader and a computer."[75]

It is fair to say that library resources are critical to academic programs and that the current state of the libraries is in precipitous decline. Unless new funding can be found for the library systems as a whole and for each and every academic program, the research and teaching capacity of the universities will become increasingly impoverished.

Notes

1. Stephen C. Crites, scribe *The Religion Major: A Report/The American Academy of Religion Task Force for the American Association of Colleges*, (Atlanta: American Academy of Religion, 1990), 7.
2. Department of Religious Studies Self Study, 1989.
3. Ibid.
4. Universities founded by churches or religious orders that are now governed by independent Boards of Governors are, from the point of view of government funding, treated as public universities in Nova Scotia and New Brunswick.
5. "Mi'Kmaq is actually the correct spelling, but over the years, Micmac has become the more commonly used name. Other variations are Míqmaq, Míkmaq, and Mi'mkaq. Their name comes from a word from their own language meaning 'allies.' Other names used for Micmac were: Cape Sable Indians, Gaspesian (Gaspesien, Micmac of Gaspé), Matueswiskitchinuuk (Malecite 'Porcupine Indians'), Shonack (Beothuk 'Bad Indians'), Souriquois (French), and Tarrateen (British)." http://www.dickshovel.com/mic.html, date 15 December 1999.
6. *Mount Saint Vincent University Calendar*, 1992-93, 9.
7. Departmental study, 1989.
8. Ibid.
9. Ibid.
10. Ibid.
11. Ibid.
12. Dalhousie University's Department of Comparative Religion declined to participate in the discussions and the resultant agreement to cooperate. The department argued, among other things, that its hierarchically structured program and commitment to provide courses for the Dalhousie international development studies programme precluded admitting more students to its courses.
13. *The Framework of the Metro Halifax Universities' Business Plan*, (1995): 3-4.
14. "Rationale for the change of the name of 'Department of Theology' to that of 'Department of Religious Studies,'" 18 April, 1994.
15. Ibid.
16. Ibid., 2.
17. *St. Francis Xavier University Academic Calendar*, "Introduction," v.
18. "Rationale for change of name."
19. Ray Hart, "Religious and Theological Studies in American Higher Education: A Pilot Study," *Journal of the American Academy of Religion* 59/4 (1991): 715-827.
20. Cited in MacDonald, "Rationale for Change of Name,"
21. In January 2000, Margaret MacDonald, Chair of Religious Studies, informed me that the university had refused to allow the replacement of the world religions specialist in the department who had taken early retirement in 1999. Rather, the university created a two-thirds position in Catholic Studies and left one-third to religious studies. The prospective appointee must teach an introductory course on world religions for religious studies.
22. *St. Thomas University Calendar*, 1998-99, 2.
23. Ibid., 2.
24. Memo from Dr. Thomas Parkhill to Roger Barnsley, 8 November, 1993, 1.
25. Ibid.

26 Ibid.
27 Crites, *Religion Major*, 9.
28 Memo from Dr. Thomas Parkhill in a memo dated November 8, 1993: 2.
29 Departmental Self Study, 7-8.
30 Final report of the Arts Faculty Planning Committee, 17 December, 1993.
31 *Atlantic Baptist University Academic Calendar*, 1997-98, 4.
32 Ibid.
33 *St. Stephen's University Calendar*, 1998-99, 4.
34 Ibid., 9.
35 Department of Religious Studies, Academic Planning Submission, January, 1991, 3.
36 Letter of nomination of Dr. Morley F. Hodder for the Position of Professor Emeritus from the Department of Religious Studies to the Committee on Honorary Degrees and Ceremonial, 29 November 1997.
37 Ibid.
38 Anderson, *Guides*, (1969 and 1972).
39 Department of Comparative Religion, Dalhousie University, "A Brief Historical Sketch" (4 January 1990), 1.
40 The original name of the department was "Department of Religion." The name was changed to "Department of Comparative Religion" in the early 1990s.
41 There was an abortive attempt to bring Dr. George Parkin Grant to the department as its new head when he was preparing to leave the Department of Religious Studies at McMaster University. The then Department of Religion rejected this appointment. While Dr. Grant finished his career at Dalhousie, his teaching responsibilities were limited to the Departments of Classics and Political Science.
42 Tom Faulkner, "Less Is More: How Religious Studies Can Foster Liberal Education." In *Religious Studies: Issues, Prospects and Proposals*, K. K. Klostermaier and Larry W. Hurtado, eds. (Atlanta: Scholars Press, 1991, pp. 105-119.
43 Department of Comparative Religion, Dalhousie University, "A Brief Historical Sketch," 1.
44 Ibid., 5.
45 Ibid., 3.
46 Ibid., 4-5.
47 Crites, *Religion Major*, 16.
48 *Maclean's* 108/47 (20 November, 1995): 32.
49 *Dalhousie University Calendar*, 1994-95, 99.
50 Departmental Response to the External Review of the Department of Religious Studies at Mount Allison University, 1996, 3.
51 Ibid., 2.
52 Ibid., 1.
53 Ibid.
54 *The Atlantic Baptist University Academic Calendar*, 1997-98, 42.
55 *St. Thomas University Calendar, 1998-99*, 39.
56 Report of the Review Team to the Department of Religious Studies at St. Thomas University, Fredericton [sic], NB, 24-25 March 1994.
57 Crites, *Religion Major*, 19-20, cited on p. 8 of the religious studies departmental study.
58 Religious studies departmental study, 9.

59 *St. Francis Xavier University Academic Calendar*, 1993-94, 11.
60 Based on 1993-1994 university calendars unless otherwise stipulated.
61 *Memorial University of Newfoundland Academic Calendar*, 1994-95, 154.
62 Ibid., 109.
63 It is difficult to know exactly what letter grade is intended by the numerical average of 2.84. The grade scale included in the calendar (p. 23) lists a B minus as 2.67 and a B as 3.0.
64 *St. Thomas University Calendar*, 1994-95, 133.
65 Complete Revised Calendar Entry: Religious Studies, 1998, 3.
66 I am indebted to my research assistant Marie Bousquet for her assistance in gathering information on library holdings and special collections in the region. Douglas Vaisey, Head of Reference Library Services at Saint Mary's University, collected the statistical information about the regional libraries and also contributed to the information on special collections.
67 The figures cited produce the following result: 7.26557% of total library holdings is in the area of religious studies and divinity schools.
68 Directory of Canadian Archives (Ottawa: Council of Canadian Archives, 1990.
69 Directory of Special Collections of Research Value in Canadian Libraries (Ottawa: National Library of Canada, 1992), 34.
70 Ibid., 29.
71 Ibid., 49.
72 Ibid., 60.
73 Ibid., 69.
74 Ibid., 144, 155.
75 Correspondence from Hans Rollmann to Paul Bowlby.

4

The Curriculum in Religious Studies

> The curriculum is the essence of any university. It consists in what students formally study in all stages from the undergraduate to the research professor. It determines the character of the university far more than any structure of government, methods of teaching, or social organization. Indeed, these latter are largely shaped by what is studied and why it is studied.
> — George P. Grant

Religious studies is best understood by its existence as a department within the contemporary university. It represents, as do all academic departments and programs, the range of subjects accredited for advanced study by the Senate of the various universities. The unique local characteristics of the universities in the Atlantic region have played a major role in the setting of priorities for the design of departments and their degree programs. Now, bearing in mind George Grant's assertion that the curriculum defines what a university is, we shall look at religious studies in the Atlantic region from the perspective of the content of each department's curriculum.

The religious studies curriculum has been a perennial topic of discussion among university teachers in the field. It has been the subject of periodic panels and frequent formal and informal discussions at the meetings of the Canadian Society for the Study of Religion/Société canadienne pour l'étude de la religion. The American Academy of Religion has for years dedicated a section of its annual conference to curriculum, course themes and pedagogical techniques appropriate to the field.

Several factors combine in the construction of a department's curriculum. The faculty in each department must determine what *can* be taught out of the whole field at the introductory and advanced levels in their curriculum. That determination is governed primarily by the training and specializations of the full-time faculty in the department. In the Atlantic region, the historic traditions of a university, particularly those institutions founded by Christian denominations or religious orders, have influenced the decisions about who has been hired to teach. Theology departments hired biblical scholars, church historians and theologians for a curriculum focused on Christianity. Their careers carried them forward into the departments of religious studies and it was only as retirements occurred or new appointments were granted that the departments could diversify the curriculum to include the contemporary study of religions. These historical factors have shaped the curriculum in religious studies throughout the post-war era.

Nonetheless, as departments have evolved, professors, particularly in smaller departments with a faculty complement of three or four, have not ignored the larger field of religious studies and its fundamental curriculum requirements. Frequently faculty teach courses at the introductory and even advanced undergraduate levels, whose subject and content are not related to their graduate training. Numerous faculty members have spent years expanding the areas of their research for teaching so that a department that has no one trained in comparative studies, for example, can offer courses on selected religious traditions, such as Hinduism, Buddhism or Islam, or on the methods and theories of religious studies. Departments have also cross-listed courses on religion from departments of philosophy, classics, sociology, psychology and anthropology as a way to incorporate diverse methods and content into the religious studies curriculum. When small departments can hire people trained in an area of world religions, it is often to teach courses about the major traditions of Asia or Africa. Such breadth of teaching assignments for the sake of the department's program can be daunting, to say the least, and can contrast sharply to narrower specializations in for example, biblical studies.

In addition to integrating required courses from the field of religious studies, departments frequently design courses to meet specific university requirements. Religious studies faculty have been major contributors to first-year specialty programs such as the Aquinas program at St. Thomas University or the multidisciplinary courses at Mount Allison University. Such specialized first-year courses can be very demanding in both time and preparation for the faculty concerned since they involve intensive individual work with students and teaching areas that may not be related to specialized training or research areas. In addition, departments may feel obligated to offer either credit or non-credit community service courses in order to enhance the relationship of the department to the local community. (For example, Mount Saint Vincent's faculty offered non-credit courses primarily for the Archdiocese of Halifax until very recently. These five-week courses were well-attended and supported by interested laity in the city. Saint Mary's regularly incorporates evening courses in religious studies for full and part-time students.) Finally, departments pay considerable attention to what students actually like to take in sufficient numbers to keep a department's overall enrolment statistics on a per capita par with those of other departments. All of these various factors are not easily reconciled, especially in the smaller departments. Frequently programs come to depend on overload teaching or part-time instructors as a way to maintain the overall curriculum for the major in religious studies.

In the discussion of the curriculum of each religious studies department, I will begin with a brief summary of the Anderson survey of courses published in 1972[1] and then indicate how the overall curriculum had changed by the mid-1990s. If the early 1970s marked the beginning of the transformation of religious studies in Canada from a predominantly Christian discipline to the more multi-religious and methodologically diverse field of study it is now, there ought to be evidence of that change in the curricula of departments by the mid-1990s.

In what follows, then, I will survey the program descriptions given in the university calendars and departmental reviews with a view to testing the extent to which the departments have diversified. We will note what changes have occurred in religious studies between 1972, when Anderson published his last survey, and 1994 when the data for this study were collected. In essence we are asking how the conversation about the nature of religious studies over the last twenty-five years has been reflected in fundamental changes to the curriculum of departments.

Religious Studies Curricula in the Atlantic Region

Departments of religious studies introduce their curriculum and program requirements to students through the academic calendar. Some departments produce a handbook each year, but that practice is not widespread. From the university calendar or departmental handbook students learn what courses are offered and what the program requirements are for them to qualify for the major and for their degree. The university calendar is a legal document in the sense that students are responsible for meeting the stated requirements and in turn the stated requirements cannot be arbitrarily changed by departments or the university. A university's academic calendar, then, will be the principal source for outlining how a department defines its curriculum.

The introductory course in religious studies is usually the first course that students encounter in the field. Most frequently it is part of a series of first-year requirements for new students. The general purposes of these requirements are to ensure that students are introduced to a number of subject areas and to test whether the students have the foundational skills in reading and writing so that they can proceed to higher levels of study. In this sense the religious studies introductory courses are part of a larger project that is either formally set up in the Faculty of Arts or informally understood to be the purpose of the freshman cluster of courses.

What do new university students need to learn at the introductory level about the study of religions? Because this question has been a significant talking point among religious studies faculty, I want to put considerable emphasis on the ways in which departments structure their curriculum in response to such a question. More advanced levels of study frequently include courses that are built on the introductory stages and, as we shall see, the advanced courses are frequently similar in topic across the region's departments. Furthermore, the introductory courses reveal a great deal about the nature and purpose of the whole departmental program and what it sets out to survey both in general and in advanced courses.

Memorial University of Newfoundland

In 1972 there were six full-time religious studies faculty at Memorial University of Newfoundland. There were nine introductory courses, two at the first-year level and seven at the second-year level. Two courses were in the area of religion and Western culture: one was on ethical issues and the other on the roles of Christianity in Western civilization. There were three world religions courses, two in biblical literature and two in Christian church history. There were twenty-eight courses at the third- and fourth-year levels of study: five in biblical studies, seven in world religions, ten in moral issues, four special topics courses and two courses for the compulsory comprehensive examination and honours thesis. At the introductory level, then, one-third of the courses were in comparative study, and at the advanced levels the proportion dropped to one-quarter of the courses listed. Western civilization, biblical courses and church history were the predominant areas covered by the curriculum.

By 1994 Memorial University's Department of Religious Studies had expanded from six to nine full-time faculty and had the largest enrolment in an undergraduate program in the region. It had also added a master's degree program, the only graduate degree in religious studies in the region.

At Memorial students are required to complete twenty full credits after Grade 12 in order to receive a bachelor's degree. To complete a major in religious studies students must take a comprehensive examination in the field and/or submit, in the case of an honours student, an honours thesis. During the formative years of the department, the unique denominationally based education system in Newfoundland continued to have a significant impact on the religious studies curriculum. This was evident in the department's general description of its curriculum:

> The curriculum in religious studies is designed to provide a basic programme in Religion as an academic discipline. Courses are open to all students on the same basis as are other courses in the Faculty of Arts. These courses are recommended for (1) students who wish to gain an understanding of the essential teachings and beliefs of one or more major religious traditions; (2) students who are preparing for careers for which a knowledge of religious thought, practices and tradition is an appropriate preparation; and (3) students who are interested in exploring this field as an area of scholarly interest and human concern.[2]

More specifically the description went on to define the fundamental link of the department's program to the training of teachers of religion for the schools:

> Those who plan to teach Religion in the schools are permitted to complete a Major or Minor or Concentration in Religious Studies under the degrees of Bachelor of Education (Primary) and Bachelor of Education (Elementary), under the Conjoint degrees of Bachelor of Education and Bachelor of Arts for High School teachers, and under the Conjoint degrees of Bachelor of Physical Education and Bachelor of Education.[3]

It was to be expected, given the emphasis in the department's requirements on supporting professional education degrees for people preparing to teach in the denominational school systems, that there would be an emphasis on Christianity.

In 1994 the department offered two layers of introduction. First, there were the general introductory courses for the first year of study. Then, in the second year, the department introduced the four areas of the department's curriculum: biblical studies; Christian thought and history; world religions; and religion, ethics and modern culture. The three general introductory courses at the 1000, or primary introductory level were followed by twelve secondary or 2000-level introductory courses that corresponded both to the specialized areas of the faculty's training and to the newer areas coming into the field of religious studies.

In the first level of introductory courses there were three 1000-level courses: "Religion in the Modern World," "Christianity in Western Civilization," and "Myth, Ritual and Religious Experience." The three courses were intended as large-enrolment courses capable of attracting students to the religious studies major. These courses did not serve as prerequisites for further study in the field since only two of them counted toward a major in religious studies.

What is striking by way of change since 1972 is the shift to a religious studies focus in the primary introductory level. In 1994 one-third of the courses were on Christianity and two-thirds dealt broadly with religion in the world and the question of what constitutes religion and religious experience.

The second level of courses provided a foundational introduction for students doing the major and for those in education who were pursuing a concentration in religious studies. The department recommended the two introductory courses on the Bible and the introduction to Christianity for both types of program. In addition to biblical studies, the introductory courses covered three areas of study: Christian thought and history; world religions; and religion, ethics and modern culture.

Overall the department listed sixty-six courses in the 1993-94 calendar, up substantially from the thirty-seven listed in 1972 according to the Anderson survey. Of the sixty-six courses, fifteen were at the two introductory levels. Of those fifteen, seven dealt with the Christian Bible, and eight with world religions and topics focused around the comparative study of religion.

Again, it is striking, given the student market served by the department, that the curriculum provided such a high number of courses on world religions. There were three, including a course on women in Eastern religions, a topic that rarely, if ever, appeared in the curriculum of other religious studies departments in 1972. Beyond the introductory level the department managed to construct a balance between courses related to Christianity and those dealing with either world religions or the field of study. There were twenty-one courses covering biblical studies, church history and theological topics, including two courses on biblical Hebrew. There were fifteen courses covering world religions (six), methods in the study of religion (four) and ethics (five). In addition, there were some fifteen cross-listed courses such as folk religion, special topics courses, and advanced courses in both languages and the curriculum areas of study. Among the required courses that were not area-specific were the comprehensive examination for honours students and the thesis for honours students, both separate courses.

Of special note in the courses of the department were the two dealing with religion in Newfoundland and Labrador. These courses made extensive use of research materials posted on the Internet (www.ucs.mun.ca/˜hrollman/index.html). The postings provided students with a remarkable set of historical and textual materials on the diverse religions and Christian denominations found in the province.

Between 1972 and 1993-94 there was a significant transformation of the religious studies curriculum at Memorial. In 1972, there were only nine courses at the introductory level, compared to fifteen in 1994. What is interesting is the continuity of courses and areas of study. In 1972 approximately one-third of the introductory courses dealt with world religions. That proportion had expanded in the 1994-95 calendar, with many more advanced-level courses in the area. The strong biblical studies courses were maintained and also expanded, and the study of methodologies and Western cultural traditions had also been maintained. It is a measure of the founding vision of the department that it maintained a strong commitment to providing local service courses connected to the denominational education system and an equally strong commitment to the diversity of the field of religious studies.

The University of Prince Edward Island

In 1994 the religious studies department at the University of Prince Edward Island offered both a major and a minor in the degree program of the Faculty of Arts. In its introduction to the field in the calendar, the department stated that

> Religion is one of the vital elements of human existence. Religious inspirations and aspirations help to shape the personal, cultural and social life of human beings; in turn, religious systems reflect and respond to the historical and social settings in that they find themselves.[4]

Since the University of Prince Edward Island was created from the amalgamation of denominational colleges, it was important for the department to also state that "The Department of Religious Studies is non-denominational."[5] Expressed more positively, the department understands that the study of religions implies an understanding "of truth and meaning posed by religions and the rich variety of answers professed and lived within the religious traditions of the world."[6] These descriptions made clear that the focus of the department's curriculum was on the structures of beliefs at both the cultural and the personal levels in the study of religions, a perspective that indicated both a continuity from its denominational roots and a shift to an existentialist perspective on religion.

In 1972 at the University of Prince Edward Island, there were three full-time faculty in the religious studies department. By 1994 the faculty complement had remained unchanged, but the specialists now included a person in biblical studies trained in the religious studies doctoral program at McMaster and a specialist on Asian religions trained at the University of Toronto.

In 1972 the curriculum included six introductory courses. Two of these were explicitly theological courses and two were biblical courses. There was one world religions course and one on general questions of religion in Western society. Beyond the introductory level there were fourteen advanced-level courses, of which six were in the Christian area, seven were in Western religious thought and one was a special topics course. Three of these courses were cross-listed from other departments such as sociology and philosophy.

In 1994 there was a twofold structure of introductory courses in a four-year degree program. The introductory-level courses were all required for the major and the minor, as well as serving as general elective courses. The field of religion was introduced by two courses: "Religion and the Person: An Introduction to the Study of Religion" and "Religions of the World." Two half-courses that introduced students to biblical Hebrew were also at the introductory level but were clearly introductory to the languages and not to religious studies. They were likely to be taken by particularly good students who were already at a more advanced level of study.

The content course introducing students to the Bible was listed for the second-year level of study along with the other more detailed introductions to the field of religious studies. In any given year the department could offer a general introduction to Asian religions, Buddhism and the philosophies of Asia, along with courses on Japan and China. These comparative religion courses were accompanied by two courses in biblical studies, and two in the area of Christianity, one theological and the other more sociological, dealing with denominational histories.

What was significant about the range of courses that characterize this introductory level of instruction was the preponderance of courses in the area of world religions or comparative religions. All of these courses were not taught every year, but the choice and distribution of courses fulfills the purpose of the department to offer a general survey of the field of religious studies.

New Brunswick Universities

In New Brunswick the four-year, twenty-credit program was standard for the bachelor's degree. In 1972 there were three religious studies or theology departments in the province: at Mount Allison University, the Université de Moncton and St. Thomas University. In 1994 the same universities continued to offer religious studies. But, by 1996 the United Baptist Bible College[7] had been incorporated by the province of New Brunswick as the Atlantic Baptist University with a religious studies major. St. Stephen's University, incorporated in 1998, does not teach religious studies, but offers a course of study on lay ministry and missions. In what follows, then, we shall survey the departments of religious studies, including the program at the Atlantic Baptist University.

Mount Allison University

In 1972 in the religious studies department at Mount Allison University there were two full-time faculty and one introductory course entitled "Biblical Literature." Beyond that there were seven courses: one world religions course; two language courses in Hebrew and Greek; one course on "The Religious Quest in the Modern World"; and three courses on Christianity. There were two cross-listed courses from the departments of history and philosophy.

By 1994 the department at Mount Allison had three full-time faculty and a major in religious studies. Mount Allison's historic connection with the United Church of Canada could have suggested to students that the only people likely to study religion at the university were those preparing to train as church ministers, or that religious studies courses assumed religious faith. To refute the first view, the calendar states emphatically "The study of religion was not confined to those preparing for theological studies; it has a valid and vital place in a liberal arts programme."[8] To address the more general suspicion about religious studies the calendar stated:

> Such a programme does not exist to advocate one faith rather than another, and least of all to proselytize on behalf of one denomination. But it is designed to encourage students to study a most important aspect of human existence, and it may help them to focus and clarify their own thinking on these matters.[9]

It may well be that the department protested too much with all of this comment in defence of its program. Nonetheless these comments are similar to other introductions to religious studies programs in the region and therefore must have spoken directly to concerns widely shared by students, and perhaps also faculty in the university who took the view that the study of religions could be nothing but apologetic.

With a faculty of three people whose doctoral training was in biblical studies, church history, and philosophical theology, respectively, it was not surprising that the emphasis was on the Christian tradition. In 1994 the department introduced religious studies using a two-tier model. In the first year, students could take introductory courses on the Old Testament, the New Testament and religions of the Near East and the Far East. These general courses could be taken as open electives in a student's program. To take the second level of introduction, students must have completed the first-year courses. This level included four options in which the emphasis was to connect the subject matter with contemporary issues. "World Religions and World Concerns," for example, focused on both Christianity and other religions in connection with current issues such as "food, population, pollution, peace, the arms race, the role of women."[10] A similar emphasis on contemporary issues was found in two other second-tier introductory courses. One was called "Christianity Today" and the other, a unique course in the region, "The Christian Tradition and the University." This latter course instructed students on the relations "between the Christian tradition and the origins and philosophy of the university, science, education and the liberal arts."[11] The emphasis on Christianity and what might be called religious ethics was evident throughout all the introductory courses.

Beyond the seven introductory courses, the department listed twenty-seven advanced-level courses that were taught by the full-time faculty as well as by part-time lecturers. The department offered basic courses on traditions such as Judaism, Hinduism and Buddhism. Paralleling the courses on the traditions were courses on themes that highlighted the department's stated concern with contemporary issues. "Enlightenment/Transformation in World Religions," "Death and Afterlife in World Religions," "The State in World Religions" and "War and Peace in World Religions," "Women in World Religions" and "Oriental Thought" illustrated the topics covered that connected the various religious traditions and issues of contemporary interest.

Without specifying distribution requirements for the curriculum, the department offered a series of advanced courses in biblical and textual studies. "New Testament Greek" provided language study in support of courses like "The Faith of the Bible," "The Bible and Literature," "The Bible in Literature," "The Interpretation of Jewish Scriptures." There were eight courses on Christian theology and/or church history. Special areas of focus in the area included a full course on the history of "The Church in Canada" and "Women in the Christian Tradition."

"Contemporary Issues" had a series of advanced courses on "Contemporary Ethical Issues," "The Ethics and Ethos of Business" and "Faith and Doubt." As with most small programs, directed reading or special topics courses provided faculty with the opportunity to work intensively with students majoring or doing an honours degree. The honours thesis course was the keystone of the honours degree offered by the department.

It is apparent that the department made a significant effort to expand the curriculum beyond the limits of the study of Christianity evident in 1972. Strategic use of part-time instructors as well as individual retraining permitted the department to offer a curriculum that provided students with the opportunity to study in the areas of teaching and research strength available from the full-time faculty, as well as to engage in the study of world religions.

It is a matter of great significance that the department moved to strengthen the "world religions" component of the program when retirement replacements were possible between 1996 and 1998. By hiring a person whose specializations included both biblical studies and Islam and a second person who specialized in Asian religions, the department built on the priorities established in its own departmental study and external review.

Mount Allison's Department of Religious Studies has planned for both the present and the future by integrating the local characteristics of the university, the strengths of the full-time faculty in teaching and research, and a clear engagement with the requirement of the field to study religions comparatively. The careful work done in preparation for the retirement of two of the three full-time faculty made it possible to preserve the parts of the curriculum that acknowledge the institution's history and culture while including new areas of study and methodologies in the field.

The Université de Moncton

The Université de Moncton is a public university and in 1972 its Département des sciences religieuses had four full-time faculty. All were Roman Catholic. One course from religious studies was required for the Bachelor's degree "parmi les courses de culture générale."[12] There were three introductory courses for the first-year, one on the meaning of religion, one on world religions and the third on Christianity in the modern world. At the second-year level of introduction there were three courses, all of them dealing with theological themes. At the advanced level there were nine courses: two in the anthropology of religion, one on world religions, and the remainder dealing with Christianity.

By 1994 the religious studies department at the Université de Moncton had seen its full-time complement reduced to two full-time professors, only one of them tenured. The reduction included the retirement of the professor in the department who had completed a doctorate in a religious studies department and had taught comparative studies and world religions. He was not replaced. As a result the major in "sciences religieuses" was effectively suspended and the courses subsequently offered were primarily service courses providing electives for students in other programs. The effects of the retirements on the program were eloquently described by the department chair:

> Nous avons élaborés un programme de majeure en sciences religieuses mais il est impossible pour nous d'offrir ce programme puisque nous ne sommes que deux professeurs à plein temps. Nous avons de très grands groupes d'étudiant-e-s (moyenne de 50 étudiante-e-s par cours) et nous donnons près de 13 cours chaque année avec la participation de chargés de cours venant de l'extérieur. Le département ne peut donc offrir que le programme de mineure et celui de concentration en sciences religieuses étant

donné le manque de professeurs. Nous offrons également un certificat en études pastorales; il s'agit d'un programme réservé à l'éducation permanente et les cours sont donnés par des chargés d'enseignement qui ne font pas parties de l'équipe régulière.[13]

Despite the discouragement of having to suspend the major in religious studies, the two members of faculty continued after 1994 to offer a significant range of courses in the department curriculum. The first-year level of courses introduced several areas of study: world religions, the Bible, new religious movements and a course on the "phénomène religieux" which surveyed the thematic characteristics of religion. By name the courses covered the core areas of the field of the study of religions. The department gave a preponderant emphasis to the Christian tradition in its courses. Nonetheless at the more advanced levels of the program the department offered a considerable variety courses in biblical studies, religion and psychology, and science and religion, as well as courses on various themes in Christianity such as mystical experience and women and spirituality.

The elimination of the major in religious studies was clearly a critical decision. Other departments with two faculty, such as Dalhousie University's Department of Comparative Religion, have continued to offer a major despite their limited complement. While declining university enrolments contributed to the decision not to replace retiring faculty, it appears that the department has substantial enrolments in the remaining courses. Given the capacity of the Dalhousie department to offer a major, it is legitimate to ask whether or not the decision to terminate the major will, in the long run, result in the elimination of the department as a whole.

St. Thomas University

In 1972 there was a theology department at St. Thomas University. Identified with the Roman Catholic Church and the Archdiocese of Fredericton, the university was affiliated with the University of New Brunswick and located on its main campus in Fredericton. The Anderson *Guide* listed six faculty but it is unclear how many were full-time. The department listed twenty-four courses in the university calendar, of which eight were cross-listed from the departments of English (1), philosophy (5), psychology (1) and sociology and anthropology (1). Students were required to take at least one course in the theology department during their first two years of study at St. Thomas.

In 1972 all four of the introductory courses were about Christianity, as were all but one of the advanced courses. The exception was one course on world religions. The cross-listed courses from English, sociology and psychology brought some non-theological courses into the program such as "Literary Symbolism and Myth," "the Psychology of Religion," and "The Sociology of Religion."

By 1994 the name of the department had been changed to "Religious Studies" and the curriculum had evolved in a dramatic way. It may be fairly stated that the documentation representing the distilled efforts of years of work to revise the curriculum[14] is a model of its kind for careful research and thinking through of the various elements—the field of religious studies, the university with its local history and requirements, the specializations of the faculty, the interests of the students—that we have identified as essential to an understanding not only of what religious studies is, but also of what the curriculum should include.

In 1994 St. Thomas offered a major and an honours in religious studies. Students could also register for a minor in the field. That year St. Thomas University's Department of Religious Studies was in the final stages of a complete curriculum and program review in anticipation of an external review. The curriculum in place and the one proposed had two very different designs. Not the least of the differences was the kind of introduction to the field of religious studies.

In the model of the curriculum in place in 1994, the first tier of introduction was simply a course entitled "Introduction to Religious Studies" that focused both on the human experience of being religious and on the teaching of selected world religions. The second tier of introduction was divided between six courses introducing Christianity, and Roman Catholicism in particular, and five courses that introduced Judaism, Islam, the religions of India, China and Japan, and the Native American religions.

In the proposed restructuring of the department's curriculum, which came into effect in 1995, the department worked out one of the most systematically planned curricula in the region. At the most general level of introduction, "Religious Studies 100," the department planned a course that focused on a "thematic, issues-oriented introduction to the study of religions."[15] The course description described the content: "Some of the themes and issues encountered were prejudice, sexuality, death and after death, problems of God, evil and suffering, the purpose of life."[16] The purpose of the course was "to foster in students an active appreciation of the religious dimension of life and to share with them the tools to think critically about it."[17] The course was intended to catch the interest of students and give them a taste for the study of religions.

The second level of introduction was identified as providing "the tools" for the study of religions. The proposal described these basic courses as follows:

Students of religions engage in the analysis of two main categories of expressions of religious experience: sacred texts or narratives and sacred performances or rituals. The intent of these courses is to investigate selected texts and rituals in order that students might become familiar with the disciplinary conversation swirling about these two general categories. In order to underscore the importance of the Christian, and especially the Roman Catholic, traditions at St. Thomas, one of these two courses will each year be focused on Christianity. In order to underscore the importance of the multicultural character of the study of religions, one of these courses will each year be focused on a range of religious traditions (not, of course, excluding Christianity).[18]

The second level of introduction included courses on the Hebrew Bible, the New Testament and the Qur'an and courses introducing the study of ritual. Beyond the introductions, at the third-year level there were five categories or "streams" of advanced study: world religions; ethics; Roman Catholic traditions; Western Christian traditions; and themes and issues. The final or fourth-year level of study was the senior seminar, the purpose of which was to integrate what had been learned. The course was revealingly titled "Religious Studies: Scope and Method."

The structure of the religious studies curriculum at St. Thomas integrated the continuing courses on the Roman Catholic tradition of the university within a religious studies framework. More frequently the strategy had been to set courses that reflected the denominational history of the university side by side with the more religious studies aspects of the curriculum.

The Atlantic Baptist University

The Atlantic Baptist University offers a major in religious studies and a separate major in biblical studies. The introduction to these majors include two courses on the Bible: The Old Testament and a parallel course on The New Testament. In addition there is an introductory course on Eastern philosophy. The second tier of introductory courses includes seven half-credit courses which are focused primarily on biblical textual studies and church history. Two of the courses provide a two-part introduction to "non-Christian religions of the world."[19]

The Atlantic Baptist University was, and will continue to be, an explicitly denominational university. In its religious studies degree program and curriculum, nonetheless, it has chosen to identify its major as "religious studies" and not Christian studies. Having done so, it has a considerable distance to go to implement what the name requires. The language used in the calendar to describe other religions is not appropriate to religious studies, as the wording makes clear that the course content is intended to be a Christian theological reflection on the meaning of the world's other religions. One can hope for and look forward to a continuing exchange in the university with the field of religious studies in Canada and elsewhere so that the comparative religion courses offered as religious studies courses are offered by specialists in the field and are designed to teach Hinduism and Buddhism according to their respective fundamental presuppositions and not as part of a Christian theological critique.

Nova Scotian Universities

Nova Scotia has the largest number of universities in the region. Overall there were some eighteen degree-granting institutions. Religious studies was or has been an integral part of the degree programs of six of the universities during the benchmark year for this study, 1994-95. Acadia University was in the process of closing down its Department of Comparative Religion as these data on religious studies were being collected. Since that academic year, Mount Saint Vincent University has allowed three religious studies faculty to retire with only one full-time replacement. Further, the University College of Cape Breton that had two full-time faculty has seen that number reduced to one and the major program set in limbo. At all three institutions, however, some courses on religious studies continue to be offered and at least at Mount Saint Vincent there has been the vigorous work of Dr. Randi Warne who is revising the curriculum with a view to building a new and very different future for the program.

One of the unique and debilitating factors about the degrees offered by the universities in Nova Scotia has been the continuation of the three-year baccalaureate degree after Grade 12. Most universities offer students a choice between a three-year and a four-year "Advanced" major degree. Nonetheless the majority of students complete only the three-year, fifteen-credit degree. The most significant limitation of this three-year degree for the curriculum of religious studies is the absence of the second level of introduction to the field beyond the general courses of a student's first year of study.

In what follows we shall survey the curriculum in religious studies at the six universities where such programs are offered. We shall include Acadia and University College of Cape Breton, where both of these programs existed as this study began.

Acadia University

In 1972 Acadia University was a Baptist university. The Department of English Bible that was founded in 1947 had been replaced by the Department of Comparative Religion in 1969. It offered a major program overseen by two full-time faculty. It offered eleven courses, of which three were cross-listings from other departments, including English, history and sociology. The department began its program with a course on "Judaism and Christianity" and at the second level of introduction to the field there were three courses, two in biblical studies and one in the philosophy of religion. All of the advanced courses were in biblical studies, church history and Christian thought. With the exception of the introductory course dealing with both Judaism and Christianity there were no courses on world religions.

In 1994 there were three full-time faculty in the department, one of whom had been on administrative leave, to serve first as dean of the Faculty of Arts and subsequently, as president of Acadia University. Of the two faculty working in the Comparative Religion Department, one specialized in Buddhism and the other in philosophy and philosophical theology. The biblical scholar of the department was on administrative leave and was never replaced, although he did offer a course in some academic years. While some part-time support came from individual faculty based in the Acadia Divinity College on campus, the undergraduate program was certainly limited in both the number and the range of course topics it could offer because of the small complement of full-time faculty. Nonetheless the department had both a major and an honours program on the books. Many of the courses in the curriculum continue to be taught today, but students at Acadia have been denied the opportunity to pursue a major in comparative religion.

The curriculum had undergone significant revision since Anderson's 1972 *Guide* was published. With the addition of a specialist in Buddhism the department had shifted from its exclusive focus on Christianity to a more inclusive curriculum that began with a survey of world religions. The course combined an introduction to the various religious faiths with an exploration of methodologies for studying world religions and for comparative study. The second level of introduction focused on selected traditions and approaches to the study of religions that were possible given the limited number of faculty. Courses on Islamic civilization, biblical studies, the civilization of South Asia and philosophy of religion provided students with a varied starting point for advanced study.

Beyond the six courses that were part of the introduction to comparative religion, the department offered an additional ten courses. Of those, four were in biblical studies, two were on modern philosophy of religion, and four were in the area of world religions. The honours year of study was done primarily through individual reading courses such as "Readings in World Religions" and "Comparative Religion."

Maintaining the major with only two faculty in the department proved to be impossible. As was the case with the Université de Moncton, enrolment was not the primary issue leading to the closure of the department. Rather, it was the limited number of full-time faculty. When the specialist in philosophical theology requested a transfer to the philosophy department, the fate of the comparative religion program was sealed. The committee on academic planning in the Arts faculty determined that the program was no longer viable.

Dalhousie University

In 1972 the Department of Comparative Religion at Dalhousie had not yet come into existence. Anderson noted that a Faculty of Arts motion dating back to 1969 had been passed recommending the establishment of a department of religious studies but the motion had not been acted on.

In 1972 it was, however, possible to construct an "interdepartmental major in Religious Studies."[20] That major drew courses from the departments of classics, philosophy and sociology and had one course entitled "The English Bible" that had no departmental affiliation. A program that a student could put together for a major in religious studies focused on the Mediterranean civilizations of the Ancient Near East, Greece and Rome with two additional courses on medieval thought. From the perspective of philosophy there were two introductory courses on the philosophy of religion and advanced courses on contemporary topics in the same area. There was one introductory-level course in the sociology of religion. There was no course on world religions.

By 1994 the Department of Comparative Religion at Dalhousie was established with two full-time faculty. When chaired by Wilfred Cantwell Smith, the department had three faculty, but with his return to Harvard in 1978 the complement reverted to two and remained at that level.

The study of religions in the department "aims at an intellectual understanding of this more than intellectual reality" and by "understanding," it meant "grasping simultaneously both the meaning of faith in the lives of participants, and the critical analysis of outside observers."[21] With that description in mind, the department constructed a highly integrated major. Unlike those of most other departments in the region, the program was structured around a hierarchical prerequisites system based on a two-tiered introduction. At the first level of general introduction, students could choose between three courses. The first was an introduction to world religions that combined both a survey of the religions and a close reading of religious texts from at least two of the traditions studied. The second course was entitled "Introduction to the Study of Religion" and centred on the exploration of what it means to "understand" religion and the methods used in its study, both social-scientific and humanistic. A third introductory course was "Explorations in Religion" that served a similar purpose to the one just noted except that it was not a prerequisite for advanced levels of the comparative religion major. It was designed to be a large-enrolment, half-credit course intended to appeal to students simply seeking an elective in their degree program. Such courses were important to the overall enrolment of the department because students at Dalhousie were permitted to take their electives at the introductory level. Courses like this one also permitted the department to focus its strategies for large-enrolment classes at the introductory level and thereby allowed the courses for majors to have hierarchical prerequisites.

At the second level of introduction students completed the course prerequisites for further study at the advanced level in the department. The second-level introductory courses emphasized the introduction to the religions of the world. Here, Christianity was explicitly one of the religions taught in parallel with other religious traditions. Thus, students at this level of introduction were able to choose between courses in a series that introduced them to the religions of the world. The courses included half-credit courses on Judaism, Christianity, Islam, Hinduism, Chinese and Japanese religions, Buddhism and a thematic course entitled "Religion and War" that in 1994 was cross-listed with a similar course at Saint Mary's University. In any given year the department offered a selection of these courses.

In the design of the Dalhousie curriculum the introduction to world religions in the second year was the foundation for the study of thematic courses at the third- and fourth-year levels of study. Thematic courses such as "Religion in Story," "Religion in Canada," "Western Spirituality," "Love and Death," "Myths, Symbols and Rites," "The Rise of Modern Science," "Mystical Consciousness and Modern Science" or "Spirituality and Ecology" illustrated the kinds of courses that were then approached comparatively. The approach assumed that students had completed at least two of the introductions to religions and, before they completed their major, four of the introductions to world religions. The keystone course of the program was a thematic seminar for majors in which the students used the cumulative content of the curriculum as a basis for study.

Like the department at St. Thomas University, the Dalhousie department has devised a hierarchical curriculum designed to teach students to study comparatively by the third year of the program. With only two faculty, and only five courses required for the major in the three-year degree, it is an ambitious goal to provide students with sufficient theory, methodologies and world religions content to be able to study themes comparatively.

Mount Saint Vincent University

The religious studies department at Mount Saint Vincent University had three full-time faculty in 1972. It offered two half-credit introductory courses, one on the Old Testament and one on the New Testament. At the second-year level there were eight courses: one on world religions, one on moral problems, and the remainder dealing with Christianity. There were six courses at the advanced level, all of which dealt with Christian topics. The cross-listed course from the sociology department brought one methodological course into the program.

In 1994 there were still three full-time faculty in the department—a specialist in Hebrew Bible, another in New Testament and a third in Christian Spirituality. The departmental focus was on Christianity and biblical studies. The emphasis seemed appropriate for an institution founded by the Sisters of Charity and one whose secularized identity was the only university in Canada dedicated to the education of women.

The bulk of the courses in the religious studies curriculum were at the second level. The rationale for this was to be found in the degree regulations of the university that required students to take many of their elective courses beyond the first-year level of study. The Department of Religious Studies therefore had no prerequisites for any of its courses either at the introductory levels or at the tertiary level of its curriculum. The specialized work with majors was reserved for selected topics courses, directed studies and a course entitled "Great Religious Thinkers," all of which required the permission of the instructor for enrolment.

Of the fourteen full- and half-credit courses at the second-year level of study, nine were primarily on the Christian interpretation of the Bible, Old and New Testament, and four dealt with the introduction to world religions and women in world religions. The other course that was cross-listed in the professional school of business was "Business Ethics" one of the courses with the highest enrolment in the department's curriculum.

Every year the Department of Religious Studies taught a series of non-credit, five-week courses in the evenings. These courses ranged from introductions to Christian meditation to introductions to the Bible and theology.

These courses were supported by the Archdiocese of Halifax and were well-attended by adults from the community.

Mount Saint Vincent University has seen all of its religious studies faculty retire since 1994-95 and has hired only once during that period. The effect of these changes has been dramatic. The new member of the department has brought a substantial shift in focus toward topics on religion and gender in relation to both religion in Canada and world religions. The shift has brought a welcome change to the department's mandate. While Christian studies can continue in the curriculum, the focus of what was actually being taught is centred much more on themes basic to the field of religious studies.

St. Francis Xavier University

St. Francis Xavier in 1972 had seven full-time faculty. At the first and second-year levels, the department offered three courses, one introducing the Bible and two introducing students to Christian theology and moral theology. At the advanced level there were twelve courses, one of which dealt with world religions and the rest of which centred on Christian history, biblical studies and ethical themes.

In 1993-94, the department listed four full-time faculty and a year later, added a new member trained in a department of religious studies. The department was also in the process of submitting to the Faculty of Arts and the Senate a proposal to change its name to the "Department of Religious Studies." During the initial research for this project it was still formally a department of theology. St. Francis Xavier University offered both the three-year fifteen-credit degree program and the "Advanced" degree or four-year, twenty-credit program for a Bachelor of Arts degree. The department of theology identified the goals of its curriculum as follows:

> As a department of theology, the program offered an undergraduate program in the study of the Christian Tradition and in the use of language about God. The aims of the various courses are to acquaint the student with the basic concerns of this tradition, to equip the student with a methodology for treating the sources of this tradition and to consider the relation of the tradition to other world religions.[22]

To meet these goals, introductory courses required for the major included an introduction to Christianity followed by a required course in moral theology. Another first-tier introductory course was "World Religions 1" which focused both on Mesopotamia and "briefly" on the other religious traditions of the world.

At the second level the courses focused on biblical studies, introducing the Bible as a whole, the Gospels and the Pauline letters. Among the more advanced courses were the second part of world religions, a specialized course on biblical archaeology and one on church history and theology. Building on the introduction to moral theology, the department offered tertiary-level courses in medical ethics for the nursing degree students and a course on the "Christian Approach to Sexuality."

The curriculum for the newly named "Department of Religious Studies" at St. Francis Xavier has barely begun the transition to the study of religions. With very strong faculty in biblical archaeology, biblical studies and philosophical theology in the program, it is now a question of how diversified the program can become, given the current specializations of the faculty. Unfortunatley, a damaging blow to the process of diversification came in 1999. With the retirement of John Berridge, the specialist in world religions, the department was forced to share an appointment with the multidisciplinary program in Catholic Studies. The loss of a full-time position in world religions was a fundamental blow. Until such time as the department can hire at least one full-time person in the area of world religions, the curriculum will be seriously weakened, no matter how well the rest of the program is taught.

Saint Mary's University

According to the Anderson *Guide,* Saint Mary's University had nine full-time faculty in 1972. The curriculum was divided into three areas: "Religion in Western Civilization," "History of Religions (Comparative Religion)" and "Religion in Contemporary Society." There was one general introductory course "Man's Experience of the Sacred." At the second-year level, each area of the curriculum had its introductory course or courses. "Religion in Western Civilization" was introduced by a course on belief and unbelief and a course on the Bible. "History of religions (Comparative Religion)" was introduced by "Comparisons of Religion." "Religion in Contemporary Society" began with "The Measure of Man." At the advanced level there were thirty-one courses, in some cases rather arbitrarily assigned either to the Western civilization or to the contemporary religion stream.

By 1975 the Department of Religious Studies had seen its full-time faculty complement reduced to four. One of the four positions was partially endowed as a "Chair in Religious Studies." The department had a minor, a major (three years) and a four-year honours program.

When Saint Mary's was operated by the Society of Jesus and owned by the Archdiocese of Halifax it had a theology department with courses that fulfilled compulsory components in the arts degree. After the Archdiocese of Halifax handed the administration of the university over to a newly constituted Board of Governors in 1968 pressure was immediately placed on the Department of Theology not only to relinquish its privileged position in the degree requirements but also to reduce its faculty complement. The department underwent an external review in 1969 and as a result was renamed the "Department of Religious Studies." It retained its tenured faculty, but saw several who had not yet been tenured resign or be dismissed without replacement.

In 1994 the department's curriculum was divided into three areas: comparative religion, thematic studies and the Christian tradition. The latter area of the curriculum was identified with the chair in religious studies which was designated to provide courses on Christianity and Roman Catholicism in particular. The three areas of the curriculum were described as follows:

> Comparative Religion: The Comparative study of religion includes courses on the major religious traditions of the world as well as courses which compare characteristics of religious life across several religious traditions.
>
> Thematic Studies in Religion: Thematic courses are offered as a way to explore various disciplines and their approach to the study of religion or to engage in a debate around a theme structured to include both religious and non-religious views. Such courses may examine a theme comparatively in order to show the views of different religious traditions or a theme may be presented in terms of a debate between religious and non-religious understandings.
>
> The Christian Tradition: By virtue of its charter and history, Saint Mary's University has a special responsibility to teach courses on Christianity. The Religious Studies Department fulfills that purpose by offering a number of courses on the Bible, on issues of debate within the Christian tradition and on the formative role of Christianity in Western Culture and Tradition.[23]

The explicit reference to the university charter and the history of the university related the curriculum to the charter's designation of the university as a "Christian" institution and to the historic support of the archdioceses of Nova Scotia and subsequently of the Archdiocese of Halifax for Saint Mary's. The three areas of the department's curriculum also showed the shift away from biblical studies and Christian theology toward a greater emphasis on comparative religions, methodologies in the study of religions and ethical issues arising in contemporary, popular culture.

The department introduced the study of religions with courses that corresponded to the three areas of the curriculum. "The Religious Dimension of Human Life: Introduction to Religious Studies" introduced the thematic area.

The "Introduction to Comparative Religion: When Great Religions Meet" introduced both the theories of comparative religion and the major world religions. The Christian area of the curriculum was introduced by two half-credit courses on the Old and New Testaments.

Students from across the university in the faculties of arts, science, and commerce all required electives that could be taken beyond the introductory level. The Faculty of Arts, in particular, required that all arts students complete a minimum of eight courses in the fifteen-credit degree beyond the introductory level. As a result, the department placed no prerequisites on any of its courses until the 400 level. All of the 400-level courses were reserved for religious studies majors only. These courses were taught conjointly with the 300-level courses but included group meetings and more advanced assignments. The system permitted controlled enrolments for the purpose of serving both the students seeking electives and advanced credits for the majors and honours students. The "Advanced Seminar in Religious Studies" dealt with hermeneutical issues in religious studies and was the first course offered by the department exclusively to majors in religious studies. Commencing in 2001, the department will also require a course on "theory and methods" at the 400 level exclusively for its majors.

Within this curriculum there was no second tier of introduction. There were thirty-two half-credit courses beyond the introductory level. Eleven of the courses were in the area of comparative studies and focused on the various world religions and topics dealing comparatively with Hindu and Buddhist religious art, myth and story or themes of non-violence. The thematic area dealt with both methodologies for the study of religions and themes such as love and death, ecology and religion, religion and science and various ethics courses. The methodologies aspect of the area included cross-listed courses from sociology, anthropology, psychology and classics. There were twelve courses in the Christian area of the curriculum and these included biblical studies courses beyond the introductory level and courses on church history, in particular on Roman Catholicism.

Overall the curriculum looks at issues from the viewpoints of several religious traditions in two of its three areas of study: the comparative and the thematic. The department has moved its curriculum and degree programs away from the theological roots evident in 1972 and this will continue as new faculty are hired in the department. The department has managed a reasonable compromise between the service function of the department to provide electives for students at the advanced level with the need to provide courses specifically for its majors.

University College of Cape Breton

The University College of Cape Breton came into existence as a full degree-granting institution in 1982. From its inception it had a small religious studies department and program. With only two full-time faculty members the program was very small, but by incorporating cross-listed courses from other departments and hiring part-time lecturers, the department was able to offer a major in religious studies. In 1994 the faculty complement was reduced to one. In that same year, the calendar listed five introductory-level courses. Two dealt with Old and New Testament literature, and with world religions; one focused on Judaism, Christianity and Islam; and the other on Hindu, Buddhist and Muslim traditions. The final introductory course was entitled "Religious Experience" and dealt with the "many forms and styles of religious behaviour in a developmental fashion."[24]

The introductory courses were the foundation for three additional tiers of study, the entire focus of which was Christianity and Western religious traditions. There were five second-tier courses, one of which was entitled "Women in Western Religious Tradition," and five third-tier courses that were predominantly biblical and theological. At this level there were two courses unique in the region, on "topics in religious toleration" that were cross-listed from the history program. The senior-level course was on ecumenical theology.

It was clear that the program at the University College of Cape Breton was governed primarily by the specializations of the limited number of faculty in the program. Given the constraints of there being only one full-time faculty member, the program offered courses that were as diverse as possible.

Patterns in the Curriculum

The religious studies departments in the region have in general followed a very conventional pattern of curriculum development. With the exception of the department of comparative religion at Dalhousie and the religious studies department at Memorial University of Newfoundland, most departments have evolved either from a theology department or from a starting point that emphasized the study of Christianity. In his book *The Religion Major*, Stephen Crites argues that in curriculum design "local institutional circumstances were bound to be decisive."[25] Those circumstances have included the historical characteristics of the universities in the region and the areas of specialization of the faculty in a given department.

While Christianity and biblical studies have been central to most of the curricula in the Atlantic region, all departments have made an effort to ensure that their particular programs go beyond the study of Christianity. The principal influence here has been the evolving field of religious studies itself both in Canada and internationally. In that field the sometimes acrimonious debates about the nature and place of the study of Christianity have sharpened awareness that to be a religious studies department it was essential to offer courses that provide students with the opportunity to study world religions and the methodologies of comparative inquiry about religions. Most of the departments in the region have in this respect made dramatic changes in their curriculum since the Anderson study of 1972. This was evident both in the number of courses offered and in the distribution of the courses across the areas of study in the field of religious studies.

As a measure of the changes it was worth recalling the general format that Stephen Crites and his committee proposed as a hypothetical organization for a curriculum in religious studies. The proposed areas of study included "Studies in Historic Traditions," "Critical Approaches to the Study of Religion," and "Themes and Theories."[26]

In the proposed area of historic traditions a department would offer courses on *all* of the religions that its faculty were capable of teaching. There would be no special category for the study of Christianity, as we find in numerous programs in the Atlantic region. It seems reasonable to assume that those religious studies programs that continue to offer area studies specifically on Christianity in contrast to a world religions or comparative religions area do so for compelling reasons. The department at St. Thomas University does so at the third-level of its curriculum because of the university's continuing connection with the archdiocese of Fredericton. The department at Saint Mary's does so for several reasons: the university's charter describes the institution as a Christian university; there is a continuing relation between the university and the Archdiocese of Halifax and because one of its faculty positions is a partially endowed chair in religious studies. Memorial's program has put considerable emphasis on biblical studies and Christianity to serve the needs of the denominational school boards, which want trained teachers to offer courses on religious studies. The fact that until recently the department at St. Francis Xavier was called a department of theology points to the continuing intimate connection of the university with its Roman Catholic heritage. These are compelling local circumstances that give departments powerful reasons to give a special place to the study of Christianity.

We have surveyed the calendar listings of courses offered by departments during the Academic years 1993-95. While not all of these courses could be taught in every academic year, most departments rotated courses across several academic years, permitting students to take a broad diversity of courses in the three or four years of study for their bachelor's degree. In the area of the historic traditions we found a total of 259 courses. Of those, 175 courses were on Christianity or the Bible. This amounts to 67 percent of the total number of courses. There were twenty-eight world religions courses that for the most part were introductory survey courses.

Table 4.1
Courses on Historic Traditions[27]

Historic Traditions	Number of Courses	Percentage of Total
Christianity and Bible	95 + 80 = 175	67.56
Judaism	8	3.08
Islam	7	2.7
Hinduism	9	3.47
Buddhism	7	2.7
China/Japan	12	4.63
Aboriginal Traditions	4	1.54
Canada	9	3.47
World Religions	28	10.81
Total Courses	259	

These data provided in Table 4.1 show overwhelmingly the disproportionate emphasis on the teaching of Christianity and the Bible. When departments do teach more courses on Christianity they do so in almost every case[28] from a religious studies point of view and not from a confessional point of view. Most religious studies departments in the region consciously avoid the theological or pastoral role in the classroom. Biblical studies courses emphasize the methodologies for the study of religious texts that incorporate archaeology, and linguistic and critical methods. This is true from basic introductory courses on the Hebrew Bible or the New Testament to the most advanced courses. Similarly courses on ethics, moral philosophy and even classical theological topics are taught from the point of view of an outsider trying to understand the viewpoints of the Christian insiders. These distinctions are important, and most especially so when it was clear that courses on Christianity and the Bible clearly have a privileged position in the religious studies curricula in the region.

Where courses have confessional content there were usually explicit institutional contexts that make the content of the courses clear to the student. The

Atlantic Baptist University, for example, has a religious studies major that is taught by faculty who share an institutional confession of faith published in the university calendar. Students have chosen to enrol in a Baptist university, which espouses in all its programs the Baptist Christian perspective. Saint Thomas University has made use of Roman Catholic priests to teach courses on the Bible and on Roman Catholic church history and theology. Until 1996 Saint Mary's University had a member of the Society of Jesus holding the chair in Religious Studies. At the Université de Moncton one of the full-time faculty in religious studies was also a Roman Catholic priest who has since retired to the pastorate. In simple terms the Christian heritage of the universities in the region has frequently continued into the religious studies phase of the department's history.

New appointments result in changes in areas of specialization of the faculty, which results in changes in the curriculum. The data we have presented about the departments suggest that given the opportunity to make new appointments they have been moving in the direction of comparative studies and appointments of faculty trained in religious studies departments. Once specialists in one or more of the world religions are appointed, the curriculum begins to add new courses and perspectives on the study of religions. The department at the University of Prince Edward Island demonstrated this in its two religious studies appointments. The departments at Memorial University, St. Thomas University, and Mount Allison University represent just a few of the case studies that have illustrated the direction of change in the curriculum of religious studies. There is no reason to believe that the direction was going to be changed.

Furthermore, it is clear from the composition of the population in Halifax and, to a lesser extent, the other major cities of the Atlantic region that the society in the region was undergoing profound changes. There is significant emigration from the region, mostly of young people from families that have been involved in the traditional occupations of fishing and forestry. At the same time there is significant immigration of professionals from Middle Eastern and South Asian countries which is transforming the social makeup. The percentage of the population in the region who are Hindu, Muslim, Buddhist or "other" is growing significantly. As the local society becomes increasingly multicultural, religious studies departments will have to reconsider the way in which they structure their programs and Christianity's position in the curriculum. Such changes in society will necessitate reconsideration of what kind of specialists are to be hired to teach religious studies in the region. It is essential that religious studies become an active participant in the interpretation of the meaning of multiculturalism in Canada. As this becomes clearer as a fundamental mandate of religious studies, the continuation of the shift to a curriculum dominated by comparative studies seems to this author as inevitable. In addition to offering courses on religions identified first with India, China or countries in the Middle East, departments will be offering courses on Hinduism, Taoism, Buddhism, Confucianism and Islam because they are also expanding religious traditions within Canada.

The second area of study suggested by Stephen Crites as essential for a religious studies department was "Critical Approaches to the Study of Religion." He rightly pointed out that all courses in the curriculum already implement critical methods as the historic traditions are taught to students. There were in the curriculum of every department some courses that focus on the methods of study in the field. The debate about these courses centres on whether they should be taught at the introductory level or at a more advanced level. Departments such as that at St. Thomas University have made the introductory level the place for critical studies so that students can test the theories and techniques as they advance through the historical studies of different traditions. Other departments such as that at Saint Mary's have situated the courses on hermeneutics and critical methods at the advanced level so that students can bring their experience in the study of different historic traditions and their experience in the study of themes to critical examination of what these methods offer. There are clearly advantages on both sides. What is important is that departments have developed strategies to examine fundamental methods of study in religious studies.

Representing this area statistically is difficult. Instruction on methodologies integrated into topical courses could not be included. We have, however, charted in Table 4.2 courses on the study of religions and religious studies, language courses offered by departments, directed reading and special topics courses that were frequently the setting for teaching students critical methods.

One of the most important developments since 1972 in the curricula of religious studies departments has been the gender-critical approach to the study of religions.[29] Mount Saint Vincent University has made this approach central to its new mandate for the department—a development that is entirely appropriate at Canada's only university primarily dedicated to the education of women. Most departments have moved to bring this field of study into their curriculum. Two strategies have been employed: the integration of gender-critical issues into the discussion of every historical tradition and potentially into every course offered by the department; and the development of courses, variously titled, that have as their subject women and religion. Such courses offered by religious studies are also frequently cross-listed multidisciplinary programs in women's studies.

Table 4.2
Critical Approaches to the Study of Religions

Course Title	Number of Courses	Percentage of Total
Religious Studies	9	8.4
Seminars and Topics	30	28.3
Language Courses	9	8.4
Psychology	6	5.7
Philosophy	21	19.8
Sociology	3	2.83
Anthropology	3	2.83
Political Theory	2	1.88
Development	2	1.88
Myth	6	5.7
Gender	15	14.15
Total Courses	106	

The implementation of the first strategy was nowhere complete. There are many reasons account for that. There are faculty who refuse to acknowledge the point of view that argues that there is a difference between the religious experience of women and that of men. It is also difficult to find textbooks on world religions that systematically integrate the distinctive contributions of women and men in the different religious traditions. Nonetheless this strategy is going to be more and more central to the study of religions for students and for faculty study and research.

There has been a very significant growth in the number of courses on women and religion. In 1972 none of the departments had any courses in this area. In 1994 there were fifteen courses across the region dealing explicitly with topics related to women and religion.

The social-scientific methods of study were not well represented in religious studies curricula. Of the 116 courses we have assigned to the area there were only sixteen courses covering the classical areas of sociology, psychology, anthropology, political and development topics. There is clearly a desperate need for faculty in the region to bring the social-scientific methods into the study of religions. This will be particularly important for religious studies departments if other departments such as psychology, anthropology, and sociology do not make appointments specializing in the social-scientific study of religion. In order to ensure that this is available in the curriculum it may be essential for religious studies departments to make appointments in this area.

The third area of study proposed by Stephen Crites was "Themes and Theories." Thematic courses permit the integration of historic traditions and critical methods with the study of specific ethical or cultural themes. It is possible to compare patterns of spirituality across different religious traditions; to study the diverse ways by which religious traditions influence the arts, from music through sculpture, painting and architecture. Religion and science courses can permit students to understand the historic debates in the West, to ask why science and religion are not perceived to be opponents in the context of Hinduism or Buddhism and to explore the interpretive power of the scientific method, its limitations and its influence on all other methods and theories of knowledge. Courses in the ethical area are not only popular with students who want an opportunity to look at current ethical dilemmas from diverse points of view, but also provide an opportunity for students to understand the significance of religious diversity within their own society.

Table 4.3
Themes and Theories in Religious Studies

Course Area	Number of Courses	Percentage of Total
Love	2	2.94
Sexuality	6	8.82
Death	5	7.35
War	7	10.29
Human Identity	3	4.41
Science	6	8.82
Ethics	16	23.52
Aging	1	1.47
The Arts	9	13.23
Atheism	1	1.47
New Religions	5	7.35
Culture	5	7.35
Spirituality	2	2.94
Total	68	

At the same time as the thematic area is important to the curricula of religious studies departments, describing the area is rather difficult because it appears in the calendars of the universities of the region in such a diverse and fragmented way. The particularities of the topics and how they were combined with other topics make them difficult to categorize. Suffice it to say that Table 4.3 will only give an impression of some of the topics in general and their place in the overall curriculum.

It is clear from these data that ethical issues were the dominant thematic component of religious studies curricula. Indeed, if one takes the courses that were explicitly designated as ethics and combines them with the courses on war, aging, and even love and death, it is clear that the thematic component of the curriculum is one that was very important to the departments. These can be high-enrolment courses, exciting for faculty to teach and for students to study.

Overall, by looking at the courses offered in the region through the patterns identified by Stephen Crites, we can see probable directions for future change in the curricula of departments in the region. There must be a greater balance in the courses on the historic traditions. Courses on Christianity and biblical studies will inevitably diminish in number as this change comes about. For example, textual studies will be seen more and more as requiring courses on both methods and content in the study of the Qur'an, the Bible, and Hindu and Buddhist religious texts. Christian church history can benefit from comparative studies in the histories of the institutions of religions elsewhere. Theory and methods courses are going to become more prevalent in religious studies departments as they integrate social-scientific methods into the specializations of faculty in the department. The study of new themes and new religious movements is also likely to grow as society incorporates more religious diversity into its midst. The test will be to look at the faculty complement and the courses offered in 2010, when many of the current faculty will have retired. Who replaces them will be the foundation upon which the curriculum for each department across the region will be changed.

Notes

1 C. P. Anderson, *Guide to Religious Studies in Canada/Guide des sciences religieuses au Canada* (Corporation for the Publication of Academic Studies in Religion in Canada, 1972).
2 *Memorial University of Newfoundland Academic Calendar*, 1994-95, 153.
3 Ibid.
4 *University of Prince Edward Island Academic Calendar*, 1993-94, 141.
5 Ibid.

6 Ibid.
7 In the Anderson *Guide* of 1972 there was no reference to the United Baptist Bible Training School or Atlantic Baptist Bible College that replaced the training school in 1970.
8 Ibid., 110.
9 Ibid.
10 Ibid.
11 Ibid.
12 Anderson, *Guide*, 1972, 129.
13 Denise Lamontagne, Directrice, Départment des sciences religieuses, letter to author, 27 February, 1998.
14 Religious studies departmental study of 1994 and the application for increased staffing dated 8 November 1993.
15 Religious studies departmental study, 19.
16 Ibid.
17 Ibid.
18 Ibid.
19 *Atlantic Baptist University Calendar*, 1997-98, 43.
20 Anderson, *Guide*, 1972, 73.
21 *Dalhousie University Arts and Social Sciences, Education, Health Professions, Management and Science Calendar*, 1994-95, 163.
22 *St. Francis Xavier University Academic Calendar*, 1993-94, 72.
23 *Saint Mary's University Academic Calendar*, 1993-94, 160.
24 *University College of Cape Breton Academic Calendar*, 1993-94, 134.
25 Crites, *Religion Major*, 20.
26 Ibid., 20-21.
27 In these data I have not distinguished between two-semester and one-semester courses. For the most part departments have converted their curriculum to courses lasting one semester only, with the exception of introductory or first-year courses, which frequently remain two semesters long.
28 There were individuals in religious studies departments who continue to adopt a confessional point of view in their theological courses. The research for this report indicates that these instances are the exception rather than the rule.
29 Unlike Stephen Crites, I have included women and religion courses and gender studies in the area of "Critical Approaches to the Study of Religion." I have done so because this subject has been so influential in the field through the critiques of method and theory.

5
Faculty in Religious Studies

> Each campus must have religion scholars who are also academic statesmen/entrepreneurs, who will establish the conditions under which the teaching of religion will have an audience, although it goes without saying that there must be first-rate scholar-teachers who may well lack gifts of entrepreneurship but all of whom can and do deliver in the classroom. — Ray L. Hart

In his report on "religious and theological studies in American higher education," Ray Hart quotes an anonymous "senior scholar and statesman"[1] who outlines three primary roles of the religious studies professor: "statesman," "entrepreneur," and "scholar-teacher."[2] These terms capture the multiple and sometimes daunting facets of the task facing faculty in the contemporary university.

The role of statesman is primarily assumed by the department chair, though all faculty share in the role as they serve on committees or speak in public about religious studies and related issues. A department chair, especially in a small department, is the manager of the department, student advisor and principal advocate of the department within the administrative systems of the university. She or he participates in administration as a member of an arts faculty executive, the university Senate or of the seemingly endless committees that come and go within the university. No small part of the statesman's role is figuring out appropriate strategies to defend or enhance the study of religions in the curriculum. So, too, the department chair must attend to the larger community, explaining the place of the study of religions in the schools of the provinces.

It is the professor as "entrepreneur" who understands that a subject such as religious studies requires more than just being part of the university curriculum. Faculty must create course titles and write descriptions that will be heard and understood by students while expressing the substance of the scholar's understanding of the topic. Where the choice exists, faculty must try to gauge which timetable slots are best for course offerings for the department's majors and for students seeking electives. With computers and administrators now registering students in their courses, faculty must determine what kind of marketing is required in the high schools and in the university so that students will actually know what religious studies is.

As the word "marketing" passes from thought onto the page, it grates. It offends faculty members' sensibilities about the importance of the subject they teach and on which they do research. Yet the days of the compulsory theology credit in the denominational university are long gone. All of the historic denominational universities are now public universities, recipients of the diminishing funds coming from the federal and provincial governments.[3] In such public settings it is no small pedagogical shift to recognize that the majority of students who take the introductory courses, or even the advanced courses, are not coming to the field with any prior knowledge of what the field is, nor with much, if any, experience of religious traditions.

Students in the Maritime provinces have not had the opportunity to study religion in the high schools. Newfoundland has been the exception because of the denominationally administered school systems. With the recent constitutional change permitting the province to create a single public education system, there will be a protracted period of adjustment that will determine the extent to which the schools, from primary to secondary, will continue to offer courses about religion. The precedent set in the other Atlantic provinces is not encouraging on that front. Religious studies has never been a teachable subject as determined by the provincial departments of education in the three Maritime provinces. Despite that, some high schools in Nova Scotia offer a world religions course, but it is only an elective. Further, there is no guarantee that a teacher of such a course has any advanced university courses in religious studies as a qualification to offer such a course.

As a result of minimal exposure to religious studies in the public education systems, students who enrol in a religious studies course at university are there for a variety of reasons, some of which are not very gratifying. Some may say directly that it was the only course left open during registration that fitted their timetable. Some want to know up front, "Does this religious studies course require a lot of essays or have a final exam?" Naively, a student may ask, "Is this a hard course?" or worse, standing at an office door with an expectant look, may say simply, "I need an easy credit. Is your course open?"

Much more exciting for the professor are the students who come with an initial curiosity and who want to test all the public stereotypes of religion derived from the news or televangelists. There are also going to be students in class who have a religious background, or who are reacting against one and simply want to explore the field of religions. There are mature students coming back to university after many years. Their seriousness about their education can be the leaven in a classroom of eighteen-year-olds.

In the face of such a complex audience, it is not surprising that the professor as "entrepreneur" must employ a variety of strategies to inform students about courses in religious studies. These strategies begin with the calendar and skillful descriptions of courses in a language which can be understood by high school students entering the university. Department handbooks and publications by the arts faculty can also introduce students to the study of religions. However, the best marketing device for religious studies courses is the reputation of the courses taught by the religious studies department. Word-of-mouth from student to student is often the best recommendation.

An essential component of a course is the teaching skills of the instructor. These skills are an integral part of another of the fundamental tasks of the university professor: the scholar-teacher or research and teaching. Graduate schools prepare their students to do independent advanced research. Teaching is not taught as part of graduate programs and experience of teaching is frequently limited to leading tutorials and marking exams. Nonetheless, good teaching is dependent upon the quality of research skills acquired in graduate school and no professor's career can advance without the cultivation of both research and teaching.

Professors require innovative methods to teach students. It is no easy task to figure out how to present good scholarship in such a way that the interest of the students is stimulated by both the content about religions and the methods of critical appreciation of that content.[4] In the end it is good teaching that is the most important form of marketing for religious studies. Good teaching has brought more majors into religious studies than any other form of advertising.

But what is good teaching? For the teacher and scholar, the days when the formal in-class lecture was the exclusive means of instruction in the university classroom are a distant memory. While lectures may still play a part in the instruction of students, particularly for very large classes, no matter how well they are prepared, lectures are among the least satisfactory means of engaging students in the study of a subject. Professors can now draw on a rich array of video materials on religions and on the Internet as a source of information and contending viewpoints. Faculty can use discussion groups and group projects or field visits to the temples and churches in the community. Integrating all these methods and sources of information into the classroom is no easy task and most certainly not one for which professors have been trained in graduate school.

The classroom and what happens in it is now the subject of frequent and heated discussion in universities and academic conferences. It constitutes the principal area of professional development for the professor following graduate school. Many universities have now established offices for instructional development, and faculty can receive funding to do research on teaching methods and go to conferences specifically about methods of instruction in the classroom. These sources of professional development deal with numerous vexing questions: How are computer technology and the information on the Internet to be integrated effectively and critically into a course? How is the misinformation on the Internet to be critically analyzed so that students are aware of how much there is on the Web? In sum, university teachers complete a long doctoral training in research and suddenly, if a university teaching opportunity emerges, are then plunged into a new apprenticeship to learn to teach what they know.

Education takes place best in the mutual interaction of teacher and student. Perhaps the most difficult pedagogical issue has to do with discovering the appropriate diversity of means by which students can begin to take charge of their own education.[5] Here, the task is to move students beyond the notion that there are simply course requirements to be met, be they written assignments, participation in debates, field assignments or readings. To grasp the notion that a course is, in its most important respect, a structure within which students discover and expand their own skills and their capacity to learn and critically assess ideas and concepts is the primary goal of today's university.

No matter what idealistic notions a professor of religious studies may have about teaching, the development of teaching skills is now a professional requirement. There is little room in the modern public university for the eccentric professor, closeted with books in some obscure corner. Since the 1960s the professor as teacher has become one of the primary requirements for appointment, tenure and promotion. Student course evaluations are routine and taken seriously at all levels of evaluation.

In addition to the roles of statesman, entrepreneur and teacher, there is also that of the research scholar within the small department of religious studies. In spite of the immediate necessities of university citizenship and teaching, there is the professor who yearns for the time to continue reading and studying, the applicant for research grants, the collector of new information on religions, the writer who presents papers at academic conferences, the scholar who publishes articles in journals or writes books. It is these aspirations that bring a person to graduate school and immersion in a life of study and academic writing. Becoming skilled in research is the substance of academic training and the source of much of the excitement about learning that motivates professors in their role as teachers.

"Statesman," "entrepreneur" and "scholar/teacher" might best be understood as headings in a job description. It is an interesting, and perhaps ironic, comment on the reality of the contemporary tasks of the professor that these terms would never appear in a job posting in *University Affairs* or the *Bulletin* of the Canadian Association of University Teachers.[6] There, the advertisements for positions in religious studies departments are most likely to define an area of expertise sought by a department, such as Christianity or Buddhism, and then itemize requirements such as a completed doctorate, demonstrated research competence beyond the doctorate in the form of publications and evidence of successful teaching experience. Such advertisements focus exclusively on the skills of the scholar-teacher, and predominantly on the former of the two roles. They leave the capacity for statesmanship, entrepreneurship and teaching to an intuitive reading of applications and the interview.

Publication and teaching, in that order, are the areas of university work that, more often than not, are the primary bases for empirical measures of success as a university professor. Renewal of a first contract, tenure hearings and promotion applications involve procedures that consume hundreds of work hours on the part of both the applicants and their colleagues in the university. In every one of these procedures teaching is evaluated, but it is the potential of a person to carry out research and to publish the results of that research that constitutes more than half of the weighted measures of success for a university professor at every stage of a career.

Typical of the kinds of evaluation procedures faced by a university professor are those connected with the quest for a tenure-track appointment. Success depends upon recommendations from supervising faculty in the applicant's graduate program, experience in teaching and publication in peer-reviewed journals. The competition for tenure-stream positions can be ferocious. For a recent new position in the department at Saint Mary's University, over eighty-five applications were submitted. Normally at least three candidates are interviewed for such positions and interviews can take up to two days. Interviews involve public demonstrations of teaching ability, presentations of research, and meetings with university presidents, vice-presidents, deans and faculty in the department. It is a gruelling process for all concerned and one that in the end involves the appointment of one candidate and the rejection of others who frequently are no less qualified for the position.

Of particular concern in all academic fields are the years that many people with completed doctorates spend in part-time teaching and in short-term contracts. Universities everywhere have used doctoral graduates either as part-time instructors teaching one course or as short-term lecturers offering a full load of courses in return for eight or nine months of contractually limited pay. In the Atlantic region, remuneration for teaching a single university course over two semesters averages approximately $7000. The normal course load of a tenured, full-time professor is three courses. In Metro Halifax, where there are several universities in close proximity, part-time instructors may teach the same number of courses for less than a third of the salary earned by a full-time faculty person.

The job market crisis for people with completed doctorates has been well documented by Russell McCutcheon.[7] In the period that has seen almost constant cuts to the total faculty complement of universities, there has emerged an exploited class of excellent researchers and teachers who have not been able to secure continuing, tenured positions anywhere. The hopes of such young, and not so young, doctoral graduates for employment have been resting on the expectation of retirements and the consequent opening up of full-time positions. That many universities have not made replacement appointments when faculty have retired has damaged such hopes and created a severe employment crisis for young scholars. There seems to be no immediate remedy for this crisis short of retirements among baby-boom generation of scholars combined with the universities" approval of replacements. The expectation is that by 2010 demand for university professors in all fields will far exceed supply in both Canada and the United States. For unemployed or part-time instructors, that is a long wait indeed.

When a person with a doctorate is appointed to a tenure-stream position, usually as an assistant professor, he/she faces five to seven years of frequent and onerous evaluation. The first of these comes in the form of application for a contract renewal within two or three years of the initial appointment. Following that is a tenure application after four or five years of employment. If the the application is successful, there follows an application for promotion from the rank of assistant professor to that of associate professor. Of these three stages of review, the tenure decision is the most crucial, since it determines whether or not the applicant will continue to have a permanent, continuing university appointment. Applications for promotion to full professor usually take place after fifteen or more years of employment. Some faculty are never promoted to this rank.

Each of these evaluations varies slightly from university to university, but essentially all of them involve a departmental review of teaching and research as well as a review of involvement in university citizenship. The department's assessment and recommendation are forwarded to a dean for a further evaluation and recommendation. The application then proceeds either to a Faculty of Arts committee or, more likely in smaller universities, to a university-wide committee, the membership of which is drawn from the science, arts and professional faculties found in a particular university. The committee makes a formal, and usually final, recommendation to the President regarding the application for renewal, tenure or promotion.

At every stage of the renewal, tenure or promotion process a faculty member is evaluated in at least three, and sometimes four, areas. The applicant must have a completed doctorate and demonstrate continuing active research in the form of conference papers, peer-reviewed publications in journals or published books. Almost all academic books published in Canada must have at least three, and sometimes more, peer reviews completed, especially if the books are supported by the Aid to Scholarly Publications Programme of the Humanities and Social Sciences Federation of Canada.[8] Peer-reviewed journal publications and books carry the most weight in the evaluations.

It is now commonplace for two or three assessors to be sought from outside the university for tenure and promotion reviews. Specialists in the applicant's field are sent a body of research material and a curriculum vitae and are invited to evaluate the quality of the research and publication material. These assessors are asked to recommend the candidate for tenure or promotion or to reject such a recommendation. These letters from external assessors carry very substantial weight in the tenure and promotion reviews.

Secondly, there is an evaluation of teaching based on student course evaluations and may also include visits to the applicant's classroom by colleagues. Thirdly, there is a review of the applicant's university and community service for which notice is taken of administrative contributions, committee memberships and general participation in university governance. Community service beyond the university may also be considered in the review.

The realities of the contemporary university and its demands leave the professoriate excited and intimidated, stimulated and wearied. There is a seemingly endless variety of new opportunities to explore the field of religious studies as teacher and as scholar. The sheer diversity of what can now be part of a faculty member's job description also places huge pressures on everyone. What can reasonably be done well by the faculty at a particular university? What are the effects on careers when faculty are part of a small department, geographically distant from colleagues in their particular specialization in religious studies and from the major research libraries in Canada and elsewhere? In the face of these kinds of questions all religious studies professors have to set priorities and make choices which over time define their particular characteristics as a professor in the field. Such career decisions also have a major impact on departments and how they are able to fulfill their mandate.

In what follows I want to summarize briefly the reports I received about how the women and men teaching religious studies in Atlantic Canada have resolved the question of priorities. On the basis of responses to questionnaires that were circulated I will report on the full-time faculty first as scholars and teachers by identifying their qualifications, areas of research and areas of teaching responsibility. Beyond that, I will survey some of the responses to the qualitative questions that were part of the questionnaire circulated to each department and each member of faculty which relate to the roles as entrepreneur and statesman.

Demographics and Gender in the Professoriate

According to the survey of faculty completed in 1994, there were forty-one full-time faculty in religious studies in the Atlantic region. Of the forty-one, three were on term appointments. This total needs to be qualified in a number of ways. Acadia University's Department of Comparative Religion is included despite the fact that the department was in the process of being closed. Its faculty were either retiring or transferring to other departments for the duration of their careers. Several departments were on the verge of faculty retirements, the effect of which at Mount Saint Vincent University was the reduction of the faculty complement to one. Some departments, like that of Mount Allison, were dependent upon the availability of regular part-time instructors to offer parts of the comparative religion component of their degree program. Further, the total of full-time faculty does not include those whose appointments were in other departments such as psychology, sociology or anthropology and whose courses were cross-listed in religious studies. For the purposes of analyzing this total and the issues based on it, we will be focusing on the full-time faculty in religious studies.

Of the forty-one full-time faculty, six were women. In the state-of-the-art review of Ontario universities the low percentage of full-time women faculty was identified as a fundamental issue for religious studies in the province. The Ontario report showed that 92.2 percent of the professoriate in 1987 were men.[9] That percentage was significantly higher than that given in the national survey of Canadian humanists done by the Canadian Federation of the Humanities in 1986: it showed that males constituted 82.8 percent of the professoriate.[10] In the Atlantic region the percentage was close to that given in the national survey of humanists, with 85.4 percent of the total full-time faculty in religious studies male and 14.6 percent female.

Two factors have altered the percentages since 1994. First, there have been new appointments following retirements. The majority of the new appointments in the region since 1994 have been women. As of 1998, seven new appointments had been women: one at Memorial University of Newfoundland, one at St. Thomas University, one at Mount Saint Vincent University, two at Saint Francis Xavier, and two at Saint Mary's University.

The second factor affecting the percentages is from the losses in the overall number of faculty in the field. The Acadia department no longer exists. Mount Saint Vincent University has seen its religious studies department of three reduced to one full-time faculty member, effective 31 December, 1998.[11] The number of faculty in religious studies at Memorial University has consolidated at nine instead of the eleven counted in 1994. By this count, then, there are now thirty-seven full-time faculty,[12] of whom nine are women. Therefore 24.32 percent of the faculty in religious studies are female and 75.68 percent are men. With twenty-five percent of the full-time faculty female and a pattern of hiring women to fill vacant positions, significant progress has been made toward the necessary goal of gender equality in religious studies in the region.

The most likely occasion for change both in areas of expertise and in the gender makeup of departments is faculty retirement. It is also the case that retirements are the moments of greatest risk for religious studies departments. Very few universities have automatic replacement policies. Indeed, quite the opposite is the case. Departments in the humanities and social sciences have experienced very high reductions in full-time faculty at times of retirement. University administrations have the prerogative to determine where new appointments will go. In that process small departments are frequently at a significant disadvantage, no matter how well their enrolments may compare with those of other departments seeking faculty replacements.

The most discouraging and demoralizing aspect of the loss of faculty due to retirement is the resultant weakness in long-term academic planning in arts faculties. The arbitrary use of age as the basis for academic planning means that some departments can experience a series of cuts in faculty complement while others with wider distributions do not experience anything like the same effect on their programs. Because provincial allocation of funds to universities has frequently been determined for each year's budget, universities have not been able to do long-term planning. All the blame for endless short-term academic planning, however, cannot simply be assigned to insecure annual funding. It has never been more difficult, it seems, to formulate an effective set of academic planning priorities, which can be used to defend the existence of small departments and programs.

Two facts are evident. First, small departments of two or three faculty that are reduced in size by retirements see their entire program put at risk. The Université de Moncton stopped offering its major when one of the three full-time faculty retired. With two out of three faculty not replaced at Mount Saint Vincent University, the major degree program is at risk. Secondly, religious studies departments that have argued successfully for the replacement of retiring faculty have moved to hire faculty in new areas of study and have taken significant steps to reduce gender inequality in the professoriate both within particular departments and indirectly in the region as a whole.

Earned Doctorates among Full-Time Faculty

In 1994 all the full-time faculty teaching in religious studies, except three new appointments, had a doctorate or an equivalent. By 1998 the three new appointments had completed their doctorates. To have 100 percent of religious studies full-time faculty in the region with earned doctorates is remarkable, especially given national statistics in this area. In the Ontario state-of-the-art review, William Closson James summarized the comparative data on faculty qualifications:

> In 1967 only 45% of those teaching religious studies in Canada had an earned doctorate, a figure which increased to 70% by 1972 (Anderson, 1972, 14). Claude Welch reported in 1970 that 63% of faculty in North American religious studies departments had doctorates (1972, 185). In 1987, of 203 faculty in Ontario religious studies departments, 154 held the Ph.D. degree and 22 the Th.D.—a total of 87% with an earned doctorate.[13]

It is clear from this summary that there was a significant number of faculty in religious studies who did not have an earned doctorate. The minimum academic degree required for university teaching was frequently a master's degree in the field throughout the post-Second World War period. In addition to that, religious studies and theology departments, it appears, were deemed to be a special case since significant numbers of faculty did not hold an earned doctorate even in the early 1960s and 1970s. In many cases the absence of an earned doctorate for professors of religious studies correlated with the hiring of local clergy to teach in religious studies programs.

It is clear that in the Atlantic region over the last twenty-five years, the minimum requirement, if not for an appointment, then certainly for tenure and promotion in religious studies has been an earned doctorate. It is a significant fact that the most senior faculty in the region in terms of experience were not appointed at less than the current normative university standard for appointment and tenure.

Our survey did not collect data on the departments from which faculty earned their doctorate. It is difficult to determine, therefore, whether a significant number of faculty were trained at the graduate level in religious studies departments or if they obtained their doctorate from seminaries or theology departments. However, a review of the lists of faculty in the 1994 university calendars in the region suggests that a very significant number of religious studies faculty in the region held doctorates from graduate programs *in religious studies*. For example, by correlating universities with known religious studies departments, it appears that of the forty-one full-time faculty surveyed, fifteen or 36.58 percent were trained in religious studies departments or an equivalent, such as the Islamic Studies program at McGill. Of the fifteen faculty, thirteen were trained in religious studies departments in Canada. Of those, the majority earned their doctorate at either the University of Toronto or McMaster University.

With the surveys used, it is not possible to estimate the impact of Canadian training compared with that of degrees obtained from major graduate programs in the United States, the United Kingdom or Europe. What these data suggest, however, is that Canadian universities from the late 1960s onward were producing skilled graduates in religious studies who competed on the open job market for positions in universities and that a significant number of them were employed in the Atlantic region.

Table 5.1
Years of University Teaching Experience

Number of Years	1 to 10	11 to 20	21-30	30 plus
Number of Faculty	15	5	15	6

Teaching Experience and Retirement Patterns

No data were collected on the age of faculty in the region. However, information was collected on the years of teaching experience and the year of retirement at age sixty-five among those teaching religious studies in 1994. (Table 5.1). Among the forty-one full-time faculty surveyed, there were two clusters of fifteen—one in the first ten years of their careers and the other with more than twenty years' experience. In an interesting parallel, the most senior faculty and the group in the middle of their careers, with eleven to twenty years' experience, were virtually identical in number. Across the region, then, there was a reasonable distribution of faculty at different stages in their career. This is important since an age distribution makes programs less susceptible to closure if one member of a department retires and is not replaced.

In theory there ought to be a correlation between the number of years of experience and the expected pattern of years until retirement. Several significant factors make the parallel unlikely. First, there is the possibility of new appointments being drawn from a population that is entering a second career, with the result that the year of retirement may be earlier than might otherwise be expected. For example, for two of the new appointments surveyed their university appointment was a second career and consequently they will retire shortly after they have completed twenty years. Secondly, these data are based on obligatory retirement at age sixty-five. It may well be that some faculty will choose to retire earlier.

Table 5.2
Retirement by Year

Year of Retirement	1994-99	2000-04	2005-09	2010-14	2015-19	2020 +
Number of Retirees	10	4	7	6	5	9

Table 5.2 shows that, between 1994 and the year 2000, ten faculty have retired or taken an early retirement package. Four were not replaced. In the face of a forty percent cut in the number of faculty, it is doubly important to remember the places that have made reappointments and the extent to which those departments went to ensure a multicultural, multireligious curriculum for their students. They include Memorial University (one), Prince Edward Island (one), Mount Allison (two) and Saint Mary's University (two).

As retirements approach, it is crucial for departments to plan carefully the case that must be made to obtain a replacement. One of the stated reasons for success in obtaining reappointments at both Mount Allison and the University of Prince Edward Island was advanced planning, which included a departmental study followed by an external review. With these documented reviews in place the departments established a credible foundation for their applications for new appointments. The process appears to have won administrative support for the department as the reviews showed a clear direction for the department.

On the basis of the evidence there is no necessary link between the size of departments and cuts in religious studies faculty complements at the time of retirements. Nonetheless the effect of cuts in small departments of two or three faculty is enormous. It takes a powerful case to ensure continuity when there are only one or two faculty trying to carry forward a degree program. Enrolment is clearly an essential component of such a case. However, it is also essential to demonstrate the nature of the field and its importance for a multicultural society.

Distribution by Rank

Faculty appointments in the university fall within four ranks: lecturer, assistant professor, associate professor and full professor. Years of teaching experience and proximity to retirement are not necessarily parallel to rank. The distribution by rank of the forty-one faculty surveyed is given in Table 5.3:

Table 5.3
Distribution of Faculty by Rank

Rank	Lecturer	Assistant Professor	Associate Professor	Full Professor
Number of Faculty	5	9	6	21

Fifty-one percent of the professoriate in the region in 1994 were at the rank of full professor. It is difficult to assess this statistic in any kind of comparative way as different universities apply different standards for promotion between the ranks. There is no evidence to suggest that religious studies faculty receive any special treatment either positively or negatively within the procedures normally used for consideration of contract renewal, tenure or promotion. All universities take very seriously the criteria they do use for assessing faculty for tenure or promotion. In unionized settings there is considerable emphasis on the common application of the criteria for all faculty without exception.

Teaching and Research

One of the key factors determining the characteristics of religious studies in a particular department is the area of specialization of each faculty member for teaching and research. Faculty want to be able to teach their area of specialization both at the introductory level as part of a general introduction to religious studies and at the advanced level for majors and honours students. As we shall see from the tables below, many faculty developed new areas for teaching and research that went well beyond their original specializations in graduate school.

Finding the correct balance of specializations for teaching and research is crucial both for a department as a unit and the individual faculty member. From a department's perspective it is crucial to have diversity in the areas of specialization while maintaining a collegial atmosphere in which dialogue across specializations can be preserved. In this mix faculty have to find those areas and issues that permit them to offer general courses at the introductory levels and advanced courses for the majors. From the individual faculty member's perspective, working in a small department creates the necessity of offering a broad range of courses from the introductory to the advanced and across several areas of the curriculum. To do this requires active and continuing research both on the pedagogies for creative teaching and in the course areas for which a professor may have little graduate-level background. While cultivating these areas may become an exhilarating research activity, it can also be so time-consuming that research in the faculty member's area of specialization can be seriously affected.

The tensions that are characteristic of the demands on the professor as statesman, entrepreneur and scholar-teacher working in a university are indicated by the way in which priorities are set and estimates of time allocated to teaching, research and other activities required of a professor are made.

Table 5.4
Priorities for Teaching, Research and Service

Ranking of Priorities	Teaching	Research	University Service	Public Service
First	29	7	2	1
Second	10	22	2	4
Third	1	6	25	4
Fourth	0	1	7	24

In our questionnaire we asked faculty to indicate their priorities among four areas of work: teaching, research, university service and public service. In reporting their priorities, twenty-nine respondents indicated that their first priority was teaching (Table 5.4). In contrast, seven stated that research ranked first in their career. A university administrator who was also a member of a religious studies department placed university service first, and one person, a professor and priest, indicated that public service was his first priority. The faculty member who ranked public service first did so with an explanatory comment that family in his view ranked first above all other priorities. These are specific cases. Overall, it is clear that the overwhelming priority for faculty was the work required to provide quality teaching to students.

Research, while not the first priority for many of the faculty in the region, clearly ranked very high in the report. Twenty-two of the respondents indicated that research was their second priority, indicating that of the forty-one faculty in the survey, research ranked first or second for twenty-nine. The third priority was university service. It was ranked first or second by four respondents, usually because they were involved in extensive university administration, either as department chair or dean. For twenty-five faculty, this was a third priority following teaching and research. Community or public service ranked last of the four choices. Where it did not rank fourth, it usually involved specific circumstances such as priestly duties or family ranking first as a matter of principle. For the most part the assigning of priorities by the faculty in the survey follows a conventional ranking with teaching and research taking precedence over university and public service.

The data on setting priorities were echoed in the responses to the question of how individuals allocated their time across the four basic areas of activity for a religious studies professor. Teaching occupied 70 percent of the time for nine of the respondents and 50-69 percent of the time for nineteen faculty. By comparison for most faculty research occupied somewhere between 29 and 50 percent of the time.

In Table 5.4, thirty-nine faculty members indicated teaching was their first or second priority. How that priority was translated into the allocation of time spent on teaching showed considerable variation in the data in Table 5.5. Of the thirty-nine respondents to this question, it appeared that a first or second priority for teaching could translate into an allocation anywhere from 30 percent to over 70 percent of time at work. It is possible to account for some of this variation by recognizing that research for the classroom and research on topics for publication might well overlap, making it very difficult to separate precisely research done for teaching from that other types of research. It is nonetheless surprising that the very high ranking of teaching among the respondents could result in such variation in time allocations.

Table 5.5
Allocation of Time for Teaching, Research and Service[14]

Percent of Time	Teaching	Research	University Service	Public Service
Over 70%	9	0	1	0
50-69%	19	2	1	0
30-49%	9	13	2	1
29% or Less	2	25	36	25

Research was the first priority for seven individuals, and second priority for twenty-two. What is striking about the time allocation responses is that no one allocated 70 percent of their time or more to doing research and only two suggested that they spent over 50 percent of their time on it. For the vast majority of respondents the most time that they could allocate to research was 30 to 49 percent. In other words it is reasonable to suggest that most faculty spend approximately one-third of their working time on research.

The time allocated to research occurs primarily during the months outside the principal teaching semesters, which run from September through December and January through April. It is significant that two-thirds of the year is allocated primarily to teaching and the remaining one-third is generally free of teaching obligations, permitting a focus on research.

Areas of Specialization in Doctoral Studies[15]

A faculty member's doctoral research is the foundation for his or her research for both teaching and publication. It was therefore important to determine the areas of specialization in doctoral studies among the faculty holding full-time positions in religious studies in the region. We asked all full-time members of faculty in religious studies to indicate the area in which they completed their final degree, the areas in which they conducted research and the areas in which they taught. We also asked them to indicate their specialized areas using their own terminology. We employed thirty-two[16] categories derived from the *Religious Studies Review: A Quarterly Review of Publications in the Field of Religion and Related Disciplines* and one entitled "other." The overlap across the questionnaire was deliberate and was intended to compensate for generalities of the categories offered in the survey. The level of choice within categories was very broad.

The data on the areas of specialization are organized into the three general categories used by Stephen Crites to describe a hypothetical curriculum in religious studies: "Studies in Historic Traditions," "Critical Approaches to the Study of Religion" and "Themes and Theories."[17] Since the area of doctoral research is foundational for every faculty member's career, I have listed all of the areas of doctoral study as each faculty member reported them on his or her questionnaire. For the discussion of research and teaching, however, the categories "History of Christianity," "Christian Origins" and "Theology" have been subsumed into the sub-category "Christian Studies" under the general topic of "Historic Traditions." I have placed biblical studies, dominated as it is by critical and historical methods, along with the social-scientific and other methods, under the general topic of "Critical Approaches." Under "Themes and Theories," I have included ethics, the arts, literature, and religion, gender studies and society and religion, among others. The threefold structure was particularly useful for measuring the adaptation of doctoral specializations to the necessities of teaching and research in the context of the small departments that characterize the region.

When religious studies departments advertise a vacant position, they normally specify the areas of specialization that will be considered. Applicants can determine the appropriateness of their application by comparing the advertisement's categories with the areas of their graduate course study and more specifically with the area of research for their doctoral dissertation. For small departments of two to five faculty positions, it is paramount that an applicant have an established research and publication area and be willing, for the good of the curriculum as a whole, to be a generalist.

In the survey of full-time faculty in religious studies in the Atlantic Region, each person was asked to identify the area of her or his doctoral research. Most of the faculty identified this in relation to specific historic traditions (See Table 5.6).

Of the forty-one respondents to the questionnaire, thirty had specializations appropriate to the category "historic traditions." Of those thirty, twenty-one or 70 percent specialized in Christianity and, together with the specialist in Western religious thought, 73 percent of the faculty in the region were specialists on Christianity and the Western religious traditions. Specialists in non-Western religious traditions included seven faculty or just 23 percent. The overwhelming preponderance of specialists trained to teach Christianity illustrates more clearly than any other data what religious studies was in 1994. It was overwhelmingly about Christianity and themes related to that tradition.

Table 5.6
Doctorates on Historic Traditions

Area of Specialization	Number of Faculty
Christianity	21
Western Religious Thought	1
East Asia	2
Islam	1
Hinduism	3
Buddhism	1
Ancient Near Eastern Traditions	1

The historical background of the universities and departments of religious studies goes some distance toward explaining the high percentage of faculty who were hired on the basis of a specialization in Christianity. Many of the faculty were hired in Theology departments. Having acknowledged that historical fact, there was a clear imbalance in the distribution of expertise across the fields of religious studies. Hindu, Buddhist or Chinese religious traditions are no less complex historically or textually than Christianity. The notion that a department can get by with several faculty teaching Christianity while comparative religions has only one specialist is no longer tenable. Clearly, with small departments it is impossible to have expertise that covers all of the religious traditions of the major continents of the world or the major historical epochs of each tradition. Having said that, the overall emphasis on specializations on Christianity cannot continue if religious studies is to fulfill its mandate.

Table 5.7
Doctorates in Critical Approaches to the Study of Religion

Area of Specialization	Number of Faculty
Biblical Studies (Christian Origins)	8
Methodology and Theory	1

I have deliberately included biblical studies under the grouping "Critical Approaches to the Study of Religion." Biblical studies integrates archaeological, textual, exegetical and historical methods without reference to consequences for beliefs within one or other of the Christian churches. With eight faculty in the region trained in biblical studies there was again a significant emphasis on this type of textual study (Table 5.7). It is not clear whether those specialists in the East Asian or South Asian areas were trained primarily in the study of religious texts. It is not possible, therefore, to indicate accurately what proportion of textual studies dealt with the sacred literature of traditions other than Christianity. At best, based on a review of curricula vitae of faculty in the region, there could have been as many as six scholars trained in non-Christian textual studies: two in the Hindu tradition; one in the Buddhist tradition; one in the Muslim tradition and two in the Chinese tradition. These scholars are included in the historic traditions area. Here the various topical refinements in the study of Christianity included in the questionnaire were not paralleled within Eastern religious traditions. Textual studies were not distinguished from historic traditions. This lack of refinement in the survey parallels the fact that those trained in comparative religion or Eastern traditions tend to be solitary specialists in the departments of the region, while there are several specialists in departments dealing with various aspects of Christianity.

Interpretation of religious texts has been a primary way to study religious traditions in religious studies departments. With eight biblical scholars in the region, 19.5 percent of the region's faculty are trained to do biblical scholarship. If we add the six faculty whose publications indicate that they studied Eastern religious texts to this total, we have 34 percent of the region's faculty trained to study religious traditions through sacred texts.

One of the most important consequences of the debates about the nature of the study of religions was the suggestion that there are many other ways to study religious traditions beyond the textual. It is probable that there will not likely be such a preponderance of biblical scholars in religious studies departments in the future, but it is also plausible to suggest that textual studies itself may become less significant as a source for interpretation of religious traditions. In their place will likely be the many different kinds of approaches to the study of religious experience, from ritual studies to the sociological and anthropological methods of interpretation. These kinds of specializations permit research and teaching on new religious movements, the new religions in Canada, from Hinduism and Buddhism to Islam. Nonetheless, the study of sacred texts, like all else in the field, will likely become just one of the many different approaches to knowledge about religions.

There was only one faculty member in the region whose training was specifically in the area of the diverse methodologies and theories of religious studies. This was a serious limitation. Some universities may still have faculty doing research and teaching in departments of history, sociology, anthropology or psychology whose courses are added to the religious studies curriculum. Increasingly, however, religion is not a high priority topic in some or all of these departments. Religious studies departments are going to have to integrate these areas into their curriculum by means of full-time positions. The religious traditions of the Atlantic region, from Aboriginal traditions through new religious movements to the historic patterns of Christian diversity, are all areas that require scholarly study. As departments review their options for new appointments it is essential that these areas be considered.

Instances of people who have been trained in one area but have become research specialists in another are limited. Hans Rollmann, a biblical scholar at Memorial University, has become an internationally recognized expert on the religious traditions of Newfoundland. Thomas Parkhill, trained in the Hindu religious tradition, has published on Maliseet history. Religious studies in the region has benefitted from this kind of adaptation to local research needs. These scholars and others like them are to be commended for their contribution to research in these areas.

Table 5.8
Doctorates in Themes and Theories

Area of Specialization	Number of Faculty
Society and Religion	1

The survey showed that there was only one person whose doctoral work was in the area of society and religion (Table 5.8). This statistic is somewhat misleading in terms of its impact on the shape of religious studies in the region. It would seem to imply that there is precious little attention paid to ethical and other religion-related issues of social significance in the region. The study of the curricula of the departments made clear that this is not the case. Many faculty have used their doctoral research as a basis upon which to do research and publish in the area of religion and society. Further, the terms used in the questionnaire did not cover specialists on environment and religions (Saint Mary's University), gender and religions (Mount Saint Vincent University), or minority and new religious movements (Memorial University of Newfoundland). All of these specialists fit into the area of "society and religion," but did not respond to the questionnaire indicating that their doctoral training most appropriately belonged in this category.

It is fundamental to any society to provide its members with as much of an opportunity as possible to acquire a critical understanding of their own tradition. Having said that, the advent of Canada's official multiculturalism policy in the early 1970s and the much more complex immigration patterns resulting from the arrival of many more immigrants from Asia, Africa and Latin America make clear that the acquisition of an understanding of society's traditions will require more specialists in non-Western religious traditions. Hindus, Buddhists and Muslims, to mention only three groups, now constitute major religious communities in the larger cities across Canada. To teach and do research on religions in Canada and the West requires a knowledge of Asian, African and Latin American traditions as much as of Christianity and Judaism. The challenge facing religious studies is to make this case as a basis for new areas of specialization.

Areas of Faculty Research

In reporting the data on areas of faculty research there can no longer be a one-to-one relationship between the total number of religious studies faculty in the region and the areas of research. The data shows that, both in research and teaching, faculty moved deliberately into new and different areas of study after they had taken up a full-time university post. The questionnaire permitted each person to designate primary and secondary areas of research. We have assumed that the area of doctoral study remained the primary area of research. What we wanted to accentuate was the diversification of research areas as faculty careers unfolded. To do this we have combined the primary and secondary areas. It was also the case that the faculty filling out the questionnaire adopted many more of the categories provided in order to describe their research areas.

Table 5.9
Research on Historic Traditions

Areas of Research	Number of Faculty
Christian Tradition	17
Religion in Canada	6
East Asia	2
South Asia	2
Buddhism	1
Hinduism	2
Islam	1
Judaism	1
Native American Traditions	1

In the reporting of research areas, there were several refinements. The Christian tradition remained the predominant area among the historic traditions. Of the twenty-nine faculty reporting, 58 percent did their research in the area of Christianity (Table 5.9). The fact that the largest number of faculty were doing research on Christianity is a consequence of the kinds of specialization sought by departments of religious studies across the region during the 1960s and 1970s. Much more interesting that this predictable result is the extent to which faculty have developed new areas for research and publication. Several new research areas on historic traditions appeared in the responses to the questionnaire, suggesting that a very high percentage of faculty were expanding into new areas of study. Religion in Canada was not indicated as an area of doctoral research, yet there were six faculty, or 20 percent of the total, doing research in the area. One faculty member had developed the area of Native American Traditions. Another had developed Judaism as an area of expertise and publication. Even when the number of faculty doing research in an area decreased, as was the case with Hinduism (a reduction from three to two) this could be interpreted as part of the diversification of faculty research areas.

Table 5.10
Research on Critical Approaches to the Study of Religion

Areas of Research	Number of Faculty
Biblical Studies	8
Methodology and Theory	5
Gender Studies	1
Anthropology of Religion	1
Sociology of Religion	3
Ritual, Cult and Worship	1
Comparative Studies	4
Psychology and Religion	1
Religion and Science	2
Philosophy and Religion	1

The most interesting and dramatic change in research areas is evident in the responses to the questionnaire which show the work being done on critical approaches to the study of religion (Table 5.10). At the same time, some continuity exists. The number of faculty doing research in biblical studies remains constant at eight when compared to the doctoral research areas in Table 5.7.

In the data on doctoral research, we reported that nine faculty were involved in the "Critical Approaches to the Study of Religion." Among those who are continuing their research in full-time positions in the region, twenty-seven reported that they are doing research in that area—a 300 percent increase.

It is difficult to imagine that any faculty member actively doing research would not get caught up in questions of methodology and theory as part of the research. It is clear that the categories offered permitted a significant range of responses that cut across the social-scientific approaches to the study of religions and philosophy of religion.

In 1994, when the questionnaire was circulated, there was only one respondent who indicated that he or she did research on gender and religion. This is a startling result. It is fair to say that the debate about gender has been the most influential and controversial issue within all fields of study in the field over the last twenty years. The debate about gender and religions has occurred annually at the meetings of the Canadian Society for the Study of Region/La société canadienne pour l'étude de la religion and its impact has changed teaching and research. The most important consequence has been the recognition that departments must create gender equality in religious studies departments and in departments across the university. Furthermore, courses on all of the historic traditions are now seen to be incomplete if they do not deal with the differences in the religious experience of women and men within those traditions. In sum, no aspect of religious studies has remained unaffected by the gender debate. As a result, the fact that only one person reported that he or she was doing research in the in the area indicates a serious weakness in the field. What mitigates this conclusion is the data we have already reported in which there has been a significant increase in the number of women teaching in the field since 1994. Were the questionnaire to be circulated now, the results would in all likelihood be strikingly different.

In the report on doctoral research areas under the topic "Themes and Theories," there was one person who was doing work in the area of society and religion (Table 5.11). Again there was a dramatic increase in faculty doing research in this area—600 percent. Ethics and the arts were the two areas where there was evidence of a significant diversification in scholarly work. The other new area was study of popular religion and culture.

Table 5.11
Research on Themes and Theories

Areas of Research	Number of Faculty
Arts, Literature and Religion	2
Popular Religious Themes	1
Sects, Cults and Occultism	1
Society and Religion	1
Ethics	2

Academic Societies

Academic societies are professional organizations that have two principal functions: they hold annual conferences where scholars give papers and, no less important, meet and socialize with other scholars in the field; and they publish scholarly journals in the field. In Canada, the publishing arm of the academic societies is the Canadian Corporation for Studies in Religion/Corporation Canadienne des Sciences Religieuses, which publishes books in the field and the Canadian academic journal *Studies in Religion/Sciences Religieuses*.

We have argued that the impact of the academic societies on the development of religious studies in the region has been significant. The kind of debates that have dominated the societies have contributed substantially to the changes that have taken place in religious studies departments. Of the forty-one faculty who responded to the questionnaire, twenty-seven answered the question about memberships in the academic societies. Of those, four indicated that they held no memberships and rarely or never went to academic conferences. On the other hand, the remaining twenty-three reported membership and/or participation in over thirty-six different societies with three people indicating active memberships in a total of twelve different academic societies. All but two of the twenty-three respondents indicated they belonged to at least one Canadian learned society and twenty-five indicated a membership in an international society. Given that these memberships now cost on average approximately $100, the individual commitment to society memberships was quite significant.

Participation in the annual conferences of academic societies is also an indication of research activity. Of the twenty-six faculty responding to the question about conference attendance, sixteen indicated that they attended an academic conference every year. In addition to that number, two attended every second year, four every third year and four rarely or never.

Conference participation has become increasingly difficult for faculty. Universities no longer fund the full cost of attending a conference and most will pay nothing unless the faculty member is presenting a paper. That faculty attend an academic conference simply to hear the papers and meet with scholars in the field is becoming increasingly unlikely. With the annual cost of academic society memberships increasing because of reductions in support from the national research agencies and the increase in the cost of travel, faculty are having to examine their participation in academic societies as both members and conference participants. As faculty set limits on their memberships Canadian academic societies are under increasing pressure. The questionnaire provided no opportunity for faculty to elaborate on these issues. Therefore it is not clear whether or not these issues were a factor in the report on society memberships and conference participation. That they are of significant concern to the Canadian academic societies is a fact.

Qualitative Changes in Faculty Research

On the questionnaire each faculty member was asked to respond to a question about changes to their research activities that had occurred over his or her career. Their responses indicated that the most significant change has been the transformation of the means by which information is written, stored and retrieved. For those faculty who had completed their doctorate in the 1960s, the index card, newsprint, ring-binder or notebook was the storage medium for research notes. Doctoral dissertations and papers were typed on manual or electric typewriters. All of these methods of storage and writing now seem antiquated. The typewriter has disappeared, along with the hand-drawn arrows leading the typist to editorial changes in a manuscript, be it a doctoral thesis, an article or a book. In the words of one scholar, "computerization has made available revolutionary new research tools—databases, spreadsheets, word processors." In addition, libraries are storing information in new ways. Bibliographies, on-line libraries and searchable CD-ROMS with biblical and other sacred texts in original languages and translations are now routinely available from the computers that are ubiquitous in libraries and in faculty offices. And then there is the Internet, the World Wide Web, with information and communications capabilities the like of which most people did not imagine possible in the 1960s, with Web pages storing audio, visual, and written information—as well as misinformation. In simple terms, so much more information is available, and so many more technical skills need to be acquired in order to use and retrieve it, that faculty could spend their careers focused on the means of research alone.

There is no doubt that the computer has brought about profound changes in the ways in which faculty do research. Yet in the end it is the individual faculty member who conducts the research. One faculty member noted the importance of external funding for his research in Asia and that the continuation of that funding provided the most substantial means by which he was able to conduct his research over a period of twenty years. Several respondents noted the importance of sabbaticals to their research. It goes without saying that for the vast majority of faculty resident in small universities with undergraduate libraries and facilities, the development of their research is centred around their sabbaticals.

Some faculty members chose to change fields of research or incorporate new areas of research within their current field. We have noted several already. In addition, one biblical scholar described the changes in research in her career this way (point form in the original): "From historical criticism to Anthropological/Sociological study of the Bible, from Anthropological/Sociological to Literary Critical study of the Bible; Feminism-influences in both teaching and research." What is at stake here is the encounter with both the new methodologies of the study of religious texts and the philosophical issues that underpin the debates about these new methods in research. Over and over again in the responses to the question on changes in research it was evident that the scholars were engaged by the currents of study and research in the field. This is not surprising given the evidence noted above of the relatively high percentages of membership in academic societies and attendance at academic conferences.

Finally there was one respondent that spoke of an increased focus on research in his career. Such a shift in priority is striking in light of the overwhelming number of respondents who stated that their first priority was teaching and that they consequently spent half or more of their professional time devoted to it. It is obvious that young scholars in their early years of employment have to spend a great deal of time developing their courses and pedagogical techniques. That some of the faculty had reached the point at which they could shift more of their energy to research was an interesting and important comment on career trajectory.

Among the activities that divert faculty from spending the time required for both teaching and research is university administration. Becoming chair of a department or an academic dean can be an all-consuming activity, the immediacy of which limits the possibilities for doing research and academic writing.

In addition there are the inevitable political battles that faculty in religious studies have to engage in to defend the existence of their departments and programs. This was strikingly evident in Halifax between 1995-96 when the Nova Scotia government seemed resolved to amalgamate universities. The university administrations were focused almost entirely on the endless demand for reports and on how to contend with government interference in the universities. Religious studies was one of the programs likely to be threatened because of retirements, and the closure of all such departments was contemplated. That neither the amalgamation of all of universities nor the closure of all of the religious studies departments had taken place by 1999 was, in significant part, the result of seemingly endless hours of labour by university administrators and faculty from religious studies departments determined to defend their respective institutions.

Finally, responses to the questionnaire from new faculty and from the younger faculty in tenure-stream positions noted the importance of getting a job, and tenure and promotion as crucial points in their careers. The impact of the processes required for faculty career reviews is significant for research. On the positive side there is the sustained requirement to publish. It is now the norm for graduate students to present papers at academic conferences and to publish their research. As opposed to twenty years ago, applicants for university positions are now expected to include publications as an essential component of the dossier. During the initial years of an appointment there is further pressure to present papers at conferences and to publish.

Areas of Specialization for Teaching

Teaching university students is overwhelmingly the first priority of the religious studies faculty in the Atlantic region. Furthermore, the setting in which faculty teach is for the most part small to middle-sized liberal-arts universities. For religious studies the largest departmental complement is nine full-time faculty (Memorial) with the smallest complements of one (Mount Saint Vincent). The effect of the small numbers of faculty in each department is that most faculty have to teach as broadly in the field of religious studies as possible. It is not surprising therefore that the diversification of research areas that we have just noted is also reflected in the research faculty do for teaching. The responses to the questionnaire substantiate that correlation.

A comparison of the research areas and teaching areas in "Historic Traditions" shows that there is only one category in which the responses were identical—the "Native American Traditions." Ironically, only six respondents indicated they were actually teaching Religion in Canada, as opposed to nine who reported that they did research in the area. In all other areas there was greater diversity of teaching in comparison with research. Even with the preponderance of specialists in Christianity, the number of people who taught in the area exceeded the number doing research. In the cognate areas of Judaism, Islam and the Ancient Near East and Greece, where there was only one faculty member doing research, we find that fifteen faculty were teaching. As a result of the requirement of departments that courses be offered in the areas of world religions such as Hinduism, Buddhism or the religions of China, we find that there were dramatic increases in the number of faculty who were teaching in these areas in comparison with those doing research: Hinduism from two to nine; Buddhism from one to eight; and from two to five in East and South Asia.

Table 5.12
Teaching Historic Traditions

Areas of Teaching	Number of Faculty	Research Areas for Comparison
Christianity and Theology	21	17
Judaism	6	1
Islam	5	1
Ancient Near East and Greece	4	0
Hinduism	9	2
Buddhism	8	1
East Asia	5	2
South Asia	5	2
Religion in Canada	3	6
Native American Traditions	1	1

These examples of the diversification of research for the purposes of teaching into so many of the historic traditions reflected the commitment of departments and faculty to offer a curriculum that covered as many religious traditions as possible. At the same time the diversification is, and ought to be, a matter of concern to departments. Given the preponderance of faculty trained in Christianity and biblical studies, it is most likely that some of these faculty have undertaken the task of preparing courses on one or other of the world religions. It is no small task for faculty to undertake the research necessary to offer advanced-level courses in Buddhism, Hinduism or Native religious traditions when those traditions have not been part of their doctoral training. Such commitment to a diversified curriculum is to be commended.

At the same time it is necessary to raise a fundamental concern about the implications of such diverse teaching loads in religious studies departments.

The problem is directly related to the slow expansion of the number of faculty in departments who have doctoral training in the Asian or Native American religious traditions or indeed in any area that is not directly related to classical Christian and biblical studies. For the study of Christianity it is assumed that a department must have at least a specialist in biblical studies and a church historian or theologian. While religious studies was in its early stages of development, such multiple specializations in Christianity seemed appropriate even in the small departments. When a specialist was added to teach other religious traditions it was assumed, given the limitations in the number of positions, that such a person would have to teach *all* of the Asian traditions, from those of South Asia to those of China, Japan and Southeast Asia. As if geographical diversity were not enough, added to it was the necessity of covering the history of these religious traditions and introducing the sacred texts and rituals as well.

The assumption that one world religions specialist in a small department is enough is as inappropriate for the complexity of these Asian religious traditions as is the assumption that the study of Christianity, in all of its cultural, historical and textual complexity, can be taught by one specialist. Solving this conundrum is not easy, but the clear implication is that departments are simply going to have to insist that new appointments are focused on the expansion of specializations to cover more of the historic traditions.

Table 5.13
Teaching Critical Approaches to the Study of Religion

Areas of Teaching	Number of Faculty	Research Areas for Comparison
Biblical Studies	11	8
Methodology and Theory	7	5
Gender Studies	4	1
Anthropology of Religion	2	1
Sociology of Religion	3	3
Religion and Science	7	2
Psychology and Religion	2	1
Comparative Studies	9	4
Philosophy of Religion	2	1
Phenomenology of Religion	4	0
Ritual and Cult	3	1

Turning to the "Critical Approaches to the Study of Religion" we see the same pattern of diversification for teaching as was evident from the responses about historic traditions. In these areas, however, it is important to note that most faculty studied hermeneutics and diverse methodologies and theories about the study of religions in their graduate work. No historic tradition can be studied without a sophisticated understanding of the methodological debates in the field. It is entirely possible, then, that faculty were bringing graduate training to their teaching in these areas.

The most striking increase in teachable areas was in "Religion and Science." There were only two people doing research on this topic but there were seven teaching courses in this area (Table 5.13). The second most significant increase was in the area of comparative studies—from four to nine. Thirdly, four people were teaching gender studies but only one was doing research in this area.

For "Themes and Theories" the pattern of diversification is strongly evident. Out of the four topics three showed very significant increases in teachable areas, with increases in "Ethics" and "Society and Religion" the most dramatic. Regretfully, the one area that shows no increase was that of "sects, cults and occultism." This latter topic, together with new religious movements and immigrant-based religious traditions in Canada, has the potential for significant growth. There is also the potential for considerable student interest in these areas, as it relates the temples that students see in their neighborhoods, the news stories they read about cults and the new immigrants they meet on the street to the study of religions in the university.

Table 5.14
Teaching Themes and Theories

Areas of Teaching	Number of Faculty	Comparison with Research Areas
Arts, Literature and Religion	6	2
Sects, Cults and Occultism	1	1
Ethics	7	2
Society and Religion	6	1

Qualitative Changes in the area of Teaching

In their responses to the questionnaire, faculty reported a variety of fundamental changes in their teaching conditions.

- *Class size*: One of the most frequently identified concerns was the perceived loss of the small class. More and more the classrooms are filled with large numbers of students, particularly at the introductory levels. Majors in religious studies must share the classroom with elective students, resulting in many cases in a real discrepancy in background and preparation for the course subject matter. One respondent observed: "With the virtual dissolution of a humanities core-curriculum, and the shrinking ration of religion majors in over-subscribed courses, I came to accept that all my courses had to have something of the characteristics of an introduction to the discipline."
- *Student Skill Levels*: Several respondents noted that they were spending more and more of their time on remedial issues connected with student reading and writing skills. "After having striven for many years to remedy student reading skills—teaching the schematic outline, quizzing on content—I moved (with an uneasy conscience) toward a kind of resignation in the new culture and placed more emphasis upon personal appropriation of whatever subject matter they discerned—with a demand for journal keeping, structured discussions, interpretive-essay exams. Feeling somewhat defeated I gave less time to the remedial effort." The note of resignation, even defeat, in this comment caught the mood of several of the respondents, who noted the difficulty students had in reading the most elementary of university textbooks or assigned readings.
- *New Pedagogical Strategies*: One of the most common observations about change in the classroom concerned the development of new strategies for teaching. It was not surprising, then, to see several comments about the abandonment of the lecture or at least the reduction in its use as a means of teaching. One persons spoke of "feeling the need for and implementing a shift from passive to active learning; from individual/class instruction to collaborative inquiry." What is interesting about this comment by a scholar with some twenty years of teaching experience is the absence of the feeling of discouragement evident in the earlier comment about student skills. Here, the change in pedagogical approach was driven by a change in educational goals and the means to achieve them rather than by a feeling that students could not do the work that they should have been able to do.
- *Continuing Education and the Mature Student*: Two respondents pointed to a shift in the audience for their teaching. The return of many mature students to the universities is permitting faculty who choose to do so to teach

courses as part of their normal teaching load or as overloads during the evenings, weekends, and summers. With these new times for courses has come a significant constituency of new students. The mature student is, usually defined as a person who has been out of the public education system, usually high school, for a minimum of three years. The mature student constituency is often made up of women and men for whom the study of religions offers exciting possibilities. Mature students are frequently more disciplined students and more open to the study of religions.

- *New Areas of Teaching*: For one respondent coming to a small department in the Atlantic region was an opportunity to be a generalist in the field. Stated positively, this view stands over against the devastation some new faculty feel as they leave behind the academic metropolis and take up full-time employment in what they perceive to be the hinterland. It is worth noting therefore that many of the respondents spoke positively about their new areas of teaching. Some had added new historic traditions such as Islam, Hinduism or Buddhism to their regular teaching. In several instances faculty spoke of the transformation of content that occurred as they redesigned courses in the light of the gender issue. The fact that textbooks and general resources used in the classroom do not deal adequately with the religious experience of women required a radical revision of course content to integrate this perspective.

- *Computers in Teaching*: Two respondents to the questionnaire referred to the impact of the computer and the availability of audiovisual material for the classroom as significant changes. In 1994 the computer, while well established in the offices of many faculty, was not the commonplace tool in the classroom which it had become by 1999. Nor was the Internet the source of seemingly endless riches and distortions requiring careful instruction in how to read Web pages critically. Nonetheless, in 1994 there was one course offered on religions in Newfoundland and Labrador that made use of Internet communications and posted resources. Another such course was offered at Mount Allison. These courses were exceptional, but most faculty were certainly aware of the power of the computer as a writing tool for students and encouraged its use.

- *Video Resources for the Classroom*: Two respondents noted the importance of the advent of the VCR and the availability for classroom use of hundreds of thousands of films, both feature films and documentaries. It has become possible to present "images" of the religious life from a rich diversity of sources. All the National Film Board films and productions by the Canadian Broadcasting Corporation and Vision TV are readily available at a modest cost for use in the classroom. In addition, though more difficult to obtain in Canada, there are the productions done for the specialty channels such as the American Public Broadcasting System and the Arts and Entertainment network. Despite these incredible resources, relatively few textbooks, on world religions, for example, provide suggestions in the area.

Recommendations

Nothing will shape the future of religious studies both in the Atlantic region and in Canada as a whole as much as the debate about what kind of specializations will be employed in the religious studies departments over the next decade or so. Between the years 1994 and 2014, twenty-seven faculty will retire from religious studies departments in the Atlantic region alone. Among the ten who have retired between 1994 and 2000 four have not been replaced at all. To continue to lose 40 percent of the religious studies faculty every five years will ultimately spell disaster for religious studies in the region.

The most recent loss to religious studies has been the replacement of the world-religions specialist at St. Francis Xavier with a person who will offer two courses in the Catholic Studies program and an introductory course on world religions for the religious studies department. It is precisely this type of replacement that is going to have to be looked at most carefully since it diminishes the resources in religious studies overall and in the area that our data suggests is in greatest need of expansion.

Since its inception, religious studies has been founded on the premise that its subject matter is the study of the religions of the world. In reality, as we have seen in Canada and, most certainly, in the Atlantic region, this has meant that faculty in religious studies have done research on and taught courses primarily about Christianity and secondarily selected religious traditions from the world's religions. We have noted the remarkable efforts of faculty to expand their areas of specialization for research and especially for teaching to incorporate many new areas into religious studies curricula across the region. We have also noted that there is a serious problem with that process. It is simply a false and ultimately, I would argue, a fatal assumption that many experts are required to teach Christianity and only a handful are required to teach other religious traditions.

The implications of this for the future planning of religious studies departments are crucial. Departments must find ways to argue their case for replacements so that there is not simply a continuation of a retiring person's specialization in the new appointment. Specialists in Christianity are going to have to analyze how the tradition is going to be taught with far fewer people offering the courses. At the same time the positions that open up must bring an ever greater diversity of religious studies specialists into the small departments of the region.

Every religious studies department must plan its future on the basis of the fundamental presuppositions that have shaped the definition of religious studies from its inception. Departments will have to select the historic traditions, which, over time, can be included in the faculty complement. Institutional and local factors will play a significant role in that selection. Once such a plan is in place, departments of religious studies can argue for the employment of as rich a diversity of specialists in the historic traditions as possible. Such positions may focus their attention on the places of origin of the historic tradition or they can focus on the diaspora communities found in North America or elsewhere in the world.

On the foundation of selected historic traditions appropriate to a department, there needs to be significant attention to the methods by which the historic traditions are studied. Departments could benefit, at least in theory, from a range of approaches that include social-scientific methods and textual studies, historical, philosophical and theological approaches. In other words, as departments consider which historic traditions in which to hire specialists, the departments can also ensure that those same specialists conduct their research using different methodologies. For example, a department could have a specialists in Biblical studies, a specialist on Buddhist history and a Hindu specialists who uses anthropological or sociological methods in their study. A department that combined various historical traditions with diverse methods has the foundation to offer a variety of thematic courses that are deliberately comparative both in terms of their content and approach to the study of religions.

There is an enormous weight of evidence to suggest that for religious studies to continue to diversify so that it is representative of the study of as many religious traditions as faculty positions allow, will mean that religious studies will be seen as an essential contributor to the academic study of the changes occurring in Canadian society at large and the university system in particular. Canadian society is rapidly integrating people from around the globe. Multiculturalism is not only a federal policy, but also a social fact in virtually every city in the country. The decline in religious affiliations to the various churches is not yet matched by the proliferation of religious temples and shrines and new religious movements, but it is very likely that in the census of 2001 the second largest religion in Canada, after Christianity, will be Islam.

In the midst of this social change is a remarkable movement to internationalize the curriculum of the university. This is expressed in global research projects,[18] development projects and a commitment to making the university curriculum as international as possible. Many students now leave university and travel around the globe teaching English as a second language. As they do so, they experience the indigenous cultures and religions of the countries in which they work. Such students need to be prepared for what they are going to experience and see. Religious studies can and must be a part of these developments.

For religious studies to be seen as essential to the internationalizing of the university and its curriculum requires faculty who are expert in their respective area of religious studies and are also capable of working collaboratively both in research and in teaching within the new programs of the university. One of the important changes in research patterns is the development and encouragement of collaborative research teams. Parallel to this development in research patterns are the varieties of new programs such as Asian studies, women's studies and international development studies. Like religious studies, these programs are multidisciplinary in their approach to research and the curriculum. It is perhaps ironic that religious studies, which has been a university department for decades, is not seen as a model for these kinds of programs. Nor is it enough simply to offer elective courses in these programs. Religious studies needs to work to be seen as an essential component of the multidisciplinary study of Asia, gender or development. This requires that departments hire as faculty women and men who are prepared to participate in team research projects around the globe and who are capable of integrating the perspective of the religions into the dialogue about changes in culture and economics around the world.

For the small departments to make the kinds of appointments we have just discussed, it is going to be necessary for the graduate schools in both Canada and the United States to recognize that the kind of specialist required is a person who has a graduate education that includes a substantial breadth of training, not only in the historic traditions, but also in the various methodological approaches to the study of religions. All graduate students must be qualified in more than one religious tradition. All graduate students must incorporate into their understanding of their part of the field the different ways by which women and men have appropriated and expressed their religious tradition. The importance of these educational priorities is reflected in the fact that the vast majority of university positions are not in departments at large institutions like the University of Toronto or McMaster University, but in those of the smaller institutions that dot the landscape of Canada and of the Atlantic region in particular.

At the time of their founding religious studies departments had faculty of vision who could see beyond the denominational or secular roots of their universities to the possibility of departments in which the study of religious traditions could take place at a university level. Their vision meant that they had to contend with those who saw the study of religions simply as an ecclesiastical encroachment into the university or, in an opposite view, as a proper extension of the churches into the university. Both the academic prejudice against the study of religions and the priorities that centred the field on the study of Christianity have limited the vision of what religious studies is and can be. Nonetheless, religious studies has always required that its curriculum include as many courses as possible on the world's religions. That fundamental principle awaits its full expression. Hopefully in the twenty-first century the faculty in the current departments will see its fulfillment.

Notes

1 Ray L. Hart, "Religious and Theological Studies in American Higher Education: A Pilot Study," *Journal of the American Academy of Religion* 59/3 (1991): 729.
2 Ibid.
3 I am here excluding the Atlantic Baptist University and St. Stephen's University, both of which are chartered by the province of New Brunswick but are not recipients of government funds.
4 Two recent discussions of good teaching are: Michel Desjardins,"Like a Cook in a Café," *Studies in Religion/Sciences Religieuses* 27/1 (1998): 69-78 and Darlene M. Juschka,"The Construction of Pedagogical Spaces: Religious Studies in the University," *Studies in Religion/Sciences Religieuses* 28/1 (1999): 85-97.
5 I cannot recommend too highly Martha C. Nussbaum, *Cultivating Humanity: A Classical Defense of Reform in Liberal Education* (Cambridge, MA: Harvard University Press, 1997) as one of the finest reflections on the modern university classroom, its ends and its purposes.
6 *University Affairs/Affaires universitaires* is the publication of the Association of Universities and Colleges of Canada. This and the *Bulletin* are the primary sources of job advertisements for Canadian universities.
7 Russell T. McCutcheon, "The Crisis of Academic Labour and the Myth of Autonomy: Dispatch from the Job Wars," *Studies in Religion/Science Religieuses* 27/4 (1998): 387-405.
8 The Aid to Scholarly Publications Programme provides a peer-review process of evaluation for academic manuscripts and, assuming that there are funds available, assigns approximately $7,000 to the publisher to defray the costs of publication and publicity for a book that has been approved.
9 Harold Remus, William Closson James and Daniel Fraikin, *Religious Studies in Ontario: A State-of-the-Art Review* (Waterloo: Wilfrid Laurier University Press for the Canadian Corporation for Studies in Religion/Corporation canadienne des sciences religieuses), 147.
10 Ibid. 146.
11 Dr. Elizabeth Bellefontaine took early retirement in 1997 in order to take up full-time duties with the Sisters of Charity. In 1998 she was killed in a tragic automo-

bile accident in New Brunswick. Sister Betty was a beloved teacher at Mount Saint Vincent University and a tenacious advocate of religious studies there.
12 I have not included the four members of Religious studies faculty at the Atlantic Baptist University for the purposes of this comparison, but rather have considered the same institutions and departments surveyed in 1994. The four faculty members at the Atlantic Baptist University are male. Currently, there is no system of tenure at the university and faculty teach across several academic areas since there are no departments as such.
13 Remus et al., *Religious Studies in Ontario*, 154.
14 Respondents to the questionnaire frequently did not answer portions of the questions. The totals therefore do not correlate with the total number of full-time faculty surveyed (41).
15 The total number of areas of specialization in doctoral studies in this section is forty. One faculty member was originally trained to the doctoral level in physics and subsequently retrained to teach comparative religion.
16 See Appendix 2 for the complete questionnaire. The categories listed included one repetition. There were therefore thirty-one categories and the one entitled "other" available for faculty to use to describe their areas of doctoral study, research and teaching.
17 Stephen C. Crites, scribe, *The Religion Major: A Report/The American Academy of Religion Task Force for the American Association of Colleges*, (Atlanta: American Academy of Religion, 1990), 20-21.
18 Cf. William F. Ryan, S.J., *Culture, Spirituality, and Economic Development: Opening a Dialogue* (Ottawa, ON: International Development Research Centre, 1995).

6
Conclusion

> What would an education for world citizenship look like in a modern university curriculum? This education must be a multicultural education, by which I mean one that acquaints students with some fundamentals about the histories and cultures of many different groups. These should include the major religious and cultural groups of each part of the world and also ethnic and racial, social and sexual minorities within their own nation. Language learning, history, religious studies, and philosophy all play a role in pursuing these ideas. — Martha C. Nussbaum

As I began writing the conclusion to this review of religious studies in Atlantic Canada, I received a call from Dr. Randi Warne, currently the sole member of the Department of Religious Studies at Mount Saint Vincent University. She told me that the Committee on Academic Policy and Planning (CAPP) at Mount Saint Vincent had issued its report on the future of academic programs in the university. The report recommends that the religious studies department be closed and Dr. Warne be transferred either to women's studies or to another department.[1] A major in religious studies could be preserved but only as a coordinated program. There are many battles yet to be fought at Mount Saint Vincent before the plan, or some modified version of it, is made official policy. Once again a religious studies department at one of our Atlantic universities is at risk.

Dr. Warne's call reminded me that when I began the research for this review in 1994 I received a long letter from Dr. Bruce Matthews at Acadia University. His Department of Comparative Religion was to be closed on the recommendation of the Academic Planning Committee of the Faculty of Arts. While courses would remain in the curriculum, there were no battles left to fight to preserve the department at Acadia.

Along the way, as the state-of-the-art review was unfolding, the major in religious studies at the Université de Moncton was suspended, leaving only two faculty teaching elective courses. Similarly, at the University College of Cape Breton, the major was left on the books, but the single member of faculty was investing his primary energy in the introductory courses of the Faculty of Arts from his base in the Department of Philosophy and Religious Studies. In January 2000 I learned that the department at St. Francis Xavier had lost two-thirds of a position in the critical area of comparative religion. These losses are real and painful for religious studies as a field of study. A department's existence in the university is, as we have argued, a hard-won recognition and to lose it diminishes both the particular university's breadth of curriculum and the field of religious studies in Canada.

It is not clear what lessons might be drawn from these actual or threatened closures in the Atlantic region. At Acadia the enrolments were thriving when the department was shut down. At Mount Saint Vincent in 1999 Dr. Warne and part-time lecturers were teaching as many or more students both in the classroom and on televised courses as were taught when the department had three full-time faculty. Nor can one point to a lack of statesmanship on Dr. Warne's part. Since her appointment in 1996 she has proven to be an energetic and articulate advocate for religious studies. If student enrolments and lack of statesmanship are not the issues behind the threatened closure, then the problem is the department's small faculty complement. As we have seen, this issue becomes critical at the time when retirements occur. A department of three is vulnerable; a department of one is severely threatened.

There is a history here which connects the current recommendations at Mount Saint Vincent to the protracted discussions about university amalgamation versus a metropolitan Halifax consortium of independent universities. The problem was identified by the deans of arts in the metropolitan Halifax universities when they pointed out in 1995 that the small departments of religious studies were the only departments which faced a crisis from retirements.[2] Their research permitted the deans to speculate that this field of study could face closure across all of the universities in the city as retirements took place between 1995 and 2003.

The deans' report, while repudiated in the end, may have had particular effect at Mount Saint Vincent. The religious studies department there provided the most extreme instance of a department facing the retirement issue. All three of its faculty retired between 1995 and 1998. In that period only one of the three faculty was replaced. The decisions to postpone or eliminate replacements for the religious studies department created the context for the Committee on Academic Policy and Planning to recommend the department's closure.

Conclusion

A similar, though not quite identical, situation determined the fate of the Department of Comparative Religion at Acadia where there was a faculty complement of three. First, one member of the department became dean of arts and subsequently president of Acadia. He was never replaced during his protracted administrative leave. It was no surprise therefore that when the president retired he was still not replaced in the comparative religion department. Coincidently another member of the department asked to be transferred to the philosophy department. With Dr. Bruce Matthews as the only remaining faculty member, the department was closed.

While the circumstances at Acadia and Mount Saint Vincent were different, it is significant that the department faculty complements were identical. For whatever reason, when the number of faculty was reduced in any way the department was immediately at risk. If there is a lesson in these two instances, then, it would appear to be that a department in Nova Scotia and perhaps elsewhere, must be larger than three faculty or it will be at risk as retirements take place. When a department is small, it does not appear to matter how well the faculty teach, how high student enrolments are in the department's courses, how productive the department's faculty are in research and publication, or how skilled they have been politically. This being the case, it means that good programs yet to face the retirement crisis are at risk. Dalhousie University's Department of Comparative Religion has two full-time faculty and the University College of Cape Breton has one.

With only one or two faculty making up a department, the retirement of one allows the administration and the Senate to close the department or the program and to reallocate the remaining faculty to another department until such time as he or she retires. It is, from an administration's point of view, the most painless way to reallocate resources to larger programs which are perceived, by virtue of number of full-time faculty, to be more viable.

However, while a small full-time faculty complement makes the administrative decision easier, it does not explain why religious studies departments were reduced in size or not allowed to grow to approximate the median size of other programs either in the social sciences or in the humanities. At least in part, the answer, while always local and particular to individual institutions, must include the scepticism within the academy about religion as a discipline. While faculty may show in what they publish and teach that the study of religions is multidisciplinary and multicultural, it seems very often to be extremely difficult to convey the significance of that to colleagues and university administrators. It is even more difficult when a department continues to have an overwhelming preponderance of courses on Christianity and faculty trained in that area. It is this that sustains the impression that religious studies is primarily about the teaching of Christianity.

I would argue that becoming a religious studies department is even harder at institutions where the founding tradition of the university is a church or religious order. High on the hillside on which the Acadia University campus is located sits the Acadia Divinity College. It overlooks the arts complex. Similarly, at Mount Saint Vincent University the enormous mother house of the Sisters of Charity overlooks the whole campus. It is difficult to discern what role such physical and symbolic presences have on the two secularized universities. Most particularly, it is difficult to identify the role of these symbolic presences in relation to the decisions taken about the two departments. However, these dominant symbols did mean that "religion" on both campuses had a powerful symbolic significance over against which a department of religious studies or comparative religion had to define itself. A religious studies department could not be the denomination's arm in the undergraduate curriculum unless it became a department of theology.

At Acadia, the name of the department introduced its difference from the Acadia Divinity College. It was a comparative religion department. The faculty taught world religions with specializations in Buddhism, Islam, philosophy of religion and biblical studies. The department went to extremes to avoid the perception of being an extension of the divinity college in the Faculty of Arts. Such a strategy may have worked for a while, but in the final analysis the argument for difference between divinity and the study of religions did not elicit institutional support for the department once the faculty complement was reduced.

In contrast to the Acadia approach, the Department of Religious Studies at Mount Saint Vincent saw as its mandate during the 1980s and early 1990s a focus on Christianity and biblical studies in particular. One might call this approach the argument for continuity, or even identity, with the religious founding tradition rather than the argument for difference. As long as the Sisters of Charity managed the university, religious studies could offer a curriculum centred on Christianity and also non-degree, short courses for laity. When the Sisters of Charity handed over the university to a public board, effectively secularizing it, the religious studies department continued to maintain that its primary mandate was to focus on biblical studies and Christianity as a form of continuity with the founding tradition of the university. Carefully selected external reviewers endorsed that choice. The three faculty who were responsible for this interpretation of religious studies retired over a very short period, during which the university was in financial crisis. Only one replacement was made.

The crucial development at Mount Saint Vincent University was the turning of the university away from its heritage as defined by the Sisters of Charity, toward its new secular public image as the only university in Canada concerned primarily with the education of women. As a result, in 1999 a new faculty position was awarded to the Department of Women's Studies, where enrolments were very low, instead of a new position in religious studies, where enrolments were very high and increasing. There was a profound irony in this decision. Despite the fact that the university had one of Canada's outstanding specialists on gender *and religion* who had developed an innovative academic plan for the department as the only religious studies department in Canada with gender and religions as its central focus, the university's academic plan argued that religious studies was expendable. In this instance, there was among the decision-makers at Mount Saint Vincent University a commitment to the existence of women's studies department rather than support for the now much more respected model, which argues that analysis of gender must be an integral part of *all* disciplines.

What is happening at Mount Saint Vincent and what has taken place at Acadia make clear that the failure of a religious studies department to grow enough within any particular university is a prescription for its elimination. Faculty retirements have constituted the defining moment not just for the continued existence of small departments, but for change in the meaning of religious studies as it is taught in a particular university. It is the primary occasion when the debates that have animated the discipline at its conferences and in its academic journals can be reflected in new directions for the development of a department.

There are other factors always at play in decisions within a university. There is the fundamental fact of federal and provincial cuts to university funding, which have been particularly acute in the Atlantic region. In Nova Scotia the cuts have translated into the highest student tuition fees in Canada, into buildings and other infrastructure in desperate need of repair; and into universities under pressure to be technologically innovative without the funds for adequate technology or, more critically, the money to hire the skilled, highly paid technicians needed to maintain high-tech educational delivery systems. These factors are real and justify the hard decisions made about what a university can continue to offer in its curriculum. A small religious studies department facing retirements in such a context has an extremely difficult case to make for its continuance.

Whether it is a relatively easy practical decision in the face of real and perceived financial necessity, or an ideological stance, or both, the effect is that religious studies may be closed at Mount Saint Vincent University and is threatened elsewhere. To preserve the study of religions in the university curriculum is going to require heroic efforts in the face of stiff competition from every other disciplines. The question as always centres on how to achieve that end. The rest of the conclusion to this review takes that question as its focus. In drawing out the implications of the information in the previous chapters we will suggest what factors made it possible for religious studies departments to maintain their programs and even to thrive in the austere times that have dominated the 1990s.

Forces for Change in Religious Studies

It is good to remember that downsizing in the midst of a fiscal crisis was not always the approach taken by universities. When Charles P. Anderson undertook his last survey of religious studies in 1972, his central theme was growth and expansion. He developed that theme in his introductory essay, "Religious Studies in English speaking Canada 1967-1972,"[3] and Michel-M. Campbell wrote about it in "Notes sur la conjoncture des sciences religieuses au Canada français depuis 1967."[4] Taken together these two essays reveal much about the dramatic expansion of religious studies in Canada during the period of their review. For Campbell the startling innovation revealed by the 1972 survey was the adoption of the multidisciplinary philosophy underlying the creation of the Canadian Corporation for Studies in Religion/Corporation canadienne des sciences religieuses. Campbell stated:

> Un des progrès a sans doute été de renoncer à la distinction entre «sciences religieuses» [religious sciences] et théologie ou sciences confessionnelles [divinity], pour adopter la philosophie de la Corporation pour la publication des études académiques en religion au Canada. Cette philosophie s'avère oecuménique au sens le plus large du terme: au delà des confessions diverses, on veut accueillir les approches intellectuelles les plus diversifiées. Le seul critère d'accueil étant le caractère académique de la démarche.[5]

Campbell's declaration points toward a central theme in both essays, which highlighted the ways by which religious studies expanded within the universities of Canada. "Oecuménique" (ecumenical) indicated not only the diversification of Christian denominational theologies, but also the introduction of courses and research on religious traditions such as Hinduism or Buddhism into the curriculum of the universities. Just as significant was the proliferation of new methodologies and approaches to the study of religious life providing an alternative to Christian or theological approach to the study of religions. These changes permitted religious studies to enter the academy and subsequently to grow. Anderson described the change: "The main breakthrough was the acceptance by the university community of a distinction between the religious study of religion and its secular study. This important distinction was the ideological pre-requisite for the founding or evolution of several new departments of religious studies around 1960."[6]

The development of the perception of a fundamental change in understanding of what the study of religions can and should be when it is situated in the university has certainly been a protracted one! When Anderson completed his last national study, existing departments in the Atlantic region were still in the early stages of development as religious studies departments. Our description of the evolution of religious studies departments in Atlantic Canada has outlined a series of stages through which many of the departments have gone. In the initial stages it was the move from having strictly denominational faculty, often in a theology department, to incorporating an ecumenical faculty and their courses into the curriculum. Catholic universities incorporated Protestants into the faculty complement. Beyond Christian ecumenism was the development of comparative religions courses and, when possible, the hiring of specialized faculty to teach such courses. Where departments such as those at Mount Allison and St. Francis Xavier were not able to expand to incorporate world religions specialists, faculty within the department took up the task of making themselves specialists through study and research. At the Université de Moncton, one of the faculty members, Edmour Babineau, went back to graduate school to obtain a doctorate with specialization in the Hindu religious tradition. Such instances point to the dedication of faculty to teaching and the field of religious studies. Such dedication does not, however, solve the problem to which critics point when they challenge religious studies to pass beyond theological approaches to the study of religions.

In 1975 and through the 1980s the challenge for religious studies in the Atlantic region was to find ways to develop a greater diversity of content in terms of world religions courses and greater methodological diversity to include at least some social-scientific studies of religions in the curriculum. If the departments were allowed to grow, they did so by expanding their faculty complement to include scholars on world religions. Twenty years later, there are some departments, such as Mount Allison and St. Francis Xavier, that have just recently been able to make fundamental changes in their programs by hiring new faculty with new specializations. To incorporate scholars trained in one or other of the major world religions is, or has been, the major priority in hiring new faculty.

I would argue that the single most important catalyst for change in religious studies departments has been the ongoing academic debates in the academic societies and in journals of the field, both in Canada and internationally. In

Canada, the original debates on these issues began in the 1970s and early 1980s at the conferences of the Canadian Society for the Study of Religion/Société canadienne pour l'étude de la religion. There, the heated debates about the necessity for the scientific study of religions drew huge audiences and set the generations of scholars against one another. Dr. Don Wiebe, now at the University of Toronto, who was the most vocal proponent of the scientific study of religions, vigorously debated with Wilfred Cantwell Smith, then at Dalhousie University, and Charles Davis of Concordia University. The debates continued in the Canadian scholarly journal Studies in Religion/Sciences Religieuses.[7] The intensity of these academic debates was a sign of the vigour of the field of study in Canada.

At the time these debates were taking place, it was very difficult to make substantial changes in the religious studies departments in the Atlantic region. The faculty who were in place were trained for the most part in theology and biblical studies, tenured and in mid-career. There were no sociologists or anthropologists of religion except in the sociology and anthropology departments in the region. When new appointments were made, their purpose was to bring courses on new religions into the curriculum or, in the case of Memorial University, to hire comparative religion professors and to expand areas of expertise in Western traditions in order to deal with the huge enrolments of prospective teachers of religion in the schools.

In his essay on religious studies in Atlantic Canada prepared for the 1987 conference of the Canadian Society for the Study of Religion/Societé canadienne pour l'étude de la religion,[8] Tom Faulkner showed that the debate about religious studies and theology was still central both nationally and in the region. That is not surprising given the preponderance of specialists in and courses on Christianity in the Atlantic region. Faulkner took up the discussion of the relation between religious studies and theological studies, setting out to define a new relationship of theologians and historians of religions. He argued that "theologians ... do what members of departments of religious studies do, but theologians are also subject to a magisterium over and above what the university demands."[9] Faulkner was quite right that it is very difficult to discern a difference in the scholarly practices of religious studies professors and theologians in divinity schools. There is the exception of the private college, the Atlantic Baptist University, which has a confession of faith accepted by all faculty and students on the campus. Here, religious studies and biblical studies seem to be subject to the kind of magisterium that Faulkner defined. Yet, even in divinity schools in Canada and particularly in the more liberal schools, a Board of Governors would be hard pressed in this day and age to require a faith statement to which all the faculty agreed.[10]

Even with the added expectation Faulkner maintained that the scholarly integrity of theology and biblical studies as scholarly methodologies is as appropriate to religious studies as others. This acknowledges the historical reality of many of the religious studies departments whose faculty were trained in these areas and whose beginnings were as theology and biblical studies departments.

Nonetheless, in the light of the debates about religious studies in the Canadian Society for the Study of Religion/Société canadienne pour l'étude de la religion, the discussion in Faulkner's conclusion introduced the puzzling anomaly as to whether a Christian magisterium, be it a bishop or a Protestant conscience, has a presence in religious studies departments and their courses. If so, is such a presence distinguishable phenomenologically from a non-religious magisterium? In those instances in which a Christian theologian professes the content of a personal faith, it would seem to give credence to the substantial effect of the presence of a magisterium. But is this fundamentally different from those who would adopt a Marxist or other premise from which to teach in the university?

The puzzle that emerges in this discussion has been most sharply focused by those who argue that all knowledge is shaped within a horizon of particular cultures, languages, and the social and political conditions of women and men. No knowledge exists that is not so conditioned and constructed. It is at least plausible, then, that the magisterium of faith is no more and no less a presence in religious studies than the magisterium of the Enlightenment and post-Enlightenment views of religion.

The danger inherent in Faulkner's argument is that it implies that only a religious faith held by a scholar constitutes a problem for scholarly practice. Other foundational premises and assumptions about method and teaching are, it would appear, exempt from the problem. It is possible therefore for a religious studies department to compare itself to other departments in the field or in the locality and differentiate itself on the ground that only in religious studies departments in universities founded by churches or religious orders is there the problem of a magisterium. Thus departments that designate a place for Christianity in the curriculum for whatever historical reason are subject to some version or other of a magisterium while departments in secular universities are objectively grounded.[11]

In this regard the practical distinction Faulkner drew in his essay missed the point for all religious studies departments. Each interprets its place in the context of particular universities with particular histories in relation to the ongoing debates about what the field of the study of religions is all about. Both Anderson and Campbell argued for an inclusive definition that was multi-religious and employed diverse methodologies. Theologies, be they Christian, Buddhist, Hindu, Jewish or Muslim, take their place among historical, social-scientific, linguistic, biblical, archaeological and cultural studies in religious studies. This methodological diversity functions in the same way as Christianity is *one of* the traditions, along with Jewish, Hindu, Buddhist and Muslim traditions, taught in a religious studies curriculum. Religious studies takes a comparative approach as its fundamental pedagogy. On this inclusive basis religious studies grew and developed. On this basis it will continue to be an important field of study in the contemporary university.

The really important question for religious studies is the nature and extent of the comparative both in the research of faculty and in the curriculum of departments. That issue has had a pressing practical dimension. There has not been room for enough diversity, most especially in small departments. From Don Wiebe to Russell McCutcheon,[12] there have been voices arguing that there is not enough room in religious studies for the materialist, scientific approach to the study of religions. There is overwhelming evidence that they are right. The number of faculty positions held by theologically and biblically trained scholars in religious studies in the Atlantic region and elsewhere has been enormous. On the one hand such scholars taught what they knew and were trained for; they were tenured. There were few new positions and those there were were allocated most frequently to those applicants who could expand the curriculum to include introductory and advanced courses on world religions. If the more social-scientific approaches were included, it was because sociology, psychology or anthropology departments often had among their specialists a person who did research on and taught courses about religion.

For the founders and builders of religious studies departments there was, at best, a small window of opportunity to change the content of religious studies through new appointments. In addition, most departments were relatively small compared to departments of history or English. Memorial University's department is the largest religious studies department in the region with nine faculty, while the majority of departments have ranged in size from one to six. The department at Memorial is the only one in the region large enough to have several faculty teaching and doing research in a related area. In Memorial's case, that is Christianity and biblical studies. No other department has any cluster of faculty that, taken together, could be designated as constituting a departmental specialty. Rather, for the most part departments are consistent with Prince Edward Island's department's description of itself—as a group of generalists who attempt to teach as much of the field as they can.

Determining which subject areas and methodologies are to be included in a religious studies department is the central issue when a department is given

Conclusion

the opportunity to hire new faculty. The criticism from McCutcheon[13] that the theologians in religious studies are keeping out the materialist, scientific methodologists must be taken seriously in this respect. It is not so much that there are "gatekeepers" barring the way to some specializations. There have been social scientists in other arts or science departments whose courses could be incorporated into the religious studies curriculum. Historically religion has been an important topic in sociology, psychology and anthropology. As a result religious studies departments focused on the religions much more than on the methodologies for studying those religions. However, in many universities the specialists in the sociology, psychology or anthropology of religion are not being replaced. Scholars with other specializations are being hired. Therefore one of the important tests for the future of religious studies as a discipline is whether departments will choose to incorporate the social-scientific approaches as part of the diversity of faculty positions and of the methodologies for the study of religions.

What is reason for optimism here is the fact that, over the past quarter-century, religious studies departments have made important decisions to change their programs. As a result there have been significant advances in a number of important areas. Departments have hired specialists in one or other of the major religious traditions by not replacing specialists in Christianity. In addition there has been a significant increase in the number of women in the field of religious studies in Atlantic Canada and in the incorporation of scholars, trained both in Canada and internationally, who are members of visible minorities. Federal policies that prohibit federal grants to institutions which do not implement an equity policy mean that the faculty and staff of the universities are going to be more gender-equal as well as more racially diverse. Such requirements will assist religious studies' case for new faculty.

As they wait hopefully for new positions to open up, it is essential for religios studies departments, particularly those in close geographic proximity, to explore ways to cooperate through the sharing of faculty, the development of joint courses, and even the exploration of a regional graduate degree offered jointly. Cooperation could be developed most easily in the Halifax area and in the Moncton-Sackville-Charlottetown areas. It is possible for departments to explore course overloads or course exchanges to enhance their curriculum. Course exchanges, as opposed to paid overloads, are likely to be viewed with greater sympathy by university administrators since such an arrangement would be cost-neutral. A faculty member from one university could teach a course at another university in exchange for a reciprocal course offering. As an appointment opens up departments could enter into conversations about what kind of specialist would enhance the discipline in the area, not just in the department where the appointment is to be made. Cooperation of these kinds has worked in the past in course exchanges between the departments at Saint Mary's and Dalhousie. The partnership agreement between the religious studies departments of Saint Mary's and Mount Saint Vincent envisages a member of faculty from the partner university on a department's appointment committee. Senior seminars that sometimes have to be taught by faculty on unpaid overload could be taught as part of a regular load by one member of faculty for senior majors from several departments. All of these kinds of cooperation can occur where departments show a willingness to work together.

One of the most significant possibilities discussed in the interviews with the faculty at Memorial University was shared regional participation in the religious studies M.A.: the department indicated an interest in exploring ways by which faculty in the region could participate in the supervision of graduate research and even course work. Students, particularly the mature students who find it very difficult to leave an area of the region to do graduate work, could be allowed to do significant parts of their graduate study at home under the supervision of faculty in one department, or even several departments, in the region. Such a proposal requires extensive planning and a student who is able to work with multiple advisors and willing to be the first person to explore such an option.

As long as the region's religious studies departments remain relatively small, cooperation among them seems to be the only way to enhance diversity of courses. There is another dimension to cooperation that could also be explored. It is apparent that a significant new direction in research funding is based on the assumption that teams of researchers will be working together. This pattern is evident in grants awarded by the national granting agencies, as well as in grants from specialized sources of funding such as the International Development Research Centre, the Canadian International Development Agency and the Shastri Institute. Regional cooperation in research is a whole area that could be explored by scholars as a way to undertake new research and also to enhance cooperation across university and departmental lines.

While the geographic advantage of some areas of the region enhances the possibilities for cooperation, there are clearly many areas that could be explored which are not dependent on proximity. With the various forms of electronic communication, it could well be to the advantage of all of religious studies departments for such opportunities to be explored.

Multicultural Citizens and Religious Studies

The social setting of the contemporary universities in the Atlantic region is multicultural. It may be convenient to imagine the region stereotypically to be, both historically and currently, a static tradition-driven area of Canada. Reality is invariably ruinous for stereotypes. The new diversity of the region's citizens is now apparent in the major cities of the Atlantic region.

On a boulevard opposite the Victorian-style public gardens in Halifax there stands a statue of the Scottish poet Robert Burns. Beside the statue an African Muslim rolls out his prayer mat. His presence illustrates both the increasing number of Muslims in Halifax and the new racial diversity in the Muslim population of the city since the Gulf War. There are now more Muslims in metropolitan Halifax than there are Presbyterians. In the early hours of the morning, while joggers circle the Halifax Common, a Hindu descends Citadel Hill on his way home from his sunrise prayers. Every summer there is the much-awaited Summerfest at the foot of the golden domes of the Greek Orthodox church overlooking the northwest arm of Halifax harbour. The Summerfest draws thousands of visitors who share in a feast, see the entertainment and take the time to tour the church, which is so different from St. Paul's Anglican church, Saint Mary's Basilica, or St. Matthew's United church located in the old core of the city. With the ribbon-cutting by the lieutenant-governor of Nova Scotia, the Taoist Tai Chi Society of Canada opened the Fung Loy Kok Institute of Taoism High Shrine, the only one east of Toronto. Halifax is the international centre for the Buddhist *sangha* founded by Chogyam Trungpa Rinpoche. KarmeCholing, the Buddhist temple in Halifax, houses both the Shambhala programs and the shrine room for Tibetan Buddhist meditation. A Japanese Zen meditation hall recently opened in what was a Methodist church located on Windsor Street.

While these examples of religious diversity are for the most part located in Halifax, the same social diversity is a growing fact of life in Fredericton, St. John, Moncton, St. John's and Charlottetown. No place in the region, if not the nation as a whole, is exempt from the spectrum of expanding multiculturalism and, with it, a new religious diversity. Thus a walk along the streets of the university towns and the major cities reveals that the common stereotype of the region is false.

There is even a persuasive argument to be made that the stereotype was always false. Religious diversity, reflecting both ethnic origin and the denominational factions of Christianity, was always a characteristic of the region. That fact entrenched numerous social divisions and defined how many communities lived together. The fault lines between denominations were reflected in the separateness of Protestant and Catholic fishing villages along the coasts, of Africville and Preston in relation to the dominant city of Halifax, of Mi'Kmaq and Maliseet reserves from the rest of the social landscape. The Acadian French remained in all of the Atlantic provinces.

These diversities were reflected in the political parties of the region which were divided as much by religious conviction as by political allegiance. They were evident in the concrete forms of racism and prejudice that were entrenched in the societies of the region. They were manifest in the patterns of socialization and education in both the primary and secondary phases as well as in the universities. There were the religiously administered school systems of Newfoundland. There were Roman Catholic Schools and "public" schools. Roman Catholic dioceses founded universities such as Saint Mary's, St. Thomas and St. Francis Xavier to serve Roman Catholics who found it almost impossible to enter the "public" universities. Protestants founded Mount Allison University and the "public" universities with their charters prohibiting the presence of religion and its conflicts. There were the Acadian universities in Moncton, New Brunswick and Church Point, Nova Scotia. In sum, the region was never a mono-culture. It shared in and was dominated by the Anglo-European traditions, both religious and secular. These traditions were broad, complex and often contentious. We should not be surprised by this complexity. Any student of religious studies knows with certainty that every culture is multifaceted, filled with concord and contradictions and never without its contending voices and entrenched differences.

What do these expanding multicultural realities mean for religious studies in the region? They certainly raise a fundamental question about the historical dominance of courses on the Christian Bible and on Christianity in general. This dominance suited a society that was ruled by people whose religious allegiance was to one of the churches. In the midst of the waning of the influence of the churches in Canada and the Atlantic region, religious studies integrated the requirement of the field to teach world religions and to situate Christianity as one among the religious traditions in its curriculum. This is now an established characteristic of religious studies in the region.

Beyond the transition to a multi-religious curriculum in religious studies lies another. It will usually be effected by new faculty bringing new specializations into a department. For that to happen current religious studies departments need the same type of visionary leadership that led to the founding of the field across Canada. The next stage in the evolution of religious studies will, I would argue, build on the established principles of the field. The requirement that students learn about world religions will maintain a global perspective within the curriculum. Accompanying that perspective will be a focus on the religious life of the locality understood as both the immediate community and Canada as a whole. What the religious traditions of the world are is a global question. How we are to study and know about those traditions is a question of methods and theories of religion. What does it mean for the religious traditions of the world to be living traditions in St. John's, Halifax, Fredericton or Charlottetown, not to mention Montreal, Toronto and Vancouver? What kind of scholarly specialists and methodologies will permit religious studies to explore these questions?

From a negative perspective it will mean that departments cannot simply replicate the specializations that have been, or are currently, established. The implication of this is that the overwhelming predominance of specialists on Christianity and biblical studies must be diminished in religious studies departments. I am not arguing for the exclusion of the study of Christianity; far from it. However, in the Atlantic region all of the religious studies departments are relatively small. In departments of three or four faculty, for Christianity simply to be one of the religious traditions will frequently translate into one or two specialists in the area! Such specialists will have to teach not only the Christian tradition but also related Western traditions such as Judaism and Islam.

The days when a comparative religions specialist would be hired to be responsible for introducing religious traditions apart from Christianity are gone. Specialists on the religious traditions of Asia cannot simply focus their teaching on particular traditions in distant lands. It is not enough to teach world religions as if the Hindu, Muslim, Buddhist or Taoist were situated only in Asia. It is imperative that these traditions be taught as part of the mosaic of religious life in Canada. The new social diversity locally and nationally accentuates the need for research on the impact of the new religious traditions and movements. For this we need specialists trained not only in the historic traditions, but also in the social sciences. Religious studies scholars should be at the forefront of the scholarship that sets out to interpret our religious diversity to students, to fellow scholars and to the public.

As courses on global and local religious traditions are developed, we require scholars who can integrate into them an understanding of the differences in the religious experience of women and men. Ultimately—and this may be some time coming—specialized courses under titles such as "Women and Religion" will no longer be necessary. Instead every course will contain an integrated examination of the ways in which the religious understanding and experience of women and men differ, are similar, are collaborative.[14]

It is in this context of the new multicultural realities of Canadian society that religious studies has something significant to contribute. Martha Nussbaum, in *Cultivating Humanity: A Classical Defense of Reform in Liberal*

Education, provides a remarkable analysis of modern university education. She begins her study by identifying the overarching task of higher education as one of educating women and men for citizenship in a multicultural setting. The key word is "citizen." What kind of education does a person require to function in the global and local environments in which all individuals reside? Her question is an important one, and most especially in the historical context of the debates about the meaning of religious studies. For her starting point is the correct one. The issue of the differences between theologies and religious studies need to be set aside. The burden of that topic has preoccupied the discipline for long enough.

The real task is to situate religious studies in the debate about what it means to be a citizen in a multicultural society like Canada. The topic unites religious studies with all other university disciplines in their concern for literacy among students and in their concern for teaching that requires students to learn to read critically and to think rationally. Most especially it unites religious studies with research projects involving scholars in many different disciplines and subject areas. In such projects religious studies scholars can contribute an analysis of the role of religious traditions in society.

Religious studies can make a compelling case, with its research and teaching focused on the diversity of religious traditions and the nature of religious loyalties, it has an important and unique contribution to make to the understanding of the meaning of citizenship in a multicultural setting. Such a contribution requires an empirical component that identifies and interprets the ways in which the religious communities of Canada participate in the social and political landscape. It requires an extensive knowledge of the history of religious traditions both in their places of origin and in the Canadian context. It requires a skilled interpretation of the ways by which religious traditions shape human beings socially and ethically and define for them the various facets of their loyalty. It requires a subtle analysis of how and why loyalties differ and can ultimately conflict and how the same loyalties can define humanity in ways that permit sharing in projects which address common needs and aspirations. It requires a pedagogy that enables students to discover what the religions are in their society and how, imaginatively, it is possible to enter into the lived experience of religious people with whom they must live and function in all aspects of life in Canada.

Situating religious studies in the context of the university's task to educate citizens for life in a multicultural, multi-religious democratic society is, I would argue, a powerful rationale for our field of study.

Notes

1 The text of the report states:

> CAPP has concluded reluctantly that it cannot recommend another position in Religious Studies in the foreseeable future. It recommends, therefore, that Religious Studies consider alternatives to its current major, either with a program on the Canadian Studies model or integrated into an interdisciplinary program such as Women's Studies or the proposed new Cultural Studies program. Either of these models would fit with the current and anticipated curriculum proposals from the department. While student interest in current courses is high, CAPP considers that these courses could continue to be offered, and the areas of religion and culture and religion and women strengthened by integration with other disciplines and fields. Once again, this recommendation is not a reflection of the value CAPP puts on the discipline nor of the quality of the program, but is taken in the context of existing and anticipated resources across the entire University.

2 *The Framework of the Metro Halifax Universities' Business Plan,* for presentation to the Honourable John MacEachern, Minister of Education, 19 July 1995, 3-4. The deans' report estimated that the faculties of arts of the metropolitan universities would lose fifty academic positions among faculty who were fifty or older in 1995. The deans speculated that "the non-replacement of 50 positions would create problems for a range of academic departments and programs. The most severe effects would likely be experienced in the following areas: Dalhousie/Kings: Comparative Religion, Classics; Mount Saint Vincent: Religious Studies, Speech and Drama, Philosophy, Politics, Economics; Saint Mary's: Religious Studies, Classics, German, Geography." The deans then went further and developed categories that identified the programs at greatest risk. Under Category A they stated: "Programs which might have to close or experience redeployment of remaining faculty: Comparative Religion/Religious Studies." In the Saint Mary's University student newspaper following the release of the business plan, the report confidently asserted that the Department of Religious Studies at Saint Mary's would close even though there was only one retirement in the period under review at Saint Mary's. This impression was corrected by the Dean of Arts in a letter to a later edition of the paper.

3 Charles P. Anderson, "Religious Studies in English-speaking Canada 1967-1972." In *Guide to Religious Studies in Canada/Guide des Sciences religieuses au Canada,* (N.p.: Corporation for the Publication of Academic Studies in Religion in Canada, 1972), 7-19.

4 Michel-M. Campbell, "Notes sur la conjoncture des sciences religieuses au Canada français depuis 1967." In Anderson, *Guide,* 21-41.

5 Ibid., 21.

6 Anderson, *Guide,* 8.

7 Donald Wiebe, "Is a Science of Religion Possible?" *Studies in Religion/Sciences Religieuses* 7/1 (1978): 5-17; "The Failure of Nerve in the Academic Study of Religion," *Studies in Religion/Sciences Religieuses* 13/4 (1984): 401-22; "The 'Academic Naturalization' of Religious Studies: Intent or Pretence?" *Studies in Religion/Sciences Religieuses* 15/2 (1986): 197-203; Charles Davis, "The Reconvergence of Theology and Religious Studies," *Studies in Religion/Sciences Religieuses* 4/3 (1975): 2-21; "Editorial: The Fourteenth International Congress of

the IAHR," *Studies in Religion/Sciences Religieuses* 9/2 (1980): 123-24; " 'Wherein There Is No Ecstasy,' " *Studies in Religion/Sciences Religieuses* 13/4 (1984): 393-400; Gregory Baum, [Response to Charles Davis, 1974-75]; *Studies in Religion/Sciences Religieuses* 4/3 (1975): 17-24; and Lorne L. Dawson, "Neither Nerve nor Ecstasy: Comment on the Wiebe-Davis Exchange," *Studies in Religion/Sciences Religieuses* 15/2 (1986): 145-51.
8 Tom Faulkner, "Religious Studies in the Atlantic Provinces: A State-of-the-Art Review: Conclusion 1987" in Appendix 1 below.
9 Ibid., 350-51.
10 The Atlantic School of Theology has recently seen its faculty association affiliate with the Canadian Association of University Teachers. In the wake of that, the Atlantic School of Theology has released a statement on academic freedom that meets all the conventional criteria for scholars' freedom to communicate their research.
11 It was precisely this argument that the Dalhousie Department of Comparative Religion adopted in 1995 when it declined to be part of any collaborative partnership with the religious studies departments at Mount Saint Vincent University and Saint Mary's University. In the partnership agreement Faulkner identified his department's principal objection to the partnership agreement in the following statement: "By virtue of their traditions both Mount Saint Vincent University and Saint Mary's University have a special responsibility to teach courses on Christianity" (Statement of Partnership, 3). Arguing for "contextual differences" between the departments, the Department of Comparative Religion at Dalhousie stated that "The mandate of the Department of Comparative Religion at Dalhousie is to teach from a 'historical and comparative perspective;' to put it another way, we have a special responsibility *not* to give Christianity a particular place in the curriculum. But it is difficult to do both ways at once. Some would say that it is impossible." "Report on Rationalization: Cooperation Among Departments of Religious Studies in Metro Halifax," by Tom Sinclair-Faulkner, 27 May 1995, 2). Faulkner's report then went on to acknowledge: "It is, of course, true that in practice Christianity receives more attention in our classes than any other single religious tradition does. But this is true because we teach in a Canadian context" (2). What is ironic here is that "Canadian context" justified a preponderance of courses on and course content about Christianity at Dalhousie, while the historical traditions of Mount Saint Vincent University or Saint Mary's University, both also in Canada, represented a fundamentally different context, suffering, it would appear, under an implied magisterium. The report also stated that at Dalhousie "Christianity is being studied as one religion among others" (2) as if that were not the case in 1995 at Saint Mary's University or at Mount Saint Vincent University now. The deliberate use of a double standard in the argument rested upon the premise that a religious studies program at a religiously founded university, even where the university is a public institution and has been for thirty years, cannot escape this mysterious magisterium and consequently does not teach comparatively in its courses. It further ignored the preponderance of scholarly studies on the history of Christianity and the history of Israel which situate historical knowledge about Christianity routinely in its comparative relationships to Judaism and to the Hellenistic and Roman world views, to name only a few. Such an argument, dependent as it was on the notion of this mysterious magisterium at work in some

places and not others in religious studies, was simply self-serving in a potentially damaging way for the future of religious studies.
12 Russell T. McCutcheon, "My Theory of the Brontosaurus: Postmodernism and 'Theory' of Religion," *Studies in Religion/Science Religieuses* 26/1 (1997): 3-23; and "The Crisis of Academic Labour and the Myth of Autonomy: Dispatch from the Job Wars," *Studies in Religion/Science Religieuses* 27/4 (1998): 387-405. Cf. also Darlene M. Juschka, "The Construction of Pedagogical Spaces: Religious Studies in the University," *Studies in Religion/Science Religieuses* 28/1 (1999): 85-97.
13 McCutcheon, "Crisis of Academic Labour."
14 Randi R. Warne, "(En)gendering Religious Studies," *Studies in Religion/Science Religieuses* 27/4 (1998): 427-36.

Appendix 1: Conclusion 1987

Tom Faulkner

Origins

As we look back at the origins of the system of higher education in the Maritime provinces we are reminded that one of the primary motives for founding such institutions was to produce an indigenous Christian clergy. Had one asked "What is the future of the study of religion?" in the early nineteenth century, the answer would have been positive and full of confidence. Today, however, the difficulties that universities face in obtaining adequate public funding combined with the privatization of religion, the secularization of higher education, the professionalization of the professoriate and the search for economic and technological mastery leave departments of religious studies and seminaries concerned that they may be increasingly marginal in the eyes of the university in particular and the public in general. In the two centuries since higher education appeared here, scholars of religion have moved from confidence and leadership to anxiety and marginalization. The shift is clear in the observation that all of the heads of institutions of higher learning in the Maritimes used to be respected members of the clergy, while today Acadia and St. Francis Xavier are the only universities with presidents who are entitled to be called "Reverend." In most cases there is resistance to appointing a member of the clergy to a junior position on the faculty.

Perhaps this shift is more a reflection of the position of the churches in the Maritimes than of the position of religion. For example, the one English-speaking university in the region that lacks a department of religious studies is the University of New Brunswick, where the university charter forbids the teaching of "religion"—a holdover from the nineteenth century when "religion" meant the standpoint of the Church of England. Even Catholic universities, however, have distanced themselves from their church in renaming what began as departments of "religion" in the region. Following the Second

World War such units renamed themselves departments of "theology" on the grounds that "religion" is what one studies in catechetical classes lacking intellectual depth and rigour while "theology" was a subject fit for university study. A further step away from the church was taken when some of those same departments changed "theology" to "religious studies" in the wake of the Second Vatican Council, thus emphasizing their openness to new, perhaps non-Catholic, currents of thought. These changes of name served to ease somewhat the veiled antagonism of some secular-minded colleagues in other departments of the university while not discouraging central administrators from thinking of the religious studies department as a link with the religious origins of the university.

Some faculty members in religious studies departments on campuses in the Maritime provinces have responded to these observations by saying that they do not feel marginal to the life of their university. But it remains a truism that departments of religious studies are more likely to find it necessary to seek justifications for their existence than are, say, departments of English when vertical cuts are debated about campus because of increasingly severe cuts in university budgets. If it is too strong to say that religious studies departments are marginal to campus life, it is fair to say that they are somewhat eccentric.

It is also interesting to note that those faculty in religious studies departments at Maritime universities who retain a connection with some Christian church or other describe themselves as "squeezed." They find themselves caught between those who ruthlessly celebrate the Enlightenment and those who wish that the department were more Catholic, or more Baptist, or whatever.

At first glance Newfoundland seems to present a radically different picture: a school system that is thoroughly denominational capped by a major university that is one of the few non-denominational institutions in Newfoundland society. But I suggest that this is consistent in broad terms with the pattern in the Maritimes: religious origins have produced a post-secondary system in which the study of religion is detached from the churches and relatively marginal to the university. The fact that the university developed later in Newfoundland than it did in the Maritimes accounts for the apparent lack of religious heritage in the university. The Newfoundland system of education clearly has religious roots; the non-religious character of its post-secondary system is the result of its relatively late development.

Part of the explanation for the drift of the study of religion away from a central position in the universities of the Atlantic provinces lies in the patterns common to higher learning in North America: the secularization of learning and the rise of new disciplines, particularly in the sciences and social sciences. But the lingering influence of our religious origins may still be detected in the fact that not one of the full-time faculty teaching religious studies in the region may clearly be identified as a social scientist—despite the fact that other Canadian universities have departments of religious studies in which social scientists hold appointments, and despite the fact that several bona fide social scientists who study primarily religion hold full-time appointments in Atlantic universities but are not members of departments of religious studies. The study of religion began in this region in religious institutions where the humanities were central, and today departments of religious studies in the region are still clearly identified with the humanities.

The Professoriate

Twenty years ago newly appointed faculty members in departments of religious studies in the region were likely to be members of the ordained Christian clergy or former members of the clergy—in either case, their academic credentials were usually provided by graduate programs in Christian seminaries. Today newly appointed faculty members are more likely to be members of the Christian laity who have received their credentials from graduate schools of religious studies at secular universities. That is the major shift in the profile of the professoriate of the region. The two types seem to work well together—a reflection of the serious academic character of the training of the older group, the native sympathy of the younger group for religion as such despite their training at "secular" institutions, and the need to cooperate thrust upon them by the fact that departments of religious studies—like departments in the humanities generally—have not grown substantially in size during the past decade.

This diversity in training is a strength of the departments in the region. But there are other dimensions to the professoriate that are insufficiently diverse. One frequently noted by faculty members interviewed in this study was the lack of women in the ranks of the professoriate. That is a problem that can be resolved slowly and partially if it is kept in mind by those making new appointments, but thought must be given to related issues.[1]

More surprising, perhaps, is the fact that only one full-time faculty member in the region may clearly be recognized as a non-Christian. While one may argue that this comes close to approximating the profile of the general population of the Atlantic provinces, it does not fit well with the theoretical emphasis on the universal character of university scholarship, nor with the aspiration of departments with roots in one particular Christian church to be seen as places where religion in all its manifestations is studied. It certainly contrasts with the pattern in departments of religious studies in the rest of English-speaking Canada. Within the Christian tradition, of course, the professoriate shows considerable diversity. But it might be interesting to speculate why the departments of Catholic origin have tended to hire Protestant Christians more frequently than the departments of Protestant origin have hired Catholic Christians.

The lack of social scientists in departments of religious studies may reflect the relatively heavy commitment to a particular methodology characteristic of social sciences. Social scientists who study religion may simply feel more at home in a social science department than in a religious studies department, where they must rub shoulders with those who share religion as the object of study but look at it from the perspective of the humanities. But anyone committed to a diversity of ways of studying religion must regret the fact that the departments of religious studies in the region have not done more to appoint social scientists to their ranks, thus bringing the peculiar insights of social science into dialogue with teaching and research that have been dominated by the humanities.[2]

Religious Studies and Theology

Endless hours may be spent debating the distinction—if any—between theology and religious studies. In proposing to draw such a distinction I do not intend to end debate but to develop a working distinction that is peculiarly useful to a review of religious studies in the Atlantic provinces. On the whole it seems both wrong and wasteful to distinguish professors in departments of religious studies from professors in seminaries in the region on the basis of the topics that they study—the overlap is, in practice, considerable—or on the basis of academic rigour—I can see no empirically verifiable distinction to be made here when the two groups are considered as wholes. To say that religious studies is carried out in university departments while theology is practised in seminaries is to ignore broadly common areas of study and widely shared standards of academic investigation.

I propose a definition of theology that permits us to distinguish legitimately what goes on in departments of religious studies from what goes on in seminaries in the Atlantic region. Both groups are engaged in intellectual formulations of and investigations into what human beings have called "religion"; both groups are committed to meeting the academy's standards of truth; but theologians are responsible to a faith community as well as responsible to the university. In the Atlantic region, and for the purposes of this study, theologians may be considered to do what members of departments of religious studies do, but theologians are also subject to a magisterium over and above what the university demands.

The usefulness of this distinction is that it recognizes what is shared by the scholars whose work is the subject of this review while it permits their respective institutions—universities and seminaries—to hold them accountable to those institutions in ways appropriate to those institutions in their distinctiveness.

Let me underline three aspects of this distinction. First, theologians do not operate under different academic rules than scholars of religious studies do; rather, theologians operate under additional rules. Like any other university scholars, theologians are often motivated by curiosity and sheer love of learning. Theologians meet the same exacting standards of scholarship that scholars of religious studies do—a fact that is demonstrated every time one of them delivers a paper at a meeting of a learned society, publishes an article in a peer-reviewed journal or applies for a grant from the Social Sciences and Humanities Research Council. If one were to listen to an anonymous address concerning the virtues and limitations of "objectivity" in the humanities and the social sciences, would one be able to say with certainty whether or not the speaker was a theologian rather than a scholar of religious studies? Some representatives of both groups would surely argue that it is desirable for the study of a subject to bring about some change for the better in the ones who study it. In short, theologians are not distinguished by their methods or their subject matter, by their motives or their research goals; they are distinguished by the fact that they must at some point show themselves accountable for their work to a faith community-usually a particular Christian church. Scholars in departments of religious studies may do the same from time to time but they are not required to do so by virtue of their appointment.

Second, the ways in which scholars of both types are held accountable may be clear in the abstract but inconsistent in practice. The magisterium exercised by one Catholic bishop may be wielded in a different fashion by another. And as one Protestant theologian observed to me, "Our problem is not that we lack a *magisterium* but that we have too many." Likewise the university's standards of academic excellence are occasionally revealed to be unevenly respected.

Third, theologians face a tricky task when they seek to accommodate both the university and the magisterium. The university is too recently the child of the Enlightenment to be entirely free of the fear that any connection with the churches is dangerous to academic freedom. And the evangelical awakenings of the eighteenth and nineteenth centuries still leave their mark on the magisterium in its suspicion of the pernicious influence that a critical mind may have on the regeneration of a desolated heart. Of course, to the extent that theologians succeed in marrying free inquiry to communal responsibility, a critical mind to a regenerated heart, they will have pointed the way for other university scholars to preserve what is best in the university while defending it against the charges of those who criticize it for being detached from communal and practical concerns.

This characterization of religious studies and theology as essentially the same, save where they are distinguished by theology's magisterium, permits us to make a practical distinction between departments of religious studies and theological seminaries, even while the work that is done within one is indistinguishable in most ways from the work that is done in the other. And it leads to two practical recommendations. First, theological seminaries ought to seek to make greater use of the teaching and scholarly resources available in departments of religious studies where those resources are consistent with the direction given by the seminary's magisterium. There is nothing pernicious or even indifferent about what departments of religious studies do as far as seminaries are concerned. As long as the seminary remains faithful to its magisterium, it will be enriched by what the department of religious studies can provide. Second, departments ought to be wary of institutional pressure to foster a particular religious identity within their university. That should not be the goal of an academic department as such; whatever magisterium faculty members may honour in other dimensions of their lives, it cannot be permitted to govern the work of their department, any more than a particular political party may shape a department of political science or a particular industrial complex may direct a department of chemistry.

Seminaries have recently been stimulated to rethink their task by Edward Farley's *Theologia: The Fragmentation and Unity of Theological Education*.[3] Appalled by the lack of material unity in theological study and its fragmentation into numerous sub-disciplines, Farley urges theology to return to its medieval character as personal wisdom that creates interior, existential changes in individuals and that empowers and guides the community of faith. One of the most interesting critiques of Farley's proposal is provided by Joseph C. Hough, Jr. and John B. Cobb, Jr. in *Christian Identity and Theological Education*,[4] in which they argue that Farley is right as far as he goes, but that the recovery of *theologia* necessarily entails something further: "the service of God's work in and for the world."[5] I propose that departments of religious studies might well consider reflecting upon Farley's "personal wisdom" with its threefold effect as the object of study around which they might organize their teaching and research—suitably broadened to accommodate rather than to exclude non-Christian traditions. If *theologia* is the proper task of seminaries, then it is surely a fit subject for departments of religious studies. The fact that Farley speaks of *theologia* may discourage scholars in religious studies from reading him. But reminding themselves that what is distinctive about theology is the magisterium may free them to examine something that may be as useful to departments of religious studies with their welter of methodologies as it is to seminaries.

Scholarship and Research

Let us consider the departments of religious studies first. One might observe that some scholars of religious studies publish more than others do, but that in general standards of research are high in the region. But as an editor of a learned journal in which a great variety of disciplines are represented, and as a former grievance officer in a dozen tenure and promotion cases, I know that general assertions about standards rarely rest on the sound foundations that statements about particular cases do. Instead let me note that the departments of religious studies in the Atlantic region see themselves as subject to university-wide standards of evaluation, not as exempt due to some special status. They are—in the old meaning of the term—without benefit of clergy" in the modern university.

Interestingly this has not meant that their practice of scholarship has been focused within their own university community. Like virtually all modern university scholars, they do their scholarly work and their research on national and international stages. With the departure of Wilfred Cantwell Smith from the region, there are no local scholars who are internationally famous, but those who are rewarded by their universities with timely promotion have all demonstrated their competence outside the region. They are part of research networks and scholarly debates that are remarkably diverse and far-flung.

By contrast, seminary faculty tend to be more involved in regional affairs—a reflection of their responsibility to a magisterium that is focused in the region. Faculty in departments of religious studies serve a regional constituency in that their students are primarily drawn from and return to the region, but their scholarly research is relatively detached from their teaching and in any case there is no faith community evaluating the quality of their students. One of the consequences of this difference is that faculty in departments of religious studies in the region are relatively free to pursue research that may be published in one way or another on a larger stage, while faculty in seminaries have less time and less motivation to publish similarly.

Seminaries compensate for this by being relatively generous to their faculty when they seek travel grants to take them to learned meetings. In seminaries, most faculty have only to ask to be granted travel money; in departments of religious studies, faculty must generally be able to demonstrate to their deans that they will be delivering a paper at the conference to which they desire to travel. (Cynics speculate on the consequences that such policies have for the quality of papers delivered at learned gatherings held at a distance.) However, the opportunities for sabbatical leave tend to be more limited for seminary faculty in terms of both time and funding than they are for faculty in religious studies. In short, the result is that seminary faculty are expected to keep up with what is being done in the scholarly world, but they are not afforded the same opportunities to make personal contributions to it as their colleagues in religious studies are. Considering that seminaries now tend to hire young scholars who have been trained in graduate institutions of religious studies and who are therefore no doubt hoping to pursue scholarly research actively, it may well be time for seminaries to rethink their sabbatical policies and the workload of teaching and community service that their respective magisteria exact of their faculty members.

Given that those actively pursuing scholarly research are drawn to national and international gatherings, it is no surprise that there are at present only two regional research projects that engage the efforts of several scholars. One is firmly rooted in a seminary: the Baptist Heritage Project under the aegis of Acadia Divinity College; the other is the research into the *histoire du peuple et de l'Eglise de l'Acadie* sponsored by the Département des Sciences Religieuses at the Université de Moncton. The former project integrates local research with the research of Baptists from many other parts of Canada but does not engage many non-Baptist scholars of religion in the Atlantic region. Nor—despite its stated objective of improving communication and understanding between francophone and anglophone in the region—does the Moncton project draw on regional scholars outside the sponsor's natural community. These two projects would be strengthened by deliberate efforts to involve other scholars from the region in their work. And regional scholarship itself would find a counterweight to the tendency to suppose that scholarly research is something that must be done at least 1,000 kilometres away.

Lest these suggestions be taken as either naive or manipulative, let me observe that scholars in the Atlantic region seem to be remarkably responsive to invitations to redirect their work in some degree. I note as editor-in-chief of *Studies in Religion/Sciences Religieuses* that one result of my visit to various departments and schools at the outset of this study has been a sharp increase in the number of good manuscripts submitted to that journal from the Atlantic region. Upper Canadians have been heard to mutter darkly about Atlantic imperialism.

Curriculum

Seminaries are constantly forced by their certifying agencies and by those who exercise their magisteria to reflect upon how best to structure their curriculum. But for the most part the departments of religious studies in the region showed no signs of having devoted much time to corporate efforts to shape their undergraduate curricula. The notable exception to this rule was the department at Saint Mary's University, which undertook a thorough and apparently successful restructuring of the curriculum in religious studies in the face of open proposals to radically reduce the size of the department. One is reminded of Dr. Johnson's dictum that one of the advantages of knowing that you are to be hanged in a fortnight is that it concentrates the mind wonderfully.

I have sometimes been told that a useful result of my initial visits to departments of religious studies is that they provoked constructive conversation about the curriculum. It seemed so evident to me that this is a neglected but important task that I generally proposed during these visits that departments of religious studies and seminaries in the region ought to consider regular meetings to focus on the curriculum—not regional learned societies gathered to hear the results of scholarly research, but workshops in which resources for and experience in teaching could be shared effectively. Given the role that such workshops might begin to play in shaping curricula, they might best be held in January—part of the teaching phase of the academic year, yet far enough ahead of the following fall to permit faculty members to incorporate what they take from the workshops into their next full class.

Besides the question of how best to teach religious studies—with or without a magisterium—there is the question of the larger university curriculum. This has been seriously neglected by departments of religious studies in the Atlantic provinces, no doubt because faculty resources are already strained and because religious studies over the years has moved ever farther from the centre of university life as a whole. The history of the undergraduate curriculum of North American universities is one of proliferation and fragmentation. Efforts to restore coherence, even a core, to the curriculum have been many but largely unsuccessful. It is in the best interests of departments of religious studies to address themselves deliberately and immediately to the search for coherence in the undergraduate curriculum for two reasons.

First, the temptation to relate to the larger university context as a service department building a strong enrolment at the risk of being perceived as an academic unit that will offer anything that attracts students is powerful and—sooner or later—destructive for a department of religious studies. Such departments are more likely to survive and thrive in undergraduate settings where there is a strong sense of what direction or directions undergraduate studies should take. As one of the most marginal of departments in the modern university, religious studies must be relatively deliberate about finding how it fits into undergraduate education as a whole. It is a hopeful sign that most current proposals for a "core curriculum" insist on the importance of religious studies.

Second, the working experience that scholars of religious studies have in coping with several disciplines and methodologies in the midst of a field of study that is relatively lacking in coherence furnishes them with skills and insights that many other university scholars lack in considering the undergraduate curriculum as a whole. In that sense scholars of religious studies have a special responsibility to contribute to efforts to reform the undergraduate curriculum as a whole. *Sagesse oblige* . . .

Notes

1 See my comments in the CAUT *Bulletin,* February 1988.
2 Tom Sinclair-Faulkner, "Sociology of Religion," *Studies in Religion/Sciences Religieuses* 17/3 (1988): 255-56.
3 Edward Farley, *Theologia: The Fragmentation and Unity of Theological Education* (Philadelphia: Fortress Press, 1983).
4 Joseph C. Hough, Jr. and John B. Cobb, Jr., *Christian Identity and Theological Education* (Macon: Scholars Press, 1985).
5 Ibid., 4.

Appendix 2

The following two pages contain reproductions of the questionnaire used for gathering data for this study.

NAME: RANK:

INSTITUTION:

PHONE: E-MAIL

In answering the questions below, please make use of the following categories and codes for areas of research and teaching. These categories are adapted from *Religious Studies Review: A Quarterly Review of Publications in the Field of Religion and Related Disciplines* Published by the Council on the Study of Religion. Issues of the *Review* may be consulted for examples of the kind of work found under each heading.

001	Africa	017	Islam
002	Ancient Near Eastern Religions	018	Jewish Thought
003	Anthropology of Religion	019	Methodology and Theory
004	Arts, Literature and Religion	020	Philosophy of Religion
005	Buddhism	021	Practical/Pastoral
006	Central Asia	022	Psychology of Religion
007	Christian Origins	023	Religion and Science
008	Comparative Studies	024	Religion in Canada
009	Phenomenology of Religion	025	Ritual, Cult and Worship
010	East Asia	026	Sociology of Religion
011	Ethics	027	Society and Religion
012	Gender Studies	028	South Asia
013	Greece, Rome, Greco-Roman Period	029	The Americas
014	Hinduism	030	Theology
015	History of Judaism	031	Zoroastrianism
016	History of Christianity		

Other [specify]: _____

(a) In the terms that you customarily use, describe the one or two major areas of your research:
   1. _____
   2. _____

(b) Indicate, using the appropriate number(s) from the above list of categories, no more than two categories of research:
   1. Primary area of research   _____
   2. Secondary area of research   _____

(c) List, using the appropriate codes from the above list of categories, the areas in which you regularly teach:

i)   iv)
ii)   v)
iii)   vi)

(d) Using the above categories, indicate the area in which you completed your final academic degree.

(e) Indicate in percentages the approximate amount of time you spend over the calendar year in the following areas of professional activity:
i. Teaching and Course Preparation   _____
ii. Research and academic writing   _____
iii. University service and administration   _____
iv. Public service   _____
v. Other (specify) _____   _____

(f) Rank your personal, professional priorities from highest (1) to lowest (5) in the following areas:
i. Teaching and Course Preparation   _____
ii. Research and academic writing   _____
iii. University service and administration   _____
iv. Public service   _____
v. Other (specify) _____   _____

(g) How many years have you been employed in university teaching?

(h) How many years have you been employed in the university where you now teach?

(i) Assuming retirement at age sixty-five, when will you retire? (year only)

(j) To what learned or academic societies do you belong?

(k) How often do you attend academic conferences such as the Learned Societies?
Every year   _____
Every second year   _____
Every third year   _____
Rarely or not at all   _____

(l) Briefly suggest the three most important changes that have taken place in your teaching and/or research over the course of your career.

Appendix 3: Documents Provided by Religious Studies Departments

All religious studies departments in the Atlantic region provided the following documentation:
1. A curriculum vitae for all full-time faculty.
2. Completed questionnaires from full- and part-time faculty (see Appendix 2).
3. Course outlines as available.
4. Enrolment statistics as available.

1. Newfoundland

Memorial University of Newfoundland

1. Memorial University of Newfoundland Academic Calendar, 1994-95.
2. School of Graduate Studies Calendar, 1993-94.
3. Memorial University of Newfoundland Collective Agreement Between Memorial University of Newfoundland and the Memorial University of Newfoundland Faculty Association, 17 December 1992 to 31 March, 1995.
4. Memorial University of Newfoundland Fact Book, 1993.
5. Report by Dr. Terry Murphy to the Vice-President (Academic), prepared in 1992.
6. Morley F. Hodder, "MUN's Department of Religious Studies, Its Origins, Its Present Program, Its Future Plans," nd.
7. Memo, dated 29 November 1997, from the Department of Religious Studies to the Committee on Honorary Degrees & Ceremonial on "Nomination of Dr. Morley F. Hodder for the position of Professor Emeritus."
8. Draft of the complete Revised Calendar Entry for Religious Studies, 1998.

2. Prince Edward Island

University of Prince Edward Island

1. University of Prince Edward Island Calendar 1993-94.
2. Department of Religious Studies Self-Study.
3. Letter from Philip G. Davis to Dr. Paul Bowlby, dated 11 February 1998, updating current state of the department.

3. New Brunswick

Atlantic Baptist University

1. Atlantic Baptist University Academic Calendar, 1997-98.

Mount Allison University

1. Mount Allison University Calendar, 1993-94.
2. A. J. Ebbutt, "History of Department of Religious Studies (1971)," dated 6 April 1971.
3. Academic Planning Submission—Department of Religious Studies—January 1991.
4. Report of the External Review Committee on the Department of Religious Studies at Mount Allison University, 1996.
5. Departmental Response to the External Review of the Department of Religious Studies at Mount Allison University, Fall 1996.

St. Stephen's University

1. St. Stephen's University Calendar, 1998-99.

St. Thomas University

1. St. Thomas University Calendar, 1994-95.
2. Memo from Dr. Thomas Parkhill to Roger Barnsley, dated 8 November 1993, "CAAS Application, 1994-95" (application for increased staffing).
3. Religious Studies Self-Study, March 1994.
4. Report of the Review Team to the Department of Religious Studies at St. Thomas University, Fredericton [sic], NB, 24-25 March 1994.
5. Religious Studies Department Response to the Report of the External Reviewers, August 1994.
6. St. Thomas University Calendar, 1998-99

Université de Moncton

1. Letter from Denise Lamontagne to M. Paul Bowlby, dated 27 February 1998.
2. Rapport Annuel du Département des Sciences Religieuses (1992-93).

University of New Brunswick

1. University of New Brunswick Undergraduate Calendar, 1994-95.

4. Nova Scotia

Acadia University

1. Acadia University Calendar, 1994-95.
2. Report of the Programme Review Committee for the Department of Comparative Religion at Acadia University to the Senate Curriculum Review Committee, December 1992.
3. Response of the Department of Comparative Religion to the Report of the Programme Review Committee for the Department of Comparative Religion to the Senate Curriculum Review Committee, 5 January 1993.
4. Memo to the Arts Faculty Planning Committee from Subcommittee, AFPC, dated 17 December 1993.
5. Acadia Divinity College Calendar, 1983-84.
6. Update from Dr. Bruce Matthews to Paul Bowlby, dated 6 February 1998.

Dalhousie University

1. Dalhousie University Arts and Social Sciences, Education, Science, Health Professions, Management Calendar, 1994-95.
2. "Report on Rationalization: Cooperation Among Departments of Religious Studies in Metro Halifax" by Tom Sinclair-Faulkner, Chairperson, Department of Comparative Religion, Dalhousie University, 27 May 1995, pp. 1-5.
3. Self-Study of the Department Prepared for the Unit Review Committee, 4 January 1990.
4. Comparative Religion Department Unit Review: External Reviewer's Report, 6 March 1998.

Mount Saint Vincent University

1. Mount Saint Vincent University Calendar, 1992-93.
2. Department of Religious Studies: External Assessment Document, nd.
3. Religious Studies Department, Department Review, 1989-90.
4. Report of the External Reviewers of the Departments of Philosophy and Religious Studies of Mount Saint Vincent University, Halifax, Nova Scotia, 17-19 February 1994.

5. Response of the Religious Studies Department to the report "The Framework of the Metro Halifax Universities' Business Plan" written by Sister Elizabeth Bellefontaine, 12 September 1995.
6. Letter from Dr. Randi Warne to Paul Bowlby, dated 28 April 1998, outlining the changes in the program since 1994.

St. Francis Xavier University

1. St. Francis Xavier University Academic Calendar, 1993-94.
2. St. Francis Xavier University Faculty Handbook, April 1991.
3. Annual Report, Department of Theology, 1991-92.
4. R. B. MacDonald, "Theology/Religion/Theology at St. F.X." 15 October 1992.
5. Memo, dated 18 April 1994 from Burton MacDonald to Committee on Studies—Faculty of Arts, "Rationale for the Change of the Name of 'Department of Theology' to that of 'Department of Religious Studies.'"
6. Handbook for the Department of Religious Studies, 1997-98.
7. Annual Report of the Program in Catholic Studies, St. Francis Xavier, 1997-98.
8. Program Proposal for Bachelor of Arts with a Major in Catholic Studies, Approved by the Committee on Studies (Faculty of Arts) on 8 March 1996 and approved by the Faculty of Arts on 22 March 1996.

Saint Mary's University

1. Saint Mary's University Academic Calendar 1993-94.
2. Senate minutes from 1971-72 pertaining to the cutbacks in religious studies department.
3. Saint Mary's University Fact Books, 1993-97.
4. Department of Religious Studies Annual Report, 1993-94.
5. "The Framework of the Metro Halifax Universities' Business Plan."
6. Business Plan, Metro Halifax Universities, 1 December 1995.
7. Letter from Paul Bowlby to Dr. Janet Halliwell, Nova Scotia Council on Higher Education, dated 23 November 1994, on the distinction between divinity schools and religious studies departments.
8. Minutes and documents of the meetings of representatives from the religious studies departments, the Atlantic School of Theology and Acadia Divinity College of Nova Scotia.
9. Draft Proposal for Partnership in Religious Studies, dated 6 March 1995 sent to Drs. Elizabeth Bellefontaine, Barry Wheaton, Jacques Goulet, Tom Sinclair-Faulkner, Ravi Ravindra, S. Armstrong, Paul Bowlby, A. M. Dalton, and Larry Murphy, S.J.

10. Partnership Between the Religious Studies Departments of Mount Saint Vincent University and Saint Mary's University, 3 May 1995.
11. Letter from Dr. Paul Bowlby to Dr. Tom Sinclair-Faulkner, dated 12 June 1995, in response to Dr. Faulkner's document "Report on Rationalization: Cooperation Among Departments of Religious Studies in Metro Halifax," dated 27 May 1995.

University College of Cape Breton

1. University College of Cape Breton Academic Calendar, 1993-94.
2. Update fax from Dr. Charles MacDonald, dated 15.05.98.

University of King's College

1. The University of King's College Calendar, 1994-95.

Université Sainte-Anne

1. Université Sainte-Anne annuaire, 1992-94.

Appendix 4: Documents from the Nova Scotia Council on Higher Education

1. *Critical Choices: The Nova Scotia University System at a Crossroads Green paper on Higher Education, An Overview*. A Report by the Nova Scotia Council on Higher Education, October 1994.
2. *Shared Responsibilities in Higher Education*. Report to the Minister of Education and Culture, December 1995.
3. *The Institutions—Their Individual roles and Characteristics*. A Report Prepared by the Nova Scotia Council on Higher Education.
4. *University Funding Formula Technical Report*. Nova Scotia Council on Higher Education, 2 January 1998.

Selected Bibliography

Adams, Charles J. "The Development of Islamic Studies in Canada." In *The Muslim Community in North America,* edited by Earle H. Waugh, Baha Abu-Laban and Regula B. Aureshi, 185-201. Edmonton: University of Alberta Press, 1983.

Alton, Bruce. "Method and Reduction in the Study of Religion." *Studies in Religion/ Sciences Religieuses* 15/2 (1986): 153-64.

———. "On the Idea of a Quebec Society for the Study of Religion." *The Canadian Society for the Study of Religion Bulletin/Bulletin de la société canadienne pour l'étude de la religion* 11/3 (1988): 5-8.

Anderson, C. P. *Guide to Religious Studies in Canada / Guide pour les études religieuses au Canada.* Canadian Society for the Study of Religion/Société canadienne pour l'étude de la Religion, 1969.

———. *Guide to Religious Studies in Canada/Guide des Sciences Religieuses au Canada.* Corporation for the Publication of Academic Studies in Religion in Canada, 1972.

Arnal, William E. "What If I Don't *Want* to Play Tennis?: A Rejoinder to Russell McCutcheon on Postmodernism and Theory of Religion." *Studies in Religion/ Sciences Religieuses* 27/1 (1998): 61-68.

Badertscher, John M., Gordon Harland and Roland E. Miller. *Religious Studies in Manitoba and Saskatchewan: A State-of-the-Art Review.* The Study of Religion in Canada/Sciences Religieuses au Canada, 4. Waterloo: Published for the Canadian Corporation for Studies in Religion/Corporation Canadienne des Sciences Religieuses by Wilfrid Laurier University Press, 1993.

Baum, Gregory. [Response to Charles Davis, 1974-75]. *Studies in Religion/Sciences Religieuses* 4/3 (1975): 17-24.

Bibby, Reginald W. *Fragmented Gods: The Poverty and Potential of Religion in Canada.* Toronto: Irwin Publishing, 1987.

———. *Unknown Gods: The Ongoing Story of Religion in Canada.* Toronto: Stoddart, 1993.

Boisvert, Mathieu. "Le Zen et l'art de la pédagogie électronique." *Studies in Religion/ Sciences Religieuses* 25/1 (1996): 99-105.

———. "Tempête en la demeure: Réflexions sur l'état des sciences des religions." *Studies in Religion/Sciences Religieuses* 27/4 (1998): 373-85.

Bowlby, Paul W. R. "The State-of-the-Art of Religious Studies in Atlantic Canada: An Update and an Introduction." Paper presented to the Canadian Society for the Study of Religion/Société canadienne pour l'étude de la religion, 26-30 May 1998.

Boyer, Ernest L. *Scholarship Reconsidered: Priorities of the Professoriate. A Special Report for the Carnegie Foundation for the Advancement of Teaching.* Princeton: Princeton University Press, 1990.

Braun, Willi, and Russell T. McCutcheon. *Guide to the Study of Religion.* London and New York: Cassell, 2000.

Campbell, Michel-M. "Notes sur la conjoncture des sciences religieuses au Canada français depuis 1967." In Charles P. Anderson, *Guide to Religious Studies in Canada/Guide des sciences religieuses au Canada*, 21-40. Corporation for the Publication of Academic Studies in Religion in Canada, 1972.

Canadian Federation for the Humanities. "Profile of Canadian Humanists." *Canadian Federation for the Humanities Bulletin*10/1 (1987): 23.

Capps, Walter H. *Religious Studies: The Making of a Discipline*. Minneapolis: Fortress Press, 1995.

Census of Canada. *Religions in Canada*. Statistics Canada, Cat. No. 93-319. Ottawa: Statistics Canada, 1991.

Christian, William. *George Grant: A Biography*. Toronto: University of Toronto Press, 1994.

Classen, Hans George. "Religious Studies in Canada." *Queen's Quarterly* 85 (1978): 389-402.

Clifford, N. Keith. "Universities, Churches and Theological Colleges in English-Speaking Canada: Some Current Sources of Tension." *Studies in Religion/Sciences Religieuses* 19/1 (1990): 3-16.

Combs, Eugene. "Learned and Learning: CSSR/SCÉR, 1965-1975." *Studies in Religion/Sciences Religieuses* 6/4 (1977): 357-63.

Combs, Eugene, and Paul W. R. Bowlby. "Tolerance and Tradition." *Studies in Religion/Sciences Religieuses* 4/4 (1974-75): 315-34.

Conway, John S. "The Universities and Religious Studies." *Canadian Journal of Theology* 5/4 (1959): 269-72.

Coward, Harold. "The Canadian Contribution to the Study of South Asian Religions." *Revue Canadienne d'études du développement/Canadian Journal of Development Studies* 7/2 (1986): 281-91.

Cragg, Gerald R. "The Present Position and the Future Prospects of Canadian Theology." *Canadian Journal of Theology* 1/1 (1955): 5-10.

Crites, Stephen. D., (scribe). *The Religion Major: A Report*. Atlanta: American Academy of Religion, 1990.

Davis, Charles. "The Reconvergence of Theology and Religious Studies." *Studies in Religion/Sciences Religieuses* 4/3 (1975): 2-21.

_____. "Editorial: The Fourteenth International Congress of the IAHR." *Studies in Religion/Sciences Religieuses* 9/2 (1980): 123-24.

_____. "'Wherein There is No Ecstasy.'" *Studies in Religion/Sciences Religieuses* 13/4 (1984): 393-400.

Dawson, Lorne L. "Neither Nerve nor Ecstasy: Comment on the Wiebe-Davis Exchange." *Studies in Religion/Sciences Religieuses* 15/2 (1986): 145-51.

_____. "On References to the Transcendent in the Scientific Study of Religion: A Qualified Idealist Proposal." *Religion* 17 (1987): 227-50.

_____. *Reason, Freedom, and Religion: Closing the Gap Between the Humanistic and Scientific Study of Religion*. Toronto Studies in Religion, 6. New York: Peter Lang, 1988.

Desjardins, Michel. "Like a Cook in a Café." *Studies in Religion/Sciences Religieuses* 27/1 (1998): 69-78.

Despland, Michel. "Church History, History of Christianity, and History of Religions." *Studies in Religion/Sciences Religieuses* 7 (1978): 259-61.

―――. "Constructions modernes de la religion: L'exemple de Volney." *Studies in Religion/Sciences Religieuses* 28/1 (1999): 23-33.

Dillard, Annie. *Teaching a Stone to Talk: Expeditions and Encounters.* New York: Harper Colophon Books, 1982.

Dumais, Monique. "Études religieuses au Québec. État de la question." *Studies in Religion/Sciences Religieuses* 28/2 (1999): 209-12.

Farley, Edward. *Theologia: The Fragmentation and Unity of Theological Education.* Philadelphia: Fortress Press, 1983.

Fraser, Brian J. *The Study of Religion in British Columbia: A State-of-the-Art Review.* The Study of Religion in Canada/Sciences Religieuses au Canada, 5. Waterloo: Published for the Canadian Corporation for Studies in Religion/Corporation Canadienne des Sciences Religieuses by Wilfrid Laurier University Press, 1995.

Geertz, Clifford. *The Interpretation of Cultures: Selected Essays.* New York: Basic Books, 1973.

―――. *Local Knowledge: Further Essays in Interpretive Anthropology.* New York: Basic Books, 1983.

―――. *Works and Lives: The Anthropologist as Author.* Stanford: Stanford University Press, 1988.

Genest, Olivette. "L'impact de la critique féministe sur l'étude de la théologie." *Studies in Religion/Sciences Religieuses* 23/3 (1994): 331-37.

Grant, George P. "The Academic Study of Religion in Canada." In *Scholarship in Canada, 1967: Achievement and Outlook,* edited by R. H. Hubbard, 59-68. Symposium presented to Section 11 of the Royal Society of Canada in 1967. Toronto: University of Toronto Press, 1968.

―――. *Technology and Empire: Perspectives on North America.* Toronto: House of Anansi Press, 1969.

―――. "Faith and the Multiversity." In George P. Grant, *Technology and Justice.* Toronto: House of Anansi Press, 1986.

―――. "Research in the Humanities." In George P. Grant, *Technology and Justice.* Toronto: House of Anansi Press, 1986.

―――. "Nietzsche and the Ancients: Philosophy and Scholarship." In George P. Grant, *Technology and Justice.* Toronto: House of Anansi Press, 1986.

Gross, Rita M. *Buddhism After Patriarchy: A Feminist History, Analysis, and Reconstruction of Buddhism.* New York: State University of New York Press, 1993.

Guédon, Marie-Françoise. "Vingt ans d'anthropologie de la religion dans les milieux de recherche francophones canadiens." *Studies in Religion/Sciences Religieuses* 21/3 (1992): 273-81.

―――. "Anthropologie et religions amérindiennes au Canada." *Studies in Religion/Sciences Religieuses* 23/3 (1994): 265-67.

Hanington, Brian J. *Every Popish Person: The Story of Roman Catholicism in Nova Scotia and the Church of Halifax, 1604-1984.* Halifax: Archdiocese of Halifax, 1984.

Hart, Ray L. "Religious and Theological Studies in American Higher Education: A Pilot Study." *Journal of the American Academy of Religion* 59/4 (1991): 715-827.

Hough, Jr., Joseph C. and John B. Cobb, Jr. *Christian Identity and Theological Education.* Macon, GA: Scholars Press, 1985.

Janz, Bruce. "Mysticism and Understanding: Steven Katz and His Critics." *Studies in Religion/Sciences Religieuses* 24/1 (1995): 77-94.

Joy, Morny. "Levinas: Alterity, the Feminine and Women—A Meditation." *Studies in Religion/Sciences Religieuses* 22/4 (1993): 463-85.

Juschka, Darlene M. "The Construction of Pedagogical Spaces: Religious Studies in the University." *Studies in Religion/Sciences Religieuses* 28/1 (1999): 85-97.

Keegan, John. *The Face of Battle*. New York: Viking Press, 1976.

Kernan, Alvin. *The Imaginary Library: An Essay on Literature and Society*. Princeton: Princeton University Press, 1982.

―――. *Printing Technology, Letters and Samuel Johnson*. Princeton: Princeton University Press, 1987.

―――. *The Death of Literature*. New Haven: Yale University Press, 1990.

King, Ursula. "Voices of Protest and Promise: Women's Studies in Religion, the Impact of the Feminist Critique on the Study of Religion." *Studies in Religion/Sciences Religieuses* 23/3 (1994): 315-29.

Klostermaier, Klaus. "From Phenomenology to Metascience: Reflections on the Study of Religion." *Studies in Religion/Sciences Religieuses* 6/5 (1977): 551-64.

Klostermaier, K. K. and Larry W. Hurtado. *Religious Studies: Issues, Prospects and Proposals,* Atlanta: Scholars Press, 1991.

Kroeker, P. Travis. "The Ironic Cage of Positivism and the Nature of Philosophical Theology." *Studies in Religion/Sciences Religieuses* 22/1 (1993): 93-104.

―――. "Reply to Donald Wiebe." *Studies in Religion/Sciences Religieuses* 23/1 (1994): 81-82.

Lalonde, Marc P. "From Postmodernity to Postorthodoxy, or Charles Davis and the Contemporary Context of Christian Theology." *Studies in Religion/Sciences Religieuses* 22/4 (1993): 437-50.

―――. "On the Moral-Existential Facet of Religious Studies Today." *Studies in Religion/Sciences Religieuses* 26/1 (1997): 25-43.

Laperrière, Guy, and William Westfall. "Religious Studies." In *Interdisciplinary Approaches to Canadian Society: A Guide to the Literature,* edited by Alan Artibise, 9-76. Montreal and Kingston: McGill-Queen's University Press for the Association of Canadian Studies, 1990.

Lapointe, Roger. "Oracle sur les sciences religieuses." *Studies in Religion/Sciences Religieuses* 23/3 (1994): 347-60.

―――. "La religion de l'humanité." *Studies in Religion/Sciences Religieuses* 24/1 (1995): 3-17.

Lemieux, Raymond. "Sur la pertinence sociale de la théologie et des sciences religieuses." *Studies in Religion/Sciences Religieuses* 27/2 (1988): 131-43.

MacIntyre, Alasdair. *After Virtue: A Study in Moral Theory*. Notre Dame, IN: University of Notre Dame Press, 1984.

―――. *Whose Justice? Which Rationality?* Notre Dame, IN: University of Notre Dame Press, 1988.

―――. *Three Rival Versions of Moral Inquiry: Encyclopedia, Genealogy, and Tradition*. Notre Dame, IN: University of Notre Dame Press, 1990.

MacKinnon, Frank. *Church Politics and Education in Canada: The P.E.I. Experience*. Calgary: Detselig Enterprises, 1995.

Martel, Gilles. "Une voie d'avenir en sciences des religions. Une explication scientifique de la foi comme action humaine?" *Studies in Religion/Sciences Religieuses* 21/3 (1992): 283-93.

McCutcheon, Russell T. "My Theory of the Brontosaurus": Postmodernism and 'Theory' of Religion." *Studies in Religion/Sciences Religieuses* 26/1 (1997): 3-23.

———. "The Crisis of Academic Labour and the Myth of Autonomy: Dispatch from the Job Wars." *Studies in Religion/Sciences Religieuses* 27/4 (1998): 387-405.

———. "Returning the Volley to William E. Arnal." *Studies in Religion/Sciences Religieuses* 27/1 (1998), 67-68.

Neufeldt, Ronald W. *Religious Studies in Alberta: A State-of-the-Art Review.* The Study of Religion in Canada/Sciences Religieuses au Canada, 1. Waterloo: Published for the Canadian Corporation for Studies in Religion/Corporation Canadienne des Sciences Religieuses by Wilfrid Laurier University Press, 1983.

Neville, R. C. "Religious Studies and Theological Studies." *Journal of the American Academy of Religion* 61 (1993): 185-200.

Nielsen, Kai. "Naturalistic Explanations of Religion." *Studies in Religion/Sciences Religieuses* 26/4 (1997): 441-66.

Nussbaum, Martha C. *Poetic Justice: The Literary Imagination and Public Life.* Boston: Beacon Press, 1995.

———. *Cultivating Humanity: A Classical Defense of Reform in Liberal Education.* Cambridge, MA: Harvard University Press, 1997.

O'Flaherty, Wendy D. *Other Peoples' Myths: The Cave of Echoes.* Chicago: University of Chicago Press, 1995.

Page, Norman. "Au seuil du XXIe siècle/On the Threshold of the 21st Century: Introduction." *Studies in Religion/Sciences Religieuses* 23/3 (1994): 255-63.

Paper, Jordon. "Methodological Controversies in the Study of Native American Religions." *Studies in Religion/Sciences Religieuses* 22/3 (1993): 365-77.

Penner, Hans H. *Impasse and Resolution: A Critique of the Study of Religion.* Toronto Studies in Religion, 8. New York: Peter Lang, 1989.

Reid, John G. *Mount Allison University: A History to 1963.* 2 vols. Toronto: University of Toronto Press, 1984.

Remus, Harold. "Religion as an Academic Discipline: Origins, Nature, Changing Understandings." In *Encyclopedia of the American Religious Experience,* edited by Charles H. Lippy and Peter W. Williams. Vol. 3, 1653-64. New York: Scribner's, 1988.

———. "Religious Studies in Ontario 1992-1999: State-of-the-Art Update." *Studies in Religion/Sciences Religieuses* 28/2 (1999): 197-208.

Remus, Harold, William Closson James, and Daniel Fraiken. *Religious Studies in Ontario: A State-of-the-Art Review.* The Study of Religion in Canada/Sciences Religieuses au Canada, 3. Waterloo: Published for the Canadian Corporation for Studies in Religion/Corporation Canadienne des Sciences Religieuses by Wilfrid Laurier University Press, 1992.

Richard, Réginald. "Psychologie de la religion: vingt ans de recherche francophone au Québec et au Canada." *Studies in Religion/Sciences Religieuses* 21/3 (1992): 257-72.

Riley, Philip Boo. "Theology and/or Religious Studies: A Case Study of *Studies in Religion/Sciences Religieuses* 1971-1981." *Studies in Religion/Sciences Religieuses* 13/4 (1984): 423-44.

Rousseau, Louis and Michel Despland. *Les sciences religieuses au Québec depuis 1972*. The Study of Religion in Canada/Sciences religieuses au Canada, 2. Waterloo: Published for the Corporation for Studies in Religion /Corporation Canadienne des Sciences Religieuses by Wilfrid Laurier University Press, 1988.

Ryan, William F., S.J. *Culture, Spirituality, and Economic Development: Opening a Dialogue*. Ottawa: International Development Research Centre, 1995.

Said, Edward. *Orientalism*. New York: Pantheon Books, 1978.

Sharpe, Eric J. *Comparative Religion: A History*. 2nd ed. LaSalle, IL: Open Court, 1986.

Sinclair-Faulkner, Tom. "Watson Kirkconnell and the Practice of Tolerance." *Touchstone* 5/1 (January 1987): 40-42.

―――――. "Less is More: How Religious Studies Can Foster Liberal Education." In *Religious Studies: Issues, Prospects and Proposals*, edited by K. K. Klostermaier and Larry W. Hurtado. Atlanta: Scholars Press, 1991, 105-19.

―――――. "Sociology of Religion." *Studies in Religion/Sciences Religieuses* 17/3 (1988): 255-56.

Singh, Pashaura. "Recent Trends and Prospects in Sikh Studies." *Studies in Religion/Sciences Religieuses* 27/4 (1998): 407-25.

Slater, Peter. "Religion as an Academic Discipline." In Claude Welch, *Religion in the Undergraduate Curriculum: An Analysis and Interpretation*. Washington, DC: Association of American Colleges, 1972. 26-36.

―――――. "Winnipeg 1980 and Women's Studies: Response to Ursula King." *Studies in Religion/Sciences Religieuses* 23/3 (1994): 339-46.

Smith, Page. *Killing the Spirit: Higher Education in America*. New York: Penguin Books, 1991.

Smith, Stewart, M.D. *Commission of Inquiry on Canadian University Education*. Ottawa: Association of Universities and Colleges of Canada, 1991.

Smith, Wilfred Cantwell. *The Meaning and End of Religion: A Revolutionary Approach to the Great Religious Traditions*. London: SPCK, 1978.

―――――. *Towards a World Theology: Faith and the Comparative History of Religion*. Philadelphia: Westminister Press, 1981.

Stanley, Laurie C. C. *The Well-Watered Garden: The Presbyterian Church in Cape Breton, 1798-1860*. Sydney: University College of Cape Breton Press, 1983.

Taylor, Mark C. "Unsettling Issues." *Journal of the American Academy of Religion* 62/4 (1994): 949-63.

Tissot, Georges. "Identité et symbole: nous et les Amérindiens—vingt ans après." *Studies in Religion/Sciences Religieuses* 21/3 (1992): 295-300.

Tomm, Winnie. "Otherness in Self-Disclosure: A Woman's Perspective." *Studies in Religion/Sciences Religieuses* 22/4 (1994): 487-502.

"The Universities: A Measure of Excellence: Third Annual Ranking." *Maclean's* 106/46, 15 November 1993.

"Universities: The Fourth Annual Ranking '94." *Maclean's* 107/46, 14 November 1994.

"Universities 95: The Fifth Annual Ranking." *Maclean's* 108/47, 20 November 1995.

Warne, Randi R. "(En)gendering Religious Studies." *Studies in Religion/Sciences Religieuses* 27/4 (1998): 427-36.

Wasserstrom, Steven M. "Uses of the Androgyne in the History of Religions." *Studies in Religion/Sciences Religieuses* 27/4 (1998): 437-53.

Selected Bibliography

Weavers, John H. "Canadian Universities and the Teaching of Religion." *Canadian Journal of Theology* 2 (1956): 151-62.

Welch, Claude. *Religion in the Undergraduate Curriculum: An Analysis and Interpretation*. Washington, DC: Association of American Colleges, 1972.

Wiebe, Donald. "Is a Science of Religion Possible?" *Studies in Religion/Sciences Religieuses* 7/1 (1978): 5-17.

―――. "The Failure of Nerve in the Academic Study of Religion." *Studies in Religion/Sciences Religieuses* 13/4 (1984): 401-22.

―――. "The 'Academic Naturalization' of Religious Studies: Intent or Pretence?" *Studies in Religion/Sciences Religieuses* 15/2 (1986): 197-203.

―――. "Postulations for Safeguarding Preconceptions: The Case of the Scientific Religionist." *Religion* 18 (1988): 11-19.

―――. "Argument and Authority in the Academy? On Kroeker on *The Irony of Theology*." *Studies in Religion/Sciences Religieuses* 23/1 (1994): 67-79.

Wyschogrod, Edith. "Facts, Fiction, *Ficciones*: Truth in the Study of Religion." *Journal of the American Academy of Religion,* 62/1 (1994): 1-16.

Younger, Paul. [Response to Charles Davis, 1974-75]. *Studies in Religion/Sciences Religieuses* 4/3 (1975): 231-33.

Index

Abdul-Masih, Magi, 34
Acadia University, 43-44, 54-55, 58, 103, 128, 129; Department of Comparative Religion, 10-14, 44, 104-105, 159, 160-63, 172, 179; university history, 21-22
Aid to Scholarly Publication Program, 127
American Academy of Religion, 89
Anderson, Charles, P., 11-13, 51, 91, 100, 104, 105, 109, 164-65, 168
Atlantic Baptist University, 13, 22, 43, 74-75, 96, 166; curriculum, 102-103, 115; honours, 75; majors, 45, 58, 64; religious studies, 44, 64
Association of Universities and Colleges of Canada, 45
Babineau, Edmour, 165
Bachelor of Arts degrees, 54-57; graduate degree, 76-77; honours degree, 60-61, 72-75; major, 57-72; minors, 59, 60, 76; multidisciplinary programs, 78-79; requirements of, 62-63, 64-66, 68-73; service or elective courses, 77
Badawi, Jamal, 34
Campbell, Michel-M., 11, 164, 168
Canadian Corporation for Studies in Religion / Corporation canadienne des sciences religieuses, 6, 143-44, 164
Canadian Society for the Study of Religion / Société canadienne pour l'étude de la religion (CSSR / SCÉR), 6, 35, 89, 142-43, 166-67
Crites, Stephen, 27, 41, 53, 65, 113, 116, 118, 136
Dalhousie University, 11, 14, 18, 20, 49, 54-56, 80, 85, 100, 112, 170; Department of Comparative Religion, 51-53, 58, 71-72, 77-78, 105-107, 112; university history, 19, 51

Dalton, Anne Marie, 33
faculty: academic societies, 143-45; areas of specialization, 133-34, 136-43, 147-50; chairperson, 121; demographics, 128-30; doctorate, 130-31, 136-41; employment crisis, 126; entrepreneur, 121-24; evaluation, 125-27; gender balance, 128-29; job description, 125; part-time, 126; publications, 125, 137; qualitative changes, 145-47, 150-52; rank, 133; religious affiliations, 181-82; retirement patterns, 132, 153-54; research, 121-25, 134, 133-36, 137, 141; service, 135-36; teaching, 121, 123-25, 131-37, 147-50
Faulkner, Tom, 17, 51, 167-68
gender, 3-5, 12, 116-17, 128-29, 146, 181
graduate schools, 155
Hart, Ray, 39, 121
Hodder, Morley F., 50
International Association for the History of Religions, 3
James, William Closson, 130, 132
library holdings, 79-86
Library of Congress, 4, 7, 80
MacDonald, Burton, 38, 39
MacKinnon, Frank, 24
Matthews, Bruce, 44, 159, 161
McCutcheon, Russell, 126, 168-69
Memorial University of Newfoundland, 11, 13-14, 28, 49-51, 54-56, 80, 83, 115, 129, 132, 140, 147, 166, 168, 170, 180; Department of Religious Studies, 58, 60-61, 74, 76-78, 92-95, 112-13; university history, 24-25
Mi'Kmaq and Maliseet, 31, 66
Mount Allison University, 10, 13-14, 43,

/ 207

54-56, 73-74, 85, 90, 96, 103, 128, 130, 132, 165, 172; Department of Religious Studies, 46-48, 56, 58, 60-63, 77-78, 97-99, 107-108, 115; university history, 23, 34
Mount Saint Vincent University, 10, 14, 30, 31, 42, 54, 55, 58, 69, 73, 77, 90, 103, 107-108, 128-30, 140, 147, 161; Department of Religious Studies, 34-37, 58, 68-69, 73, 77-78, 116, 159-60, 163, 170; general degree requirements, 56-57; mission statement, 34; Sisters of Charity, 20, 35, 162, 163
multiculturalism, 2, 9, 42, 115-16, 140, 154-55, 161, 171-75
Murphy, S.J., Lawrence, 33
Nussbaum, Martha, C., 159, 174-75
Parkhill, Thom, 140
Ravindra, Ravi, 51
religious studies, 2, 9, 35, 47, 49, 139; courses, 3, curriculum, 2, 4, 8, 12, 27, 59, 77-78, 89-120, 136, 187-88; distribution requirements, 72-73; graduate degees 72-75; history of, 7-9, 13; honours degree, 72-75; in international curriculum, 2, 154; in public schools, 122; major, 57-59, 61-76; methodologies, 1-12, 17, 27-28, 30, 35-36, 38-39, 41-42, 47, 49, 50-51, 53, 66, 78-79, 90, 108, 116-17, 127, 136-39, 141-43, 147-150, 153-55, 161, 181-87; minor, 76
Remus, Harold, 6
Rollman, Hans, 85, 94, 140
Saint Francis Xavier University, 10, 14, 20, 30-31, 38-40, 42, 54-55, 57-58, 129, 153, 165, 172, 179; Catholic studies, 14, 40, 68; Department of Theology, 10, 58, 67-68, 73, 108-109; Department of Religious Studies, 39-40; 57, 67, 78, 108-109
Saint Mary's University, 10, 14, 15, 20, 30, 42, 54-58, 82, 91, 106, 113, 129, 132, 140, 172, 187; Department of Religious Studies, 32-34, 36-37, 58, 69-71, 73-75, 77-78, 109-112, 115, 116, 170; general degree requirements, 57; university history, 20, 31-32
St. Stephen's University, 14, 22, 43, 46, 96
St. Thomas University, 10, 13, 14, 30, 31, 49, 54, 74, 80, 83, 96, 107, 113, 129, 172; Department of Religious Studies, 32, 40-42, 58, 65-67, 73-74, 77, 78, 100-102, 115-16; general degree requirements, 56, 65, 77, 90; mission statement, 40-41; university history, 23, 40
Smith, Wilfred Cantwell, 51, 52, 105, 166, 185
State-of-the-Art Reviews, 6, 35
Steigman, Emero, 33
students, 122-23
Studies in Religion / Sciences Religieuses, 6, 35, 144, 166, 186
theological schools: Acadia Divinity College, 14, 22, 83, 104, 162, 186; Atlantic School of Theology, 14, 19, 24, 83; Queen's College, 14, 24, 83
Université de Moncton, 13, 14, 23, 54, 58, 96, 130, 160, 165; Department of Religious Studies, 99-100, 115, 186
Université Sainte-Anne, 20
University College of Cape Breton, 14, 20, 58, 103, 104, 112, 160-61
University of King's College, 10, 18-19, 49, 80, 85
University of New Brunswick, 11, 23, 49, 80, 83, 85, 100, 179-80
University of Prince Edward Island, 10, 14, 24, 30, 56, 58, 61-62, 80, 85, 132, 168; Department of Religious Studies, 27-30, 73, 78, 95-96, 115
Vaisey, Douglas, 82
Warne, Randi, 37, 159, 160
Wiebe, Donald, 166, 168
Werblowsky, R.J.Z., 3

Series Published by Wilfrid Laurier University Press for the Canadian Corporation for Studies in Religion / Corporation Canadienne des Sciences Religieuses

Editions SR

1. *La langue de Ya'udi : description et classement de l'ancien parler de Zencircli dans le cadre des langues sémitiques du nord-ouest*
   Paul-Eugène Dion, O.P. / 1974 / viii + 511 p. / OUT OF PRINT
2. *The Conception of Punishment in Early Indian Literature*
   Terence P. Day / 1982 / iv + 328 pp.
3. *Traditions in Contact and Change: Selected Proceedings of the XIVth Congress of the International Association for the History of Religions*
   Edited by Peter Slater and Donald Wiebe with Maurice Boutin and Harold Coward
   1983 / x + 758 pp. / OUT OF PRINT
4. *Le messianisme de Louis Riel*
   Gilles Martel / 1984 / xviii + 483 p.
5. *Mythologies and Philosophies of Salvation in the Theistic Traditions of India*
   Klaus K. Klostermaier / 1984 / xvi + 549 pp. / OUT OF PRINT
6. *Averroes' Doctrine of Immortality: A Matter of Controversy*
   Ovey N. Mohammed / 1984 / vi + 202 pp. / OUT OF PRINT
7. *L'étude des religions dans les écoles : l'expérience américaine, anglaise et canadienne*
   Fernand Ouellet / 1985 / xvi + 666 p.
8. *Of God and Maxim Guns: Presbyterianism in Nigeria, 1846-1966*
   Geoffrey Johnston / 1988 / iv + 322 pp.
9. *A Victorian Missionary and Canadian Indian Policy: Cultural Synthesis vs Cultural Replacement*
   David A. Nock / 1988 / x + 194 pp. / OUT OF PRINT
10. *Prometheus Rebound: The Irony of Atheism*
    Joseph C. McLelland / 1988 / xvi + 366 pp.
11. *Competition in Religious Life*
    Jay Newman / 1989 / viii + 237 pp.
12. *The Huguenots and French Opinion, 1685-1787: The Enlightenment Debate on Toleration*
    Geoffrey Adams / 1991 / xiv + 335 pp.
13. *Religion in History: The Word, the Idea, the Reality / La religion dans l'histoire : le mot, l'idée, la réalité*
    Edited by/Sous la direction de Michel Despland and/et Gérard Vallée
    1992 / x + 252 pp.
14. *Sharing Without Reckoning: Imperfect Right and the Norms of Reciprocity*
    Millard Schumaker / 1992 / xiv + 112 pp.
15. *Love and the Soul: Psychological Interpretations of the Eros and Psyche Myth*
    James Gollnick / 1992 / viii + 174 pp.
16. *The Promise of Critical Theology: Essays in Honour of Charles Davis*
    Edited by Marc P. Lalonde / 1995 / xii + 146 pp.

17. *The Five Aggregates: Understanding Theravāda Psychology and Soteriology*
    Mathieu Boisvert / 1995 / xii + 166 pp.
18. *Mysticism and Vocation*
    James R. Horne / 1996 / vi + 110 pp.
19. *Memory and Hope: Strands of Canadian Baptist History*
    Edited by David T. Priestley / 1996 / viii + 211 pp.
20. *The Concept of Equity in Calvin's Ethics**
    Guenther H. Haas / 1997 / xii + 205 pp.
    * Available in the United Kingdom and Europe from Paternoster Press.
21. *The Call of Conscience: French Protestant Responses to the Algerian War, 1954-1962*
    Geoffrey Adams / 1998 / xxii + 270 pp.
22. *Clinical Pastoral Supervision and the Theology of Charles Gerkin*
    Thomas St. James O'Connor / 1998 / x + 152 pp.
23. *Faith and Fiction: A Theological Critique of the Narrative Strategies of Hugh MacLennan and Morley Callaghan*
    Barbara Pell / 1998 / v + 141 pp.
24. *God and the Chip: Religion and the Culture of Technology*
    William A. Stahl / 1999 / vi + 186 pp.
25. *The Religious Dreamworld of Apuleius'* Metamorphoses: *Recovering a Forgotten Hermeneutic*
    James Gollnick / 1999 /xiv + 178 pp.

Comparative Ethics Series /
Collection d'Éthique Comparée

1. *Muslim Ethics and Modernity: A Comparative Study of the Ethical Thought of Sayyid Ahmad Khan and Mawlana Mawdudi*
   Sheila McDonough / 1984 / x + 130 pp. / OUT OF PRINT
2. *Methodist Education in Peru: Social Gospel, Politics, and American Ideological and Economic Penetration, 1888-1930*
   Rosa del Carmen Bruno-Jofré / 1988 / xiv + 223 pp.
3. *Prophets, Pastors and Public Choices: Canadian Churches and the Mackenzie Valley Pipeline Debate*
   Roger Hutchinson / 1992 / xiv + 142 pp. / OUT OF PRINT
4. *In Good Faith: Canadian Churches Against Apartheid*
   Renate Pratt / 1997 / xii + 366 pp.
5. *Towards an Ethics of Community: Negotiations of Difference in a Pluralist Society*
   James H. Olthuis, editor / 2000 / x + 230 pp.

Dissertations SR

1. *The Social Setting of the Ministry as Reflected in the Writings of Hermas, Clement and Ignatius*
   Harry O. Maier / 1991 / viii + 230 pp. / OUT OF PRINT
2. *Literature as Pulpit: The Christian Social Activism of Nellie L. McClung*
   Randi R. Warne / 1993 / viii + 236 pp. / OUT OF PRINT

Studies in Christianity and Judaism / Études sur le christianisme et le judaïsme

1. *A Study in Anti-Gnostic Polemics: Irenaeus, Hippolytus, and Epiphanius*
   Gérard Vallée / 1981 / xii + 114 pp. / OUT OF PRINT
2. *Anti-Judaism in Early Christianity*
   Vol. 1, *Paul and the Gospels*
   Edited by Peter Richardson with David Granskou / 1986 / x + 232 pp.
   Vol. 2, *Separation and Polemic*
   Edited by Stephen G. Wilson / 1986 / xii + 185 pp.
3. *Society, the Sacred, and Scripture in Ancient Judaism: A Sociology of Knowledge*
   Jack N. Lightstone / 1988 / xiv + 126 pp.
4. *Law in Religious Communities in the Roman Period: The Debate Over* Torah *and* Nomos *in Post-Biblical Judaism and Early Christianity*
   Peter Richardson and Stephen Westerholm with A. I. Baumgarten, Michael Pettem and Cecilia Wassén / 1991 / x + 164 pp.
5. *Dangerous Food: 1 Corinthians 8-10 in Its Context*
   Peter D. Gooch / 1993 / xviii + 178 pp.
6. *The Rhetoric of the Babylonian Talmud, Its Social Meaning and Context*
   Jack N. Lightstone / 1994 / xiv + 317 pp.
7. *Whose Historical Jesus?*
   Edited by William E. Arnal and Michel Desjardins / 1997 / vi + 337 pp.
8. *Religious Rivalries and the Struggle for Success in Caesarea Maritima*
   Edited by Terence L. Donaldson / 2000 / xiv + 402 pp.
9. *Text and Artifact in the Religions of Mediterranean Antiquity*
   Edited by Stephen G. Wilson and Michel Desjardins / 2000 / xvi + 616 pp.

The Study of Religion in Canada / Sciences Religieuses au Canada

1. *Religious Studies in Alberta: A State-of-the-Art Review*
   Ronald W. Neufeldt / 1983 / xiv + 145 pp.
2. *Les sciences religieuses au Québec depuis 1972*
   Louis Rousseau et Michel Despland / 1988 / 158 p.
3. *Religious Studies in Ontario: A State-of-the-Art Review*
   Harold Remus, William Closson James and Daniel Fraikin / 1992 / xviii + 422 pp.
4. *Religious Studies in Manitoba and Saskatchewan: A State-of-the-Art Review*
   John M. Badertscher, Gordon Harland and Roland E. Miller / 1993 / vi + 166 pp.
5. *The Study of Religion in British Columbia: A State-of-the-Art Review*
   Brian J. Fraser / 1995 / x + 127 pp.
6. *Religious Studies in Atlantic Canada: A State-of-the-Art Review*
   Paul W.R. Bowlby with Tom Faulkner / 2001 / xii + 208 pp.

Studies in Women and Religion / Études sur les femmes et la religion

1. *Femmes et religions**
   Sous la direction de Denise Veillette / 1995 / xviii + 466 p.
   * Only available from Les Presses de l'Université Laval
2. *The Work of Their Hands: Mennonite Women's Societies in Canada*
   Gloria Neufeld Redekop / 1996 / xvi + 172 pp.
3. *Profiles of Anabaptist Women: Sixteenth-Century Reforming Pioneers*
   Edited by C. Arnold Snyder and Linda A. Huebert Hecht / 1996 / xxii + 438 pp.

4. *Voices and Echoes: Canadian Women's Spirituality*
   Edited by Jo-Anne Elder and Colin O'Connell / 1997 / xxviii + 237 pp.
5. *Obedience, Suspicion and the Gospel of Mark: A Mennonite-Feminist Exploration of Biblical Authority*
   Lydia Neufeld Harder / 1998 / xiv + 168 pp.
6. *Clothed in Integrity: Weaving Just Cultural Relations and the Garment Industry*
   Barbara Paleczny / 2000 / xxxiv + 352 pp.

SR Supplements

1. *Footnotes to a Theology: The Karl Barth Colloquium of 1972*
   Edited and Introduced by Martin Rumscheidt / 1974 / viii + 151 pp. / OUT OF PRINT
2. *Martin Heidegger's Philosophy of Religion*
   John R. Williams / 1977 / x + 190 pp. / OUT OF PRINT
3. *Mystics and Scholars: The Calgary Conference on Mysticism 1976*
   Edited by Harold Coward and Terence Penelhum / 1977 / viii + 121 pp. / OUT OF PRINT
4. *God's Intention for Man: Essays in Christian Anthropology*
   William O. Fennell / 1977 / xii + 56 pp. / OUT OF PRINT
5. *"Language" in Indian Philosophy and Religion*
   Edited and Introduced by Harold G. Coward / 1978 / x + 98 pp. / OUT OF PRINT
6. *Beyond Mysticism*
   James R. Horne / 1978 / vi + 158 pp. / OUT OF PRINT
7. *The Religious Dimension of Socrates' Thought*
   James Beckman / 1979 / xii + 276 pp. / OUT OF PRINT
8. *Native Religious Traditions*
   Edited by Earle H. Waugh and K. Dad Prithipaul / 1979 / xii + 244 pp. / OUT OF PRINT
9. *Developments in Buddhist Thought: Canadian Contributions to Buddhist Studies*
   Edited by Roy C. Amore / 1979 / iv + 196 pp.
10. *The Bodhisattva Doctrine in Buddhism*
    Edited and Introduced by Leslie S. Kawamura / 1981 / xxii + 274 pp. / OUT OF PRINT
11. *Political Theology in the Canadian Context*
    Edited by Benjamin G. Smillie / 1982 / xii + 260 pp.
12. *Truth and Compassion: Essays on Judaism and Religion in Memory of Rabbi Dr. Solomon Frank*
    Edited by Howard Joseph, Jack N. Lightstone and Michael D. Oppenheim
    1983 / vi + 217 pp. / OUT OF PRINT
13. *Craving and Salvation: A Study in Buddhist Soteriology*
    Bruce Matthews / 1983 / xiv + 138 pp. / OUT OF PRINT
14. *The Moral Mystic*
    James R. Horne / 1983 / x + 134 pp.
15. *Ignatian Spirituality in a Secular Age*
    Edited by George P. Schner / 1984 / viii + 128 pp. / OUT OF PRINT
16. *Studies in the Book of Job*
    Edited by Walter E. Aufrecht / 1985 / xii + 76 pp.
17. *Christ and Modernity: Christian Self-Understanding in a Technological Age*
    David J. Hawkin / 1985 / x + 181 pp.
18. *Young Man Shinran: A Reappraisal of Shinran's Life*
    Takamichi Takahatake / 1987 / xvi + 228 pp. / OUT OF PRINT
19. *Modernity and Religion*
    Edited by William Nicholls / 1987 / vi + 191 pp.
20. *The Social Uplifters: Presbyterian Progressives and the Social Gospel in Canada, 1875-1915*
    Brian J. Fraser / 1988 / xvi + 212 pp. / OUT OF PRINT

Series discontinued

Religious Studies in Atlantic Canada: A State-of-the-Art Review

Paul W. R. Bowlby with Tom Faulkner

What is "Religious Studies" and what is its future in Atlantic Canada? How have universities founded by Roman Catholic and Protestant denominations, and public universities, differed as they approached the study of religious life and traditions?

Religious Studies in Atlantic Canada surveys the history and place of the study of religion within Canadian universities. Following a historical introduction to the public and denominationally founded universities in the Atlantic region, the book situates the departments of religious studies in relation to the distinctive characteristics of the various universities in the region, focusing on curriculum, research, and teaching.

Bowlby examines the current strengths of the religious studies departments in Atlantic Canada, and where those departments are fragile, i.e., where departments have thrived because of careful long-term planning, as well as where crises of retirements have radically affected the size and strength of departments. In conclusion, Bowlby suggests strategies for future survival and growth in the field of religious studies.

Religious Studies in Atlantic Canada is the last of a six-part series on the state of the art of religious studies in Canada, a unique account of the regional differences in the development of religious studies in Canada. Written for the general reader as well as the specialist, the book provides an introduction and an overview of religious studies curricula, faculty research, and teaching areas at the region's universities.

Dr. Paul Bowlby is chair of the Religious Studies Department at Saint Mary's University in Halifax, Nova Scotia, a post he has held for nearly twenty years.

ISBN 0-88920-361-X